World Wildlife: the last stand

BOOKS BY PHILIP KINGSLAND CROWE

World Wildlife: the Last Stand
The Empty Ark
Sporting Journeys in Africa and Asia
Diversions of a Diplomat in Ceylon
Sport is Where You Find It

World Wildlife: the last stand

by Philip Kingsland Crowe

Author of *The Empty Ark*

with a foreword by H. R. H. Prince Bernhard of the Netherlands

Charles Scribner's Sons | New York

To Irene

Contents

It gives me great pleasure to introduce this new book by Philip Crowe.

I have read his fascinating reports over the last few years with tremendous interest and it makes me very happy that they now will be available to the public. The work he has done is invaluable and what he has to tell us is of the utmost importance. Moreover, his great sense of humor makes it delightful reading. I am sure that this book will bring the cause of wildlife conservation nearer to the heart of a great number of people.

The Prince of the Netherlands.

World Wildlife: the last stand

Preface

In 1961, while visiting the island of Mauritius in the Indian Ocean, I saw in a dusty display case a replica of the famous dodo, the great bird that has become a synonym for all vanished species. Unable to fly or otherwise protect himself, the dodo was killed by men for food—though its fiesh was unpalatable—and its eggs were eaten by the rats that inevitably accompanied the early voyagers to the island. By 1681 it was extinct. Were it not for the restoration efforts of Sir Edward Newton in 1889, we wouldn't know today what the doomed creature looked like.

Birds and animals restricted to islands have always had a hard time of it, but until recently a large share of the other barren areas of the earth have been left to wildlife. By 1958, however, studies, including those by the UN, revealed that the heavily populated nations of the world were suddenly faced with the fact that they had used up all their available good land. Attempts to use the arid wastelands were not successful, because

1

the water problem couldn't be solved; nor was man able to cultivate effectively the vast tropical swamplands. But hunger is a stern taskmaster, so these last refuges of many rare birds, animals, reptiles, and fish are now being rapidly exploited. As a result, the burning of cover, the cutting of trees and the draining of the swamps means the end for some of these endangered species, unless immediate steps are taken to provide them with protected areas where a limited number can survive.

At the same time that man is using up the last of his land assets he is breeding faster and living longer than ever before. The Food and Agriculture Organization of the United Nations reported that there had been no increase in land available for cultivation in 1966 despite a net increase that year of seventy million in the world's population. By 1975, demographers predict, the well-fed, surplus-producing nations will no longer be able to feed the hungry ones. It will then be necessary to decide which of the nations of Asia, Africa, and Latin America are most deserving of the limited aid available. Certainly millions will face starvation.

Even without the terrible pressures of the present and of the coming decade, the world has lost more than 200 species of birds and animals during the past 2,000 years. Most of these have been exterminated within the last half century. Year by year, from now on, the desire of the world's hungry people for meat will rise steadily. No animal, bird, or reptile that can possibly fulfill this urge will be safe without special protection.

This grim future is not inevitable. If the leaders of hungry nations can for one thing take a firm stand on birth control, thereby reducing starvation, both wildlife and humankind will have a chance.

At the same time, governments, particularly those of Africa, should be impressed with the fact that wildlife will actually flourish on semidesert land that can never be effectively cultivated. Careful preservation of the breeding stock and annual cropping of their offspring can make an important addition to the continent's protein food supplies.

This book is a report on three missions to try to save rare wildlife in some of the world's most populated countries. In 1966 the target was Ceylon, India, and the little Himalayan kingdoms of Sikkim and Bhutan. In 1967 it was Central America and Mexico, and in 1968 southern Africa. This included South Africa, South-West Africa, the Portuguese Overseas Provinces of Angola and Sao Tomé, the newly independent

2

countries of Lesotho, Botswana, Kingdom of Swaziland, and the then Spanish colonies of Fernando Po and Río Muni.

These missions were undertaken for the World Wildlife Fund, an international organization dedicated to the survival of endangered species of birds and animals. Organized in 1962 under the distinguished patronage of His Royal Highness Prince Bernhard of the Netherlands, the Fund's international headquarters are located at Morges, Switzerland. It is also represented by National Appeals in Austria, Belgium, Britain, Canada, France, Italy, the Netherlands, Pakistan, Switzerland, South Africa, the United States, and West Germany. As a founding member of the American Appeal and an International Trustee of the World Wildlife Fund at Morges, I have been closely associated with the Fund's efforts since its inception and have made six major expeditions in its behalf. The first three of these journeys have been recorded in my book, *The Empty Ark*, published in 1967.

I am indebted to Prince Bernhard, president of the International Trustees of the World Wildlife Fund, for his foreword for this book and for his consistent interest in my missions, and to the Duke of Edinburgh, president of the British National Appeal of the World Wildlife Fund, for his letters of introduction to the various chiefs of state of many of the nations which I visited.

I am grateful to the Honorable Dean Rusk, our former Secretary of State, for advising our various ambassadors and other diplomatic officers of my schedules. Without the help and support of our diplomatic missions, my journeys in many of the earth's out-of-the-way places would not have been as comfortable or successful.

On my mission to India and the Himalayan kingdom I was accompanied by the late E. P. Gee of Shillong, Assam, a member of the Indian Board of Wildlife and one of the leading naturalists of that part of the world. Mr. Gee kindly edited the text covering those countries. I was also pleased to have with me Adrian Middleton of Sydney, Australia, who did a fine job as my aide-de-camp. Major William Phillipps and Charles E. Norris, both former presidents of the Ceylon Wildlife Protection Society, edited the chapter on Ceylon. I served as ambassador to Ceylon during Major Phillipps' last years there and found him always ready and willing to tell me about the island's wildlife.

World Wildlife: the Last Stand

The Honorable Ellis Briggs, a distinguished career ambassador who has served as American envoy to a number of nations, accompanied my wife and me, along with Mrs. Briggs, to Central America and Mexico. The late Dr. William Vogt of the Conservation Foundation, an authority on Latin America, took the time and trouble to edit the text of this mission. I am also grateful for letters of introduction furnished by Dr. Ira Gabrielson, president of the American Appeal of the World Wildlife Fund, Dr. Dillon Ripley, secretary of the Smithsonian Institution, Judge Russell Train, Under Secretary of The Interior, and Dr. Harold Coolidge, president of the International Union for the Conservation of Nature and Natural Resources.

For help during our travels in southern Africa I am most grateful for the cooperation of the government of South Africa, especially for that of my old friend The Honorable Ben Schoeman, Minister of Transport. I am also indebted to His Excellency the Marquis de Merry Del Val, the Spanish ambassador to Washington, for his introductions to the governor of Spanish Guinea, and to His Excellency Vasco Vieira Garin, the Portuguese ambassador to Washington, for his letters to the governors of Sao Tomé and Angola.

Philip K. Crowe

Easton, Maryland
February, 1969

PART 1

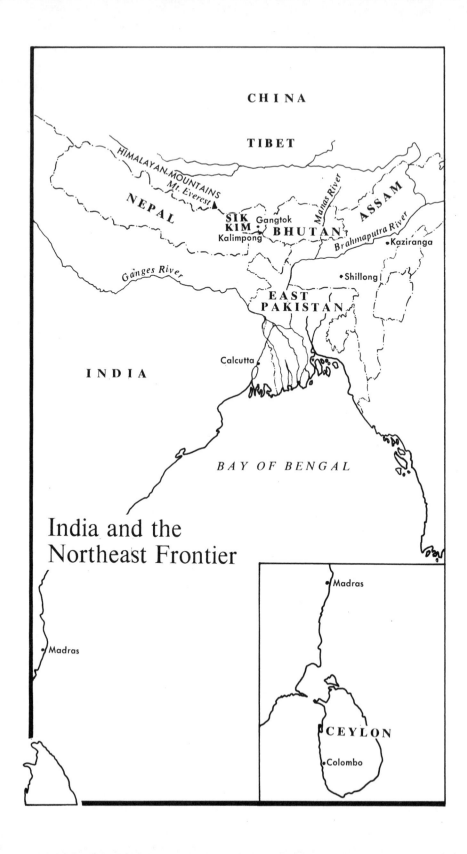

CHINA

TIBET

HIMALAYAN MOUNTAINS

Mt. Everest

NEPAL

SIK
KIM
Gangtok

Kalimpong

BHUTAN

Manas River

ASSAM

Brahmaputra River

Kaziranga

Ganges River

Shillong

EAST
PAKISTAN

INDIA

Calcutta

BAY OF BENGAL

India and the
Northeast Frontier

Madras

Madras

CEYLON

Colombo

CHAPTER I

Facts and Figures
about Conservation

In six years of wildlife missions, my wife and I have visited fifty-four countries for the purpose of persuading the chiefs of state and other decision-making men in the various governments to increase their interest in the conservation of rare birds and animals. Specifically, we urged them to grant more legal protection to endangered species and to set up parks and reserves where these scarce forms of wildlife can be domiciled. Lastly and most importantly, we explained the *sine qua non* of conservation—patrolling the designated safe havens with sufficient guards to make poaching impossible or at least difficult.

A wildlife reserve is viable only when it is protected. Unfortunately there are a good many so-called game parks around the world that exist only on the maps, or are so inadequately guarded that the wildlife in them is under heavy hunting pressure. Nor is this sad state of affairs limited to any one continent. It is certainly true that Latin America has a number of reserves that are sanctuaries in name only. But it is equally true that the parks of Buddhist Ceylon and Hindu India must withstand a great deal of poaching.

When it comes to food or profit there is very little difference among races. Illegal killing of game goes on in all of the great game parks of Africa. By and large, however, these are much better guarded than those of Central and South America and the Far East. The parks of Europe and North America are the best protected. Nevertheless, the wildlife that lives or stays outside the safety zones is apt to have a very rough time, especially in North America and Canada. No one knows how many California condors and whooping cranes are shot each year by nimrods who mistake them for geese.

Hunters, however, make a much more important contribution to conservation than most non-shooters give them credit for. If it were not for the fees resulting from hunting licenses, the states and the Federal Government would not be able to afford the game wardens who enforce the limits during the hunting seasons and protect the game when they are closed. Private hunters' organizations, such as Ducks Unlimited, have been cited for saving the wildfowl by buying breeding grounds in Canada when the ducks and geese of North America were in real danger of following the passenger pigeon into oblivion. In Africa the good white hunters—and most of them are good men in the conservation sense—function as honorary wardens, maintaining close relations with the wildlife authorities.

Rare birds and animals are, of course, much sought after by zoos all over the world. Regrettably, some zoo directors will pay fantastic prices for animals and birds whose export is expressly forbidden by the laws of the countries where they are found as well as by international agreements. These directors, often fully aware of the laws, prefer to ask no questions. The traffic in primates is particularly blatant. Endangered orangutans of Sumatra can always be bought in the Singapore black market, while the fast declining lowland gorilla of Gabon, Río Muni, and Cabinda is never in short supply if the price is right.

Zoos, on the other hand, have done conservation a priceless service by keeping alive many species that would certainly have vanished in a wild state. Père David's deer, for example, exists today only in private parks and zoos. The future existence of the Arabian oryx, too, depends more on the herd at the Phoenix, Arizona, zoo than it does on the few scattered herds that may or may not still roam the Rub al Khali in southern Arabia. The time may well come when the soaring world population crowds out of their last strongholds many of today's rare species. Then their only hope for survival will be within the constantly improving facilities of zoos.

International agreements to protect wildlife are, of course, worthy efforts. To get the countries which sign them to live up to their obligations is sometimes another matter, but there is certainly a moral obligation to do so. The mere fact that a nation has ratified such a treaty can be a great boost to the local conservationists. The first of these international agreements, known as the London Convention for the Protection of African Fauna and Flora, was brought about by Great Britain. Accredited representatives from all countries having territories of the African continent came to the meeting, held in the House of Lords in late October, 1933. The United States, India, and the Netherlands sent observers. Chairman of the meeting was the well-known American conservationist, the late Dr. John C. Phillips.

The convention became effective in 1936, when five of the original nine participating nations ratified it. These were Belgium, Egypt, the Anglo-Egyptian Sudan, the United Kingdom, and the Union of South Africa. Since then, however, the convention has become somewhat of a dead issue, for after the Second World War the former colonies fragmented into independent nations, and, if there is one thing newly sovereign countries hate, it is to be bound by agreements entered into by their former masters.

The International Union for the Conservation of Nature and Natural Resources subsequently stepped into the vacuum. In 1965 the I.U.C.N. developed a draft resolution for Africa which is both succinct and brief. At the same time, a corollary effort begun by the Food and Agriculture Organization of the United Nations resulted in a lengthy and more complicated document which may be more difficult to get ratified. As of this writing, no decision has been made as to which version the African countries will be asked to sign.

A similar international agreement, known as the Convention on Nature Protection and Wildlife Preservation in the Western Hemisphere, was promulgated in 1940 to meet the wildlife problems of the twenty-one American Republics. So far, eighteen nations have signed this convention, which marks the third cooperative step taken by the United States to further wildlife protection by international treaty on the American continent (see Appendix II). In 1916 we ratified the Migratory Bird Treaty with Canada. Twenty years later we ratified a somewhat similar treaty with Mexico.

Worthy as these international efforts are, their thrust encompasses the whole field of wildlife while the primary problem today is to save individual species of rare birds and animals before it is too late. The World Wildlife Fund, founded expressly to meet this challenge, is the only conservation organization today that exists primarily to help save threatened species and habitat areas anywhere in the world. Since its inception in 1961, the World Wildlife Fund has supported 285 projects. Among these are the acquisition of more than 200,000 acres in the United States, the United Kingdom, Spain, Colombia, Central America, Iceland, and the Seychelles Islands. (A list of the sixteen projects originated by the author is in Appendix I.)

The World Wildlife Fund has also financed surveys of rare and endangered species. These include habitat management, relocation of animals that were in endangered areas, and the establishment of breeding groups. Among the species aided were the aye-aye of Madagascar, the cheetah of Africa and Asia, the orangutan of Indonesia, the Javan rhino, the Warana sea turtle of the Caribbean, Hunter's antelope of Kenya, and the Japanese crested crane. The World Wildlife Fund has also supplied funds and equipment for thirteen reserves in Europe, Asia, Africa, and South America, including eight-four-wheel-drive cars, four patrol boats, and four light aircraft.

Contributions to the World Wildlife Fund from 1962 through 1968 have totaled more than 7.8 million dollars. More than 175 international and 100 national projects have received financial support. Yet encouraging as these figures are, they merely scratch the surface of the job to be done. There are literally hundreds of worthwhile projects that demand financing but have had to be postponed because they do not appear to deserve as high a priority as others at the present time.

The trouble with some charity organizations aimed at helping wildlife is simply that the cost of running them eats up a good deal of the money, which should go to the birds and animals. A strenuous effort has been made to keep down the overhead costs of the World Wildlife Fund both in the Washington headquarters of the American Appeal and in the international office at Morges in Switzerland. Except for these paid employees, none of the rest of us who spend a great deal of time, effort, and money on missions and other jobs for the Fund receive any financial remuneration whatsoever.

The purpose of the Washington office is only to raise money and generate favorable publicity, which will make this job easier. Although no scientists are employed there, the staff can call on a number of well-known authorities among the American directors for technical advice.

The international headquarters has a simpler problem when it comes to access to expert knowledge because it shares a building with the International Union for the Conservation of Nature, on whose staff are men who specialize in wildlife. The I.U.C.N. Survival Service Commission publishes and keeps up to date two valuable loose-leaf books known as Red Data Books, which list endangered species of birds and mammals.

The editor of the bird book is Colonel Jack Vincent. Though he has now left Morges, he will continue to edit the book from his home in South Africa. Colonel Vincent, whom readers will meet in the chapter on South Africa, is a world authority on birds, and the I.U.C.N. is extremely lucky to have his help. The birds are classified as: (1) very rare and believed to be decreasing in number; (2) less rare but believed to be threatened —require watching; (3) very rare but believed to be stable or increasing; (4) status inadequately known—survey required or data sought; (5) depleted—severely reduced in abundance and still decreasing. When new data is available, a single sheet is mailed to replace the old data sheet.

The Red Data Book on Mammals is edited by Noel Simon, who is not a scientist but who has spent much of his life in Africa and has amassed a wide knowledge of wild animals. The current list of rare and endangered species and subspecies totals 277. The descriptive pages—no individual gets more than one page—are colored for easier identification: the pink sheets are used to draw particular attention to those mammals believed to be the most gravely endangered; the green sheets are used for mammals whose survival was at one time questioned but which are now regarded as out of danger.

The Survival Service Commission, which is headed by Commander Peter Scott, chairman of the World Wildlife Fund of Great Britain, is composed of a number of well-known scientists and conservationists who meet regularly and advise the editors of the Red Books. It is the Survival Service members and the Red Book editors who furnish the International World Wildlife Office with the list of endangered species, which is then made available to the various National Appeals. All projects are scanned in the light of the necessity for immediate action to save those species that are thought to be on the edge of extinction.

Since there are today so many conservation organizations in America and England with similar names and objectives, it is well to give a brief history of the World Wildlife Fund and the ways in which it differs from other conservation efforts. According to "The Launching of the New Ark," the first report of the World Wildlife Fund (published by Collins in London and edited by Commander Scott, with the able assistance of Ian MacPhail, the director general of the British Appeal) credit for the idea came from a letter written by Victor Stolan to Sir Julian Huxley on December 6, 1960. The letter ends with an impassioned plea that "if what is left in Africa and elsewhere is to be saved, a blunt and ruthless demand must be made to those who, with their riches, can build for themselves a shining monument in history."

Sir Julian then talked with E. M. Nicholson, director general of the British Nature Conservancy. He immediately got in touch with Commander Scott, who had been thinking along the same lines for some time. As a result of these meetings, a preparatory group was formed in London under the chairmanship of Mr. Nicholson, which adopted the name World Wildlife Fund and selected the giant panda as the Fund's symbol. Soon after this the Fund was given a major boost by the offer of H.R.H. Prince Philip to become president of the British National Appeal of the Fund. At the same time, Mr. MacPhail was engaged to be secretary general of the appeal and proceeded to set up an office in London, which he ran with notable success until his resignation in 1967.

Another important step in the history of the Fund was the acceptance of the position of president of the World Wildlife Fund, International, by H.R.H. Prince Bernhard of the Netherlands. A venerable but commodious château was rented in Morges, and Dr. Fritz Vollmar, a Swiss businessman who had always been interested in wildlife, retained as secretary general.

The first move of the new organization was to issue what was known as the Morges Manifesto, a statement of objectives that was signed by sixteen of the world's leading conservationists from eleven countries. On September 11, 1961, the World Wildlife Fund was legally constituted under Swiss Law at Zurich. It was registered as a tax-exempt charitable institution on October 16 of the same year. Soon after this, a number of the promoters of the Fund met at Arusha in Tanganyika for a meeting of the I.U.C.N. They were much gratified by the willingness of Julius Nyerere, Prime Minister of Tanganyika, now Tanzania, to support the idea. The Prime Minister's words, which later became known as the Arusha Manifesto, read in part: "In accepting the trusteeship of our wildlife we solemnly declare that we will do everything in our power to make sure that our children's grandchildren will be able to enjoy this rich and precious inheritance."

The World Wildlife Fund branch in the United States was formed at a meeting in 1962 at Washington, D. C. Among those present were Dr. Ira Gabrielson, chief of the Wildlife Service of the United States Department of the Interior; C. R. Guttermuth, secretary of the North American Wildlife Foundation; Russell Train, then a federal judge, later president of The Conservation Foundation; Harold Coolidge, widely known conservationist, who is now president of the International Union for the Conservation of Nature; Kermit Roosevelt, grandson of the late President Theodore Roosevelt and secretary of the World Wildlife Fund; and the author.

Soon after this meeting the drive for funds was launched by a dinner at the Waldorf-Astoria in New York City on June 6, 1962, which was honored by the presence of both Prince Philip and Prince Bernhard. The board of directors has since been enlarged to its present total of thirty-five members. The Fund's various money-raising campaigns, under the direction of Herbert Mills, the executive director, and Kay Partney Lautman, the executive secretary, have been increasingly successful with each passing year.

As I noted above, the Fund differs from other similar organizations in that it is the only one that exists primarily to save endangered species all over the globe. It is also different in that it does not attract contributions by sending out stamps or issuing a magazine (the British Appeal does have a newsletter), nor is it a membership organization in the sense of the National Geographic Society. The message without the trimmings is clear enough. As our president, Prince Bernhard, said recently, "The new Noah's Ark we have to build is a desperate bid to save the world's wildlife and wild places, not so much at the eleventh hour, but at ten minutes to midnight."

CHAPTER II

Ceylon, India,
and the Little Kingdoms
of the Himalayas

Because the first of the three major missions described in this book is somewhat more remote in time—1966—and presented infinitely greater geographical difficulties for the wildlife reporter, I have chosen for the reader's sake to summarize the most important of our findings concerning the elephants of Ceylon, the great Indian rhino, and the conservation problems of two little kingdoms (plus Tibet) on the roof of the world, Sikkim and Bhutan. Neither spatial distance across the globe nor the seeming cultural isolation from our own environment can diminish the unfortunate facts now facing these beasts and the lands they inhabit.

ELEPHANTS OF CEYLON

Two thousand two hundred years ago the Indian Emperor Asoka prohibited the killing of animals and caused his edict to be carved on stone for all to read. The ancient kings of Ceylon also made laws against the needless slaughter of wildlife. But after these enlightened times, no strong hand came to the aid of the jungle dwellers. With the advent of gunpowder, the great herds of wild elephants, which used to roam all parts of this beautiful island, began a long decline.

But even more lethal for the elephants than the gun was the loss of their habitat. After the British put down the local wars, which decimated the island, they stamped out malaria and dysentery, two even more vicious killers, and the people multiplied. As the population surged upward, the forests were cut down for timber and agriculture, driving the herds back into more and more remote and inaccessible areas. The highlands of the island, once their favorite pastures during lowland droughts, became clothed with tea bushes. By the time I came to Ceylon as American ambassador in 1953, the elephants, estimated to number fewer than 5,000, were largely restricted to the two big game reserves of Wilpattu in the northern part of the island and Yala in the southeast.

The fate of the Ceylon elephants continued to worry me after I left the island in 1956. Consequently, I was happy to learn on my arrival at Colombo in early 1966 that a bill among the "must" legislation due for passage by the island government recommended added protection for threatened species as well as enlargement of both the Wilpattu and the Yala national parks, mostly at the expense of areas where shooting was still allowed. Many of the recommendations for protection of the island's wildlife had come from Viscount Soulbury, governor general during my term there.

I also learned that the Smithsonian Institution was prepared to undertake a two-year study of the Ceylon elephants under the direction of Dr. John S. Eisenberg, a member of the Smithsonian staff. The object of the survey was to provide the ecological and behavioral background necessary for the effective conservation of these elephants. Because such a study has never before been undertaken, no one knew exactly how many elephants there were or where their movements took them. At that time, however, the elephant study still depended on American aid, canceled during the Bandaranaike regime.

Since then American aid has fortunately been re-extended to Ceylon and all financial problems affecting the Smithsonian survey have been ironed out. As of January, 1969, Dr. Eisenberg had not yet completed his survey of the elephant population, but on the basis of his preliminary figures he reported to the Minister of State that the elephants were down to fewer than 1,500 and that he saw a distinct danger that they would be extinct in another twenty-five years. Although the Wildlife Department of the Ceylon government agreed with this bleak forecast, it thought that the present population stood between 5,000 and 6,000. Loss of habitat in addition to indiscriminate killing by cultivators were given as the reasons for the decline.

There is a faint ray of hope, however, in the studies now being conducted by Dr. Eisenberg and his Ceylonese colleagues. These scientists think that the reason Ceylon elephants do not breed in captivity may be due to the fact that they have no opportunities. The keepers or mahouts are prey to age-old superstitions to the effect that bulls permitted to mate will lose their stamina or go mad. The sexes are therefore strictly segregated during their periods of sexual urge. A campaign to enlighten elephant owners as well as their mahouts has been started.

To give the elephants a chance to prove their virility in captivity under the most benign circumstances, a breeding farm will be established at Peradeniya. After all, the domesticated herds of India and Burma have no trouble reproducing, and there is no valid reason why the Ceylon species should not also.

A young civil servant named Lyndede Alwis, warden of the Wildlife Department and director of the Zoological Garden, had the chief say on both the wild and captive fauna of the island. Both of his departments were underpaid and understaffed, but the situation in the Wildlife Department was particularly alarming. The two main parks, where most of the islands' game was concentrated, were very lightly patrolled. Wilpattu, with an area of 260 square miles, had only fifty men to guard its borders, while Yala, with 122 square miles, had to try to get by with thirty men. Only one Jeep was allocated to each park. This meant that most of the watchers had to travel by bicycle or on foot, whereas the poachers always equipped themselves with motor transport.

Among the aids which de Alwis felt he needed desperately were more Jeeps, a simple radio communications setup to connect the various stations, several so-called capture-guns, which immobilize game animals for examination without killing them, and last, but not least, a snakebite kit for each of the stations. At that time, anyone bitten in the parks by a cobra, tic-polonga, or krait had very little chance of survival.

Another frustrating obstacle to conservation in Ceylon is the inability of‘ the laws to discourage poaching. A poacher hijacks a 350-pound sambar stag and sells the meat for about 400 rupees. When he is caught, he is taken before a magistrate who is only allowed to fine him twenty-five rupees. True, the magistrate can confiscate his gun, but seldom does.

A day's drive southeast of Colombo on the shore of the Indian Ocean lies Yala, loveliest of Ceylon's national parks. As a guest of Charles E. Norris, former president of the Ceylon Wildlife Protection Society, and his wife Patsy, it was my good fortune to spend a long weekend at the park. Norris's Land-rover had a takedown top so we had a full 360-degree view of the game when we made our first safari in the late afternoon. Hardly had we left camp before we came on a herd of six elephants. There were two tiny calves, a pregnant cow, and three other cows. Although much smaller than their African cousins and lacking tusks, the Ceylon cows are just as ferocious in defending their young. It was estimated that there were about 100 elephants in the park during the period we were there. Due to the annual drought, Yala cannot carry a large resident population of elephants.

On the banks of a shimmering lagoon whose mouth was separated from the ocean by a line of dunes, we saw a big herd of axis deer. Most graceful of the ungulates, the axis, or spotted deer, is a joy to watch. Lying on the sand of a nearby island was a sight no less spectacular—the biggest crocodile I have ever seen in Ceylon. Through the glasses it looked to be more than fifteen feet. My driver, a city boy, blanched and almost stalled the car, but I have never heard of a case in Ceylon of a fresh-water crocodile attacking a human being. In fact, the village boys swim among them.

Birds of prey are among the handsomest of the park's feathered population. We photographed a crested eagle on a dead branch and caught a fish eagle on the wing. According to some authorities these eagles may, under certain conditions, utter cries that local superstition ascribes to the devilbird. While the majority of the island's most experienced birdmen think that the devilbird is the forest eagle owl, no one knows for sure.

The legend behind it all is this: A poor family, so it goes, had no food, and the husband, in a fit of hunger and anger, killed his son and gave the meat to his wife to cook. The woman, recognizing her son's remains, rushed shrieking from the house crying, "My son, my son!" In her desperation she stabbed a spoon into her head. The jungle gods then turned her into a bird and the spoon into a crest. The devilbird is said to have a cry which resembles that of a woman in agony. Those who hear it die soon, according to the legend. A reality nearly as horrible as the folklore is the native's occasional practice of catching a loris, the little big-eyed denizen of the deep jungles, and then holding it over a slow fire until it cries. The tears are said to be a sure cure for a variety of unlikely diseases.

Adding up the birds and animals seen in Yala in four treks in the jungle, two in the early morning and two in the late evening, I was very much impressed with the variety of game and other wildlife encompassed in the park's relatively small area. We saw all of Ceylon's major animals except bear. The actual count came to sixteen elephants, fourteen sambur deer, at least 100 axis deer, five pigs, three mongooses, six jackals, two tala-goya, or large monitor lizards, two crocodiles, perhaps 250 wild buffalo and two families of wanderoo, or langur, monkeys. The birds—too numerous to count—included the relatively rare painted stork, hornbills, brown-headed gulls, red-wattled lapwings, black-headed orioles, weaver-birds, and a host of others.

Almost completely lacking in minerals and with her tea- and rubber-producing areas virtually all under cultivation, Ceylon has only one important source of foreign exchange left—tourism. And tourists love wildlife. Few people would go to most countries in Africa, for example, except to watch the game animals. However, before Ceylon can exploit her tourist trade she must build a first-class hotel at Colombo. Nothing gives the tourist a poorer impression of a nation than an antiquated or rundown leading hotel. Assuming, however, that the eager tourist is willing to overlook the rickety bathroom fixtures and indifferent food of the capital, he does expect clean quarters and plain but wholesome fare in the country. At the present time these facilities are limited. Compared with 1952-55, when I stayed at virtually every resthouse in Ceylon, the amenities of these hostelries have, if anything, declined. Although the bungalows in the parks were better, they were still far below the standards of the parks in many of Africa's poorest countries. Fortunately, the government of Ceylon was well aware of these shortcomings, and negotiations were under way for a new hotel in Colombo.

We left Yala in the late afternoon and drove to Norris' tea estate, a mile high in the mountains at Naumunukula. The road, fairly good in 1955, was in bad shape. But saddest of all was the country it runs through. In place of miles of virgin jungle there stretched a strip of virtual wasteland. The incredibly desolating process of cutting the timber, burning it, sowing one crop, and moving on had laid its bleak hand on the land. The Ceylon peasants, with no money to buy fertilizer, have no alternative; yet they are ruining their country. We drove in silence past the ramshackle huts, the stark skeletons of once beautiful satinwood trees, and the weed-choked fields.

Few men in Ceylon have devoted as much time to conservation as Ted Norris. In his study was a huge inch-to-the-mile map of Yala. On it he had indicated the water holes, an analysis of the various soils, and the types of grasses. The only map of its kind in Ceylon, it is of great value to the team of scientists who are doing the elephant survey for the Smithsonian. Two other good friends of Ceylonese conservation who deserve mention here are W.W.A. Phillips, a retired tea planter, and Derrick Nugawela.

As shooting was virtually banned under the two Bandaranaike governments, many sportsmen turned to fishing and discovered that the triumph over the monsters of the deep is just as exciting, with more edible rewards, than stalking the always elusive game. However, fish, like animals and birds, suffer from poachers. Dynamiting is not only an easy way to kill fish but a terribly wasteful one. For thousands of small and useful fish are also killed, while only a small proportion of those large ones affected by the blast die immediately and come to the surface. Luckily, the use of dynamite on a large scale was restricted to the Trincomalee side of the island; there was little of it used on the Colombo side. Virtually all the one-armed men one sees in Batticaloa and the other east-coast towns are dynamiters who did not let go of their sticks fast enough.

In the old days the rivers of Ceylon teemed with mahseer, the premier game fish of the Orient. Dynamiting and poisoning, however, have so decimated these fine sporting fish that today they have vanished from some rivers and can be found only in the wildest and least accessible stretches of others. The Mahaweli Ganga, the biggest river of the island, still has ten-pounders. The Amban Ganga might also hold some mahseer, but the Heen Ganga and the Gal Oya are no longer worth fishing. The lula, a fish which looks like a catfish without whiskers and provides good sport on light tackle in the rivers, has also been sadly depleted. Even the walaya, a variety of fresh-water shark whose flesh is barely edible, is growing scarcer.

Laws do exist against poisoning and dynamiting. Yet it is extremely difficult to catch the culprits. Moreover, the fines are nominal. Another factor that hardly militates against illegal killing is the attitude of many of the local magistrates, who sometimes regard the culprits as voters rather than poachers.

I am pleased to hear that since I left Ceylon—where my visit had been made much smoother thanks to the offices of the Duke of Edinburgh and our ambassador, Cecil Lyon—many rare and seldom seen species of wildlife have finally been granted legal protection. These include the dugong, which is under great pressure by Moslem fishermen who prize the flesh because it tastes like pork, which good Mussulmen are prohibited from eating. In appearance the dugong, an aquatic animal related to the manatee, looks somewhat like a mermaid. When seen through a few fathoms of water, the females might well be taken by less finicky sailors for something quite desirable. Stupid and slow, these 200-pound weed-feeders get caught in the fishing nets and make no effort to escape. In 1953 I found one of these poor creatures in a tank in Manaar and saved it from being carved up by having it towed out to sea and released. The new laws will prohibit the sale of dugong meat.

The leathery turtle is in bad shape owing mainly to the villagers' practice of digging up its eggs after the turtle lays them in the sand. Wild pigs also dig up these eggs. Hence the only way to preserve this increasingly rare species is to patrol the laying beaches. The new ordinance, which also protects the swamp and estuary crocodiles, proclaims that they can be shot only on license. The salt-water crocodile occasionally becomes a man-eater, but I have never heard of a fresh-water crocodile being a menace. In fact, I have swum in pools with them in the Mahaweli Ganga, the great river of Ceylon.

The fishing cat, the pangolin, the loris, and the flying squirrel will get absolute protection, while the Ceylon bear and leopard can be shot only on special licenses. Since these are very seldom issued now, both these splendid animals may have a chance to recover their numbers. Because of their poor eyes, bears will occasionally attack and badly maul a human being. There are also a few cases of man-eating leopards. But the wholesale killing of the bear for "sport" by waiting for them at night over water holes will be stopped. In addition, the sale and export of leopard skins has been banned. So there is now a good chance that many of the interesting fauna of the island will be preserved for the enjoyment of future generations.

THE GREAT INDIAN RHINO

Our next great geographical leap took us to the town of Shillong, more than a mile up in the highlands of Assam. In the pine forests above it lies the home of the late E.P. Gee, one of India's best-known conservationists. Below, the rolling green hills fall away to the waters of Lake Barapani and the thin silver pencil of the Brahmaputra River, while on clear days one can see the distant peaks of Bhutan and, far beyond, the gleaming snow mountains that mark the border of Tibet. Many rise to more than 21,000 feet. Nyegyi Kangtang, or Snow Country of Delight, which towers to 23,120 feet, has never been climbed.

Born in England, Gee came to India in 1927 to become a tea planter in Assam. After retiring in 1959, he decided to make his home at Shillong in order to continue his work for the conservation of rare species of both flora and fauna. India subsequently gave him numerous appointments in the wildlife field, appointing him a member of the Indian Board for wildlife in 1952, the senior conservation agency in the nation.

Of the many studies of mammals Gee undertook, one of the most fascinating concerned the Indian wild ass, which lives in the Little Rann of Kutch. A vast salty wasteland occupying more than 1,000 square miles on the west coast, the area is one of the most desolate in India.

A handsome zebra-like creature, the Indian wild ass stands eleven to

Indian wild ass on the Little Rann of Kutch   (PHOTO E. P. GEE)

twelve hands. It has a bright yellowish color with a short mane of dark chestnut and a line of the same color extending down the back to the root of the tail. The lower parts are white. Although the inhabitants of the Rann don't harm them, the asses, which Gee estimated at about 900 head in 1962, are susceptible to various diseases, including surra (caused by a blood-infecting parasite) and South African horse sickness. Wolves, which used to prey on the herds, have become so rare that they are no longer a factor. As a result of Gee's recommendations, the Indian wild ass has been officially placed on the list of fully protected animals by the Gujarat State Government.

Another specialty of Gee's was the great Indian one-horned rhinoceros. Having studied the rhinos in Nepal, Bengal, and Assam, Gee was a leading figure in the drive to save these magnificent beasts from extinction. The high prices paid by the Chinese druggists for rhino horn make poaching most attractive. Despite the fact that possession or sale of horns in India is illegal, an underground trade route extends to the Far East via Calcutta. Although the internal use of powdered rhino horn has been pretty well disproved as a stimulant for men's sex glands, there are still

23

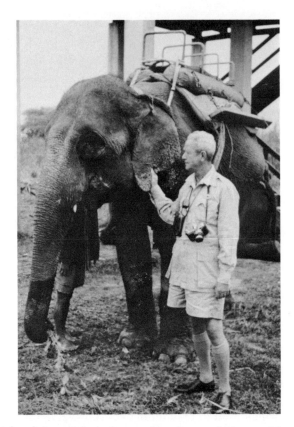

The author in
Kaziranga Sanctuary

those who believe that in ointment form it may be of some help to old men. For this reason, the rhino will always be in danger.

Gee told Adrian Middleton and me something about the Kaziranga Sanctuary to which we were to go. Situated on the southern bank of the Brahmaputra River, the preserve contains 166 square miles. Most important, it is one of the few areas in the world where the great Indian rhino still survives. At the end of the last century there were said to be only about a dozen left, but careful conservation has since built the population up to about 400.

Gee had steeped himself in the mystique surrounding the rhino horn and the beast. Besides its supposed sexual value, according to Gee, the horn is believed to help women at the time of childbirth. Whoever owns one has little trouble renting it for large sums to expectant mothers to keep under their beds. Others believe that if a rhino horn is left to soak, the water takes on elixir qualities that prolong life. Even stranger is the theory that rhino urine is a potent medicine—here the cure may be worse than the cough.

Gee also explained that in the old days the rhinos, unaccustomed to seeing visitors, often charged. Unlike the African black rhinos, which attack with their horns, the Indian species uses its tusks, then bites the victim with an upward thrust of the head. Since both the elephant and tiger are afraid of the rhino, a good case could be made to appoint him the King of Beasts. Gee tells of a hunter in 1886 who wounded a rhino and followed it up the next day. The blood spoor led to the badly hurt animal, which had subsequently been attacked by two tigers but, nevertheless, was succeeding in fighting them off. The "sportsman" missed the two tigers, though he did manage to shoot the poor rhino.

From Shillong, high in the Khasi Hills, to Kaziranga, down on the south bank of the Brahmaputra River, is a matter of some 200 miles—in all, a long day's drive but a very rewarding one. Spring had arrived in Assam, the scarlet blooms of the Indian coral tree vying with the even more vivid reds of the flame-of-the-woods. Adjutant storks gravely surveyed the paddy fields, pied harriers soared in a blue sky; wagtails, drongos and gray-headed mynas chattered in the bamboo thickets. Just as colorful were the tribal people we passed on the road: the Khasi, whose girls are lovely and whose men are lazy and henpecked; the Mikirs, who are great fishermen, and many others hard to identify among the more than fifty tribes of Assam.

We encountered many soldiers along the way, and also passed a group of Nagas, the sturdy hill people whom I remembered from the war.

Just as evening fell we arrived at the Government Guest House at Kaziranga. Over well-earned gins that night, E. P. Gee told us more about the great Indian one-horned rhinoceros, for which the Kaziranga Sanctuary was primarily established. Rhinos, according to Gee, get under one's skin. He recalled that during the war when he was serving in the Arakan an order was given warning the patrols not only to be on the lookout for the huge beasts but to report the number seen to headquarters. The commanding officer was a conservationist and wanted the facts.

Later we were joined by P. Barua, chief conservator of the forests of Assam, who gave us some grim details as to how rhinos are poached in the sanctuary. The process does not depend on guns. The criminals drift down the Brahmaputra River in skiffs, land at night, and dig a pit in a rhino trail. Sooner or later one of the great beasts falls into it. The poachers then quickly spear the beast to death, hack off the horn, bury the carcass, and depart.

The economics of horn hunting are impressive. The average black market price for a kilogram of horn is 10,000 rupees, or about 5,000 rupees ($1,000) per pound. The market is in Calcutta, where the agents for the Chinese pharmacists, the real culprits, have their offices. Occasionally the law catches up with them. Barua told us of the case of an air-line office clerk in Calcutta who noticed a strong smell coming from a package, which when opened was found to contain three fresh rhino horns. A check disclosed that both the sender's address and the address to which it was consigned were fictitious. However, the invoice marks were clear. By checking everyone who had dispatched packages on that date from that part of Assam, investigators were able to find the criminal. Barua also added to the list of health superstitions making the horns so precious. It seems, he said, that many Indians wear a rhino-horn ring on their left hands as a guard against piles.

According to Gee, the rhino's only other enemy besides man is the tiger, a pair of which occasionally attacks a mother and her calf. One tiger provokes the mother's charge while the other dashes in and kills the offspring.

Kaziranga Sanctuary, which is about twenty-five miles long, consists mainly of fifteen-foot-high elephant grass interspersed with open meadows that are more or less swampy, numerous small *bheels*, or ponds, and sluggish streams. The borders of the park are the Brahmaputra River and the main road from Gauhati to Jorhat. Soon after we set out on our trip, a brace of wild pigs *(Sua scrofa)* broke cover and charged away into the dense grass. Few animals show greater courage and determination to survive than the wild pig. When all other wildlife has gone from India, I bet the ubiquitous "soor" will still be around.

My first view of the great Indian one-horned rhinoceros *(Rhinoceros*

Indian One-Horned Rhino at Kazaringa   (PHOTO E. P. GEE)

unicornis) was as dramatic as it was exciting. We had just been in very high, dense elephant grass, so thick that even our elephants had to force their way, and had emerged into a small open plain when I saw what I thought was a brown hump of land with several egrets sitting on it. The land moved—and there was a rhino! Unlike the African rhino, whose skin is more or less smooth, the Indian species has "armor plates" giving it the appearance of some weird primeval monster that should have vanished from the earth with the ice ages. Some experts believe that the Indian rhino is larger than the African white rhino. The massive protective plates certainly give this impression. Gee told me that these plates are much less tough than they appear to be, for the rhinos bleed freely when bruised. This rhino showed massive scars from fighting with another bull. Apparently used to visitors, however, the great brute stood placidly while I photographed him. I was just as glad then that I was on an elephant.

Farther on in an open meadow we came on a magnificent herd of wild

Tiger on the prowl   (PHOTO E. P. GEE)

buffalo *(Bubalus bubalis)*. Although looking like domestic buffalo, *"arna,"* as the Indians call him, has a much finer carriage, is heavier, and infinitely braver. Against a big bull, even a tiger has little chance. Except for man and some of the big cats, the buffalo has no enemies. Both the males and cows with calves are apt to charge, so we did not go too near even with the elephants. Gee explained that the riding elephants are not always staunch to the charge of a rhino or a buffalo because of the vulnerability of their trunks.

An amusing example of the timidity of our huge mounts occurred soon afterward. We heard a scurrying in the undergrowth, and half a dozen little brown animals shot out from the cover. Squealing, our elephant, Joytara, did her best to wheel about and make off. After the mahout brought her under control with his iron ankus, he laughingly told Gee that she was afraid that the "ud," or otters, were young tigers.

Tigers *(Panthera tigris)* do inhabit Kaziranga but are seldom seen. However, in the wet clay by the side of *bheel* we spotted the pug mark of a female. Leopards *(Panthera pardus)* are seen even less frequently than tigers. So thick is the elephant grass that a fleet of great cats could hide in it indefinitely. One of the few ways to push tigers out of this formidable vegetation is to drive a herd of domestic buffalo through it.

Although we saw a total of sixteen rhinos during our two-hour trek, none of them, according to Gee, were really mature animals. In only one case was the horn developed to more than six inches. Gee thought that the total population of the great Indian one-horned rhino was only about 725—185 in Nepal, 65 in Bengal, and 475 in Assam. The two African species, on the other hand, are in less danger. Several years ago I was told by the chief warden of South Africa that he estimated the black rhinos of the continent to be in the vicinity of 12,000 and the white at 4,000.

A curious habit of rhinos is to deposit their dung at a fixed place, making it easy for the poacher to wait for them at the "toilet." However, Gee does not believe that these dung heaps indicate "territories," as might be the case for many species. Old rhino bulls "retire" to the open paddy fields on the edges of the sanctuary where they are relatively safe from the young bulls, who like nothing better than a fight with an inferior. Gee thought that one of the reasons why the rhino almost became extinct was its foolhardy nature. Almost all big animals run at the appearance of man, but the rhino charges. Since the invention of gunpowder, he has, of course, had little chance.

While rhinos are strictly preserved in India, they can still be shot in Nepal with special permission from the king, and I was shocked to hear that a maharaja of Gwalior had secured permission and killed a rhino in the Rapti Valley. His purpose was not even sporting. Some Hindus believe that if a man slits open the stomach of a rhino and crawls in while the carcass is still warm, his departed parents will go straight to heaven.

Kaziranga exports rhinos to zoos, getting 50,000 rupees, or about $10,000, for a mature animal. A rhino cow takes sixteen and one-fourth months to produce her calf as against eighteen and one-half to nineteen and one-half for an elephant. Elephants very occasionally have twins, while rhinos have never been known to produce them. Nevertheless, Gee once saw a pair of rhino calves—with a single cow—which he thinks may have been twins. As for longevity, it is thought that the rhino's life span is about the same as an elephant's, or about seventy years. On the matter of size, Gee had been measuring Perboti, a young female elephant, since she was born and had a set of growth-rate records for the past sixteen years. The mother, named Deckali, was fathered by a wild tusker from the herds which spend part of each year in the sanctuary.

The southern border of the Kaziranga Rhino Sanctuary is marked by the Mikir Hills. In the evening, when the sun is setting, the forested peaks turn deep purple, standing out starkly against the blood-red sky. These hills abound in legends, and no one knew them better than E.P. Gee, who has guided many people around Kaziranga, including such charming conservationists as Peter and Phillipa Scott. As our elephant chose his silent way among the muddy trails, Gee turned on the pad beside me to tell me the tale of the man-eating tiger of the Mikir Hills.

The lowlands at the foot of the Mikir Hills are heavily planted in tea, which must be picked by hand; hence there is always a large population of laborers working in the gardens. Just before the war, a man-eater began to haunt the hills, preying on these laborers. In the beginning, the local planters tried to get him; later, army officers came from far places to try their luck, and the Government and the India Tea Association posted a large reward. Baits were poisoned, blinds were built, and hunters sat up over human corpses—all to no avail. The man-eater, whose pug was so well known that plaster casts of it were widely circulated, defied them all. By the end of the first year the death toll was fifty people. At the end of the fifth year it had risen to over 300. The tiger, for it was an old male, covered an area of about 500 square miles. Rarely did he return to the kill for a second feed. Accurate information concerning its whereabouts was hard to get for still another reason. The Mikir tribes, being extremely superstitious, firmly believed that anyone giving information about the man-eater would be the next victim.

One night a Babu, a Bengali clerk, sat up over a dead cat with his newly obtained gun and fired at a shadow. In the morning, unaware that he had actually hit anything during his vigil, the clerk found a dead tiger nearby and duly reported the fact to the superintendent of the tea estate where he worked. The superintendent, who happened to have the cast of the man-eater's front paw in his office, took it along when he went to see the carcass. To his amazement the dead tiger was the man-eater. Sad to say, the Babu, convulsed with fear when he heard of his feat, went quite mad and ended his days in a lunatic asylum.

Back at the elephant lines as we watched the feeding, Gee shared another story, that of a bull whose mahout was dishonest and stole his food. The elephant put up with this as long as possible, but finally his patience gave out. He chased the crooked mahout across the parade ground to the hut where he lived, smashed down the hut, and killed the man by goring him to death with his tusks. The official inquiry disclosed not only that the mahout had indeed been stealing the elephant's food but that the bull was just about to go into must and was therefore in an exceptionally nervous state. The elephant was acquitted and continued to serve the sanctuary. Another tale less easy to swallow was Gee's account of the man who pulled a thorn from the foot of an elephant when it was being trained. One day years later this same man was sitting in the cheap seats of a small circus when to his amazement he recognized the elephant for whom he had done the good deed many years before. The elephant also recognized him and, reaching over with his trunk, took the man up gently, transporting him from the cheap seats to the best box.

We went out three times on riding elephants during our stay at Kaziranga and spent one of our three days there driving through another sector of the sanctuary. On the basis of these trips and my talks with the sanctuary's staff, I was able to get a pretty fair idea of the park's layout and the men who ran it. In the first place, Kaziranga's legal status as a wildlife reserve is highly vulnerable. In India, sanctuaries are created by an executive order and can just as easily be wiped out if the state government feels that the land would be more useful for cultivation. Kaziranga is much too well known for this to happen to it, but a change should be made in the law so that the reserve becomes a national park and thus "entrenched" by act of the state legislature. Gee hammered away on this important theme for years.

In addition, the staff should have uniforms to distinguish them from the locals and to improve their morale. The cost would be small. Besides, the other wildlife parks in India manage to outfit their men in distinctive garb. As to transport, there was only one vehicle for the whole sanctuary, an old truck. At least two Jeeps should be kept for the officer in charge of the sanctuary. The one fair-weather road in the park is a north-south dirt track usable for only four months in the year during the dry weather. This road should be made all-weather, and an east-west road added. Such roads would be useful in controlling poaching as well as getting visitors out quickly in case of accident.

Summing up, I think that Kaziranga is one of the most interesting game parks in the world. Any help that we can give it in the form of aid through the Smithsonian Public Law 480 would be a very good investment indeed. Funds for the purchase of at least two Jeeps would be a good beginning, I feel, plus a few outboard motors to give the game guards some mobility on the Brahmaputra.

On the extreme northern border of the Indian state of Assam where the frontier marches along the jungle-clad mountains of Bhutan there lies the seldom-visited Manas Wildlife Sanctuary. Only during the four dry months can a car reach the base camp. The 105-plus square miles of the sanctuary contain a variety of wildlife, including herds of wild elephant, ten to twenty rhinos, and numerous gaur, the largest of the bovines. Tiger and leopard prey on the sambur, barking deer, and hog-deer. Because all of these animals wander back and forth across the border, it is of great importance that protection be afforded them in Bhutan as well as Assam. Gee had discussed this at length with the king of Bhutan, who agreed in principle to the creation of a sanctuary on his side of the border of about the same size as the Manas reserve. One of our objectives in going to Manas was for me to see the layout so that I could discuss it with the King when we visited him in his capital of Thimbu in April.

The sanctuary takes its name from the Manas, a mighty river that rises in the perpetual snow mountains of Tibet and flows through Bhutan into Assam, where it eventually becomes one of the largest tributaries of the Brahmaputra. Running clear and blue over beds of golden gravel between jungle-clad banks, the Manas alternates between long deep pools and rapids with white water boiling over the boulders. In its depths swim mahseer, the premier game fish of Asia.

To try our luck against these "salmon of the Orient" we went upriver in the early morning of a hazy day in early March. On the way we saw a troupe of the rare and beautiful golden langurs which are found no place else in the world except between the Manas and Sankosh rivers on the

Mahseer caught on the Manas River in Assam, India

(PHOTO E. P. GEE)

E. P. Gee and the author

border of Bhutan and Assam. Although it carries the scientific name of *Presbytis geei* in honor of Mr. Gee, the golden langur was not actually first noticed by him, but by E. O. Shebbeare in 1907. Gee, however, was the first naturalist to photograph and study them.

A pale chestnut hue in winter, these handsome monkeys turn milky white in summer. This was their coloring when we found them in a grove of trees next to the camp being built on the bank of the Manas for the King. They will be safe in the area, but many of the larger animals may not be. For though the King was said to believe in sanctuaries, it is not certain that he applied to himself the law against shooting in them. This was a failing of many of the rulers and ex-rulers of India and the adjoining states. The King of Nepal shot in the parks of his country, while His Highness of Mysore could seldom resist a tiger even if it happened to be in one of Mysore's game refuges.

About a mile beyond the border where the river narrows we beached the boats on a rocky spit and started fishing. Here we found the skeleton of a sambar hind *(Cervus unicolor)* whose end had been a tragic one. According to our Assamese boatman, a pack of dholes, or Indian wild dogs *(Cuon alpinus)* had run her to exhaustion and then pulled her down just as she emerged from swimming the river. Hunting in silent packs with a tireless canter that they can sustain for hours, the dholes have been known to kill tiger. Kipling tells a vivid story of them in the *Jungle Books.*

Although the pool by the spit didn't yield any fish, all of us enjoyed the majesty of the river. Toward evening a flight of great hornbills sailed lazily up the gorge. With their enormous horn-shaped black-and-yellow bills, the hornbills look like a survival from another age. Their living habits are also reminiscent of the days of castles. Selecting a hole in a lofty tree, the female imprisons herself, using her bill to shore up the entrance with her droppings, which eventually harden like cement. Only a narrow slit is left through which her mate feeds her. When the young hatch, the hen breaks out. Then, after closing the entrance again so the young cannot get out, she helps her mate feed them.

With the fish on our minds again, Gee explained that mahseer are members of the barbus or carp family and come in all colors, including black, which he had taken. Some have thin and some thick lips, but all

Spotted-billed pelicans on nest   (PHOTO E. P. GEE)

have extremely hard mouths and can smash the average wire hook as if it were made of glass. Mahseer are covered with scales so large they are used for playing cards in some parts of India. Their fame as fighting fish is said to stem from the fact that they have more area of fin in proportion to their bodies than other game fish. Gee used Hardy's oval wire mahseer treble hooks, which are many times stronger than the strongest salmon hook.

Just in front of the camp, the Manas trifurcates into the Beki, the Hakua, and the stream that keeps the name of its parent. On our second day we took rubber boats and floated down the Hakua, fishing as we went. Our rods saw little action, but the banks held a variety of interesting wildlife. Huge buffalo—the Manas cows have the widest spread of horns in the world, and the record of eighty-two inches was shot here—were down at the river drinking. As soon as they saw or smelled us, however, they lumbered rapidly away, making considerable speed for such great beasts. Crocodiles, which Gee said used to lie like cordwood along the

3 5

Little Egret on Nest

(PHOTO E. P. GEE)

banks, have all gone, perhaps because of the poachers and perhaps because of increased traffic on the river due to construction of the King of Bhutan's camp.

It was not until noon at the junction where the Manas curves back and joins the Hakua that I finally caught a fish. Mahseer are finicky customers. We saw many, some like great submarines that lay dormant on the water and paid not the slightest attention to our spoons, and smaller active ones that darted away like silver bullets when they saw us. It is almost axiomatic that if you can see a mahseer it can see you and won't bite.

I was reeling in after a cast where the colder water of the deeper and faster-flowing Hakua is joined by the warmer stream of the shallower and slower Manas when the fish struck. It was no whale, but it gave me a five-minute battle in the swift current of the Hakua before I towed it in to the beach. The fish was a Himalayan golden mahseer weighing three and one-half pounds.

Later in the trip, the officials of the Manas Sanctuary reported to Gee that his efforts to stop the grazing of domestic buffalo in the sanctuary have been successful. One of the Manas officials also spoke of the possi-

Sambar Stag   (PHOTO E. P. GEE)

Indian Swamp Deer   (PHOTO E. P. GEE)

bility that the King might proclaim a sanctuary in Bhutan of 250 square miles instead of 100. If the reserved forest on the border of the present Manas Sanctuary could be included in this larger domain, the Assam-Bhutan Park would total 500 square miles.

Unfortunately, poaching continues to be a problem. The Bodo and Mech tribesmen come in on elephants after the rains when the grass is high and shoot the game. They have good shotguns, while at that time the forest guards had only a few old weapons. Since then, John Olin, former chairman of the Olin Mathieson Chemical Corporation and a member of the board of directors of the World Wildlife Fund, has presented the game guards of Kaziranga with some modern rifles. Fortunately, news of this kind reaches poachers fast. As late as 1965, however, one of the game guards was shot by poachers; but the judge fined the criminal only fifty rupees and four days in jail. The victim, who luckily recovered, was given a bonus of 100 rupees.

Like Kaziranga, Manas is a sanctuary with a legal status vulnerable to revocation. It should be made a national park possessing borders defined by an act of the Assam legislature.

38

SIKKIM AND BHUTAN

From Red China the shortest invasion route to India lies through the little Himalayan kingdom of Sikkim. When we drove up from Siliguri, the railhead in West Bengal, we passed convoy after convoy filled with Indian mountain troops on their way to meet the threat. Thanks to His Highness the Chogyal, or king of Sikkim, and to the government of India, which issued me and my party the necessary permits for this highly restricted area, we had no trouble at the various check points.

Gangtok, the capital, is built on a mountain that is flanked by the Roro and Rongni valleys. Here we first paid our respects to the Chogyal and Queen Hope at a luncheon given by their Highnesses for His Excellency, Vincent Herbert Coelho, the newly arrived Indian Political Agent for Sikkim and Bhutan. While the rulers of these two Himalayan states are sovereign, they have no armies to speak of and are completely dependent on India for defense, imports and access to the world. The Indian Political Agent, therefore, is the most powerful man in both countries.

Gyalsay Palden Thondup Namgyal is the Twelfth Consecrated Ruler of Sikkim with the title of Chogyal, or King. A young man in his thirties, he has the pleasant habit of giving his complete attention to whomever he talks with. The King, who speaks fluent English, has a broad interest in his country and its peoples. He told me he wanted to talk with both Gee and me about conservation and promised to set a time. The Queen, the former Hope Cooke, is a slender, attractive girl in her late twenties. Although she wore her hair bobbed and used eye shadow, she dressed in Sikkimese clothes.

Sandwiched between Nepal and Bhutan, Sikkim is smaller than either, with a total area of only 2,745 square miles and a population of about 170,000. The country consists almost entirely of mountains and deep valleys. Kanchenjunga, the Home of the Gods, towers to 28,808 feet, but climbers are not allowed to ascend the last twenty feet as they might disturb the deities. Down to 17,000 feet there is snow; from 12,000 to 9,000 feet, forest; and terraced cultivation below that.

Our primary purpose in going to Sikkim was to interest His Highness in establishing sanctuaries for the wildlife of his remote Himalayan kingdom. In its rugged mountains and deep valleys there still survive some rare and interesting animals, birds, and flowers. I was particularly pleased, therefore, when His Highness and Her Highness, Queen Hopela (the suffix "-la" is used for the first names of all ladies of distinction),

39

The author with Their Highnesses the Chogyal and Gyalmo of Sikkim

came for a private luncheon with us at the Palace Guest House expressly to discuss conservation.

The Chogyal began our talks by telling Gee, Middleton, and me that more than half of Sikkim is now legally a sanctuary in that all shooting, except in defense of livestock and crops, is prohibited. He added, however, that this means little because there are no wardens. Besides this, the Indian Army had shot and was shooting a great many head of game. Even so, he did not blame the commanding general, for who can police the many scattered outposts of a sergeant and a few men? Yet he said that at least fifty nyan *(Ovis ammon hodgsoni)*, the largest of all the wild sheep, have been shot by the Assam Rifles guarding the border or by the Red Chinese troops in Tibet.

The Chogyal asked Gee and me if we thought it would be feasible for him to drive the remaining sheep from the border area of northeast Sikkim to an area farther west and south. He said he has been assured of the support of the Indian Army in such a maneuver. Both Gee and I felt that the plan would not work. In the first place the terrain is such that great gaps would have to occur in the line of beaters. With an average altitude of 16,000 feet, much of the area is so precipitous that it would be impossible for men on foot to cover it. Also the beat could never be accomplished in a single day. Consequently the animals would be sure to slip back to their old haunts during the nights. Getting out a detailed map of Sikkim, which His Highness smilingly told us was classified as secret even though it was made thirty years ago, we traced the areas under consideration. The King had to agree that a drive would indeed be a major operation without any assurance of success.

The nyan are not the only wild sheep in Sikkim. In the central part of the country are found shapo, or urial *(Ovis orientalis)*, which are the smallest of the wild sheep. The Chogyal told us that when the great earthquake of 1954 occurred, a herd of shapo appeared on a mountain and warned the villagers of impending disaster by stamping their hooves and generally acting strangely. Fortunately, these sheep are safe in the area because they are protected by the Tolung Monastery, whose abbot has made it known that these sheep are particular favorites of the gods.

There are also bharal *(Pseudois nahoor)*, or blue sheep. Looking like a cross between a sheep and a goat, the bharal has rounded, smooth horns that curve backward over the neck. These sheep suffered badly at the hands of a German expedition in 1939. En route to Lhasa, the expedition stayed six months in central Sikkim and slaughtered great numbers of game, including the blue sheep. According to the Chogyal, some members of it tried to impress the Tibetans at Lhasa by drinking the blood of wild asses and serving bear steaks. The Tibetans were quite unmoved.

In addition to preservation of the sheep, we discussed with His Highness the necessity of protecting the snow leopard, musk deer, Himalayan black bear, brown bear, goral, tahr, red panda, and binturong in the areas where shooting is allowed. From N. M. Rasily, the conservator of forests, I got a copy of the game laws. They contained the startling fact that for the very nominal fee of thirty rupees ($6) one could get a license to shoot the following: one tiger, one bharal, one Tibetan gazelle, one serow, two goral, two barking deer and any number of bears, leopards, and pigs. When Gee offered to revise this list, the Chogyal said he would be glad to have him do it.

In the list of game birds that can be shot for the ridiculously small fee of fifteen rupees ($3) were included two kalij pheasants, four partridges, four blood pheasants, six luichey (wild fowl), six hare and twelve each of green and imperial pigeons. Those who wanted them could also account for twelve porcupines. With the ruler's permission, Gee also revised the small-game schedule.

Before the conversation shifted to other matters, Gee and I pressed His Highness to consider proclaiming two sanctuaries of at least 100 square miles each, one in the high altitudes for upland game and one at low altitudes for lowland fauna. He promised to give our suggestions serious thought. He added that the only such reserve now in his country is the twelve-acre deer park in Gangtok that we saw early in the day.

Sikkim is another of the fabled lands of the Abominable Snowman, but here it is not called a Yeti. Instead it is called the Meti. The Chogyal told us that the creture looks like a bear, has long hair of a dirty gray color, and resembles an old man. He did not say that he believed in the Meti; nor did he say he did not believe in it. He told us several tales of men who claim to have seen it and who died suddenly afterward. For some strange reason the Meti always throws logs of wood at the people who see him, and whistles while he does this. The Tibetans, on the other hand, say that the Yeti carries smooth round stones under its left armpit to hurl at people. In the upper Amazon jungle of Brazil I had heard an even more farfetched tale of a man-ape with a habit of throwing things at people. In this case, the missiles consisted of his own defecations.

Another semi-legendary animal of the highlands of Sikkim is the snow lion. Queen Hopela told me that it is white with greenish mane and tail. But she did not go so far as to say she had actually seen one.

In the days when there was a thriving trade with Tibet, the horns of deer in the soft stage of their annual development were exported to Lhasa, where the Chinese doctors used them as aphrodisiacs. Now that the border is closed, the deer have a better chance of keeping their horns. The two divisions of Indian troops then in Sikkim may have caused some havoc to the game, but they did stop this nasty trade.

On the other hand, I had many reports on the increasing scarcity of wildlife in Tibet. The wild yaks, wild asses, bharal, nyan, and shapo which used to delight the few western explorers who crossed the high passes have been systematically wiped out for food either by the Chinese Red Army or by the starving Tibetans.

On this mission I was greatly helped by letters of introduction by Ilia Tolstoy, an old China O.S.S. friend of mine.

As a guest of Her Majesty the Queen of Bhutan and her mother, the Rani Dorji, Gee, Middleton, and I spent a pleasant and interesting afternoon at Bhutan House in Kalimpong. My main objective here after leaving Sikkim was to urge the Queen to use her influence with the King to get him to go through with his plan to proclaim a 200-square-mile wildlife sanctuary which would be contiguous with the present Manas Sanctuary on the border of Assam and Bhutan. I had hoped to be able to persuade him myself, but I was strongly advised by a doctor not to attempt the two-day, high altitude Jeep trip to Thimbu, the capital of Bhutan, because of my health. Gee, however, agreed to make the trip, which was arranged for us by the King. I knew he would put over all our points. In addition to the reserve, it was important that His Majesty also be persuaded not to allow any shooting in the new sanctuary.

Although not the capital city, Kalimpong has strong ties with Bhutan as a whole. While there I reviewed my notes on this little-known kingdom whose present ruler, King Jigmi Dorji Wangchuck, kindly invited me and my companions to be state guests in his country. Perhaps the last of the "closed countries," Bhutan accepts no foreigners except those personally invited by the King. It was largely because of His Majesty's interest in wildlife and a letter on my behalf from the Duke of Edinburgh that I was invited to visit him.

Bounded on the west by Sikkim and on the east by India's Northeast Frontier Agency, Bhutan borders Red China on the north and India's states of West Bengal and Assam to the south. Few small nations are in such a strategic position. Unlike Sikkim, which is a protectorate of the Republic of India, Bhutan is sovereign in every respect except that of foreign affairs, which are handled through New Delhi. As a guardian of India's northern approaches, Bhutan receives a yearly subsidy of half a million rupees and the right of duty-free transport through India for her exports and imports. The chief crop is rice, which once went to Tibet and now goes to India.

As I realized earlier from my short trip in Bhutan on the Manas River, the terrain is almost devoid of flat places. Lofty ranges divided by deep, humid valleys make up the little country's 18,000 square miles. The elevation of the central valleys averages 8,000 feet. The only way to get around in most places is by the sturdy thirteen-hand horses known as tanghans.

The dominant race are the Bhotias of Tibetan origin. At one time there was considerable intermarriage between the Tibetan nobility and the ruling families of Bhutan. The name Bhutan is a contraction of the Indian name Bhotanta, meaning the end of Tibet. The dialect is Tibetan, and the Bhutanese are all Lamaistic Buddhists. Unlike the Sikkimese men, some of whom wear pigtails, the Bhutanese men and women have cropped hair. Tall and muscular, they are called "Druk-pa," or "thunder people." Despite the name, however, they possess a good sense of humor. Perhaps this helps the women carry loads of eighty pounds. The men wear loose knee-length robes bound at the waist by a sash, a costume that very much resembles the "dels" worn by the men and women of Mongolia. Every man also regularly carries a knife called a "dossum." On a ceremonial visit it is the custom to carry a sword, or "pathong." Without his sword and a shawl to show his rank, a Bhutanese cannot take part in public life.

The government of Bhutan is conducted largely by the king, whose vernacular title is "Precious Ruler of the Dragon people." Far from an oriental dictator, the King abolished slavery, emancipated women, and encouraged the formation of a national assembly of 130 members. His Majesty, however, reserves the right to veto unwise laws and impose the death sentence.

Living in Bhutan is none too healthy, owing to the reluctance of the Buddhist population to kill flies. Dysentery is virtually endemic. Some of the medicine is also a bit primitive. Persons bitten by rabid dogs are treated by a concoction of leopard's milk. Leeches abound in the damp valleys, but the application of salt or tobacco has a discouraging effect on them.

Relations between the sexes in Bhutan are almost poetically frank. The men shout from the hilltops, "Women, prepare, I am the lord of the mountain and I own the sun. Your valley is mine." "But are you a man?" yells back the practical girl.

Because my health precluded my going into the exceptional altitudes of Bhutan's interior, Gee made this trip soon after I left India. Meanwhile, I turned back to Calcutta.

The stress of our schedule subsequently forced me to cancel the balance of my mission. I was unable to keep appointments with the President of India, the Kings of Nepal and Bhutan, and with His Holiness, the Dalai Lama. I did, however, complete my work in Ceylon, Assam, and

Sikkim, having gotten a pretty fair idea of how conservation is going in general from my visits to two of India's great sanctuaries. Most important, I traveled the entire time in India with the late E.P. Gee, the acknowledged authority on wildlife in the subcontinent.

India's problems are many, with inevitable consequences for the nation's wildlife, to say nothing of the plight of her people. Threatened by Pakistan and Red China on her northern borders and at that time suffering from one of her worst droughts in history, India's 500 million inhabitants are twenty-five percent short of their bedrock nutritional requirements. Each year the population increases by twelve million mouths, more than the equivalent of adding a New York City every twelve months. Yet the Indian peasant produces only a third as much rice as the Japanese farmer on the same acreage, and only half as much as the Chinese. Although there is no market for cattle—Hindus can't kill or eat them—India has 202 million head, the largest bovine population in the world. Ironically, the untouchables are often the best fed as they can eat anything, including rats, while the orthodox Hindu cannot even eat eggs. Poverty is all-pervasive, for India, the second most populous nation on earth, contains 14 percent of the world's population but has only 2.2 percent of its land area.

Pressure on the land increases with the surging population. The few remaining uncultivated areas are diminishing yearly. Even the sanctuaries are suffering from the inroads of domestic herds. In both the Kaziranga and Manas sanctuaries in Assam, I saw numbers of cattle eating down the grass that should have been saved for the Asiatic rhinos, buffalo, and deer of the preserves. Poaching, stimulated by the immense rewards for rhino horn, takes a steady toll of these great and rare beasts. In some of the Indian sanctuaries timber cutting, which destroys the habitat for many forms of wildlife, is permitted.

An eloquent exponent of saving Indian wildlife, Gee pointed out that there are four basic reasons why conservation must be improved everywhere before it is too late. Primarily, he felt that man had no right to extinguish a species simply for sport or profit. Second, wildlife is the raw material of biological science; without nature's basic and diverse elements to work with, the biologists would have no laboratory. Third, the world would lose incalculable aesthetic values if we should allow the birds and animals to vanish from the earth. Finally, there is the undeniable economic importance of wildlife for tourism. Some East African nations make most of their much-needed foreign exchange from people who come to see their wildlife. India could vastly increase her earnings from this source if, for example, the accommodations in the sanctuaries were improved.

Gee also felt strongly about the legal position of India's sanctuaries. Like those of Ceylon, India's wildlife preserves have been set up by executive decisions but have never been "entrenched" by being upgraded to the status of "national parks" by acts of the state legislatures. Although I was pleased to hear that efforts to get the parks of Ceylon ratified by parliament were meeting with some success, many of India's wildlife reserves do not have this protection.

The legal position of wildlife reserves in the three Himalayan states of Nepal, Sikkim, and Bhutan is different in that all three are ruled by sovereigns whose decisions do not have to be approved by any existing advisory bodies. Nepal already has a wildlife reserve in the Terai. As a result of the talks Gee and I had with His Highness the Chogyal of Sikkim, there is a good possibility that a sanctuary will be proclaimed in northern Sikkim, too. I also had a long talk with the Queen of Bhutan about a park in her country which would be contiguous with the existing Manas Sanctuary in Assam.

Tibet is the domicile of a number of rare and interesting animals. The chiru, or Tibetan antelope *(Pantholops hodgsoni)*, has long slender horns which, seen in profile, give the male the appearance of a unicorn. The chiru also has a swollen snout, perhaps to enable it to breathe easier in the high altitudes of the great desert of northern Tibet. The bharal, with goat- and sheep-like features, roams the high mountains of Tibet at the 16,000-foot levels. Its color is brownish gray suffused with slate blue. The nyan also inhabits the plateau of Tibet. The largest of all wild sheep, it stands up to four feet at the shoulder, the record set of horns measuring fifty-seven inches in length. The adult rams wear a great black ruff on their chins. Tibet is also the home of the wild yak *(Bos grunniens)*, which inhabits the desolate wastes up to 20,000 feet.

Since the invasion of Tibet by Red China in 1950, disturbing reports have been filtering out, of the killing of great numbers of Tibetan wildlife by detachments of the occupation army as well as by the local population, many of whom are starving as a result of Red Chinese oppression.

Before the Chinese invasion, many Tibetans owned flocks of sheep, yaks, and cattle. In 1959, however, the Communist governor at Lhasa ordered the registration of all domestic herds. Two years later he issued a law forbidding the Tibetans to sell their livestock to anyone but the Red Army. Those who did not comply were imprisoned and often executed.

While accurate military information is difficult to get, the consensus among the best-informed refugees was that the Red Army in Tibet consisted of about 300,000 regular troops, most of whom are stationed on the borders of Sikkim, Bhutan, Nepal, and the Northeast Frontier Agency of India. Since the border areas are almost all high among the haunts of the wild sheep, antelope, and yak, it is not surprising that the troops pick off wild mutton and venison whenever they can. Despite the success of the Peking Zoo in breeding giant pandas in captivity, no effort is being made to save the wildlife of Tibet from almost certain extinction.

Since most of the wild animals of Tibet occasionally cross the borders into Sikkim, Bhutan, and Nepal, it is now doubly important that they be given sanctuary in these little nations. I discussed this at length with the Chogyal of Sikkim and outlined the urgency of the situation in letters to the rulers of Nepal and Bhutan.

While my health did not allow me to visit the gir lions in Gujarat State, I learned from Gee and others that this famous sanctuary for the last of the Asiatic lions is getting along well, with a 1966 population of about 280. Another park that I had hoped to visit was the Corbett National Park in northern Uttar Pradesh. I had called on Jim Corbett, the famous naturalist and author of the classic *Man-eaters of Kumaon,* when I was in India in 1935 about the time the park was being laid out.

Since leaving the Indian subcontinent in 1966, I have had several most encouraging follow-up reports about the progress of conservation there. In February, 1967, I received a letter from the Queen of Bhutan saying that her husband had proclaimed three parks, one in the South adjoining an existing park, and two in the North. In June, 1967, Gee wrote me that he had recently returned from another trip to Bhutan during which he had several long talks with the King. The King told him that the newly proclaimed Laya Sanctuary in the extreme north of Bhutan, near the Tibetan border, holds takin, blue sheep, and snow leopard.

PART 2

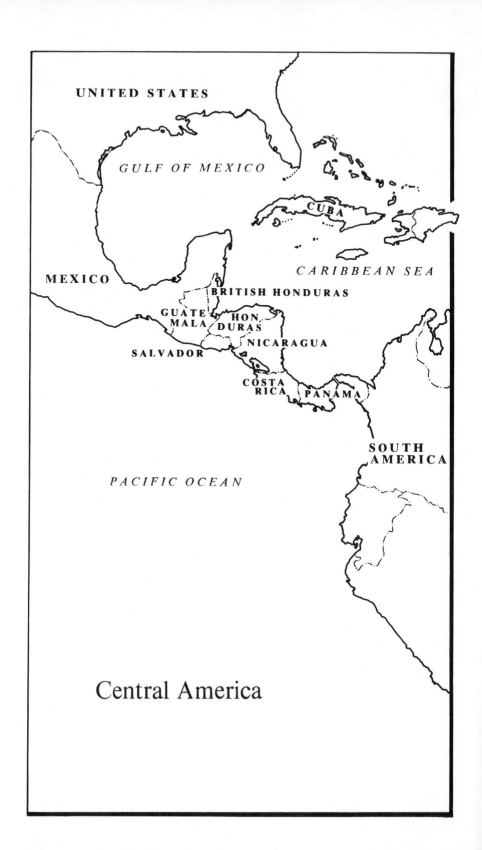

UNITED STATES

GULF OF MEXICO

CUBA

CARIBBEAN SEA

MEXICO

BRITISH HONDURAS

GUATE-
MALA
HON-
DURAS

NICARAGUA

SALVADOR

COSTA
RICA
PANAMA

SOUTH
AMERICA

PACIFIC OCEAN

Central America

CHAPTER III

Papa Doc
and the Peripatus

The journeys that my wife Irene and I have taken on behalf of wildlife during the past four years have been primarily by air. Only for the trips from Yokohama to the Siberian port of Nahodhka, and from Montevideo to the Falkland Islands far down in the South Atlantic, have we been on shipboard—and then only because there was no other way to get there. On the present mission, however, we were not confined to tossing freighters on storm-swept oceans as was the case on those two voyages. This time we embarked on the comfortable and stable Santa Maria of the Grace Line and sailed down the calm, sunny expanses of the Caribbean. Though our final destination was Cristobal in Panama, we stopped first at Port-au-Prince in Haiti, then at Cartagena in Colombia.

Discovered by Christopher Columbus in 1492, Haiti still beckoned the explorer in 1967. There is no gold to take away in galleons, but the country possesses some very rare animals whose survival is of great interest to zoologists and therefore to the World Wildlife Fund. Chief of these are: the Haitian solenodon, a ratlike creature with a nose that would be the envy of Jimmy Durante; the peripatus, a missing link between the worms and the centipedes, and, believe it or not, a wild horse. This, one well-known zoologist thinks, may be a survival from the original horses of the Americas, which have been extinct for millions of years.

Known in Haiti as the "zagouti," *Solenodon paradoxus* is a large rodent with a long cartilaginous snout and strong, curved claws for making dens and seeking food in Haiti's iron-hard earth. Except for a brother species in Cuba, its nearest relatives are in Madagascar and West Africa. It is of interest to science because it belongs to a group of insectivores that have survived from the early eras of life on earth. They are now extremely rare in both Haiti and neighboring Santo Domingo. In his amusing book, *Animal Treasure*, Dr. Ivan T. Sanderson tells about his work in the region of northern Haiti where the solenodon was reputed to live. However, he found only a single specimen—and that one very dead.

One of the reasons for the rarity of this little creature is probably the result of unfortunate publicity in the newspapers. It seems that several solenodons were caught and presented to Señor Trujillo, the dictator of Santo Domingo, who took one look at them and forwarded them to Mayor La Guardia in New York. His Honor did not fancy keeping them at Gracie Mansion, so he in turn presented them to the zoo, where they were duly displayed as rare and valuable exhibits. One paper—probably because of a slip of the Linotype—said they were worth $10,000 each. The real price in Santo Domingo, however, was only ten dollars, but the effect on the solenodon population can well be imagined.

The peripatus, the zoologists explain, is a descendant of the type of animal that evolved after the marine worms emerged from the sea and began living on land. Wine red in color and fitted with multiple little legs, its only defense is to eject a white sticky fluid.

But to me the most intriguing—if improbable—discovery was Dr. Sanderson's report that he found a herd of "wild horses" in the pine forests at the northern end of the island. He described them as a "silvered pinkish fawn with dark chocolate brown ears, manes, and tails." He added that they were considerably larger than the ponies one sees everywhere on Haiti, and looked very much like the Greek horses on ancient pottery, with stand-up manes and arched necks. When he asked about these horses, he learned that the locals feared them, claiming they attacked ordinary horses on sight.

Although it is scientifically accepted that the only horses in the new world since prehistoric times are the feral descendants of the horses brought in by the Spaniards, Dr. Sanderson advances the theory that there just might still be pockets of truly indigenous horses that have survived. He bases this on pre-Columbian rock drawings of horses found in the central plateau of Haiti and on the similarity of these horses to the wild horse of central Asia. He evidently thinks that there is a possible connection between the Przewalski of Mongolia, which I reported on in *The Empty Ark,* and the local herds of Haiti. It seems to me that if this were so, the world would have heard about it by now. But the idea is nevertheless a fascinating one.

Along with our traveling companions, Ambassador and Mrs. Ellis Briggs, we were particularly anxious to ask about these rare animals in Port-au-Prince. Although the Briggses had spent two years in Santo Domingo, during which time the ambassador covered virtually all of Trujillo's domains and much of Haiti as well, he had never heard of the wild horses. He was familiar with the name "agouti," but thought it referred to the paca, a piglike animal quite unrelated to the solenodon.

We know from Glover M. Allen's *Extinct and Vanishing Mammals of the Western Hemisphere* that the solenodon was first described by the Russian zoologist Brandt in the 1840's. It was thought to be extinct until 1907, when A. H. Verrill found it surviving in very limited numbers. Today the scientist most interested in the solenodon is Dr. John F. Eisenberg, of the National Zoological Park of the Smithsonian Institution in Washington. He believes that the species is in danger of extinction because of the destruction of its habitat, killing by man and animal, and a very low rate of reproduction. The Smithsonian plans to trap some solenodons and breed them in captivity in the National Zoo.

So it was that we greeted my old friend, Lane Timmons, United States Ambassador to Haiti, with many scientific questions. He very kindly came to the ship to welcome Ambassador Briggs and me and entertained us while we were ashore at Port-au-Prince.

The capital of François Duvalier's domain is about as rundown as possible, and his long-suffering people, even though they call him "Papa Doc," must in secret have other names for Haiti's self-proclaimed lifetime president. Most cities have certain smells, and some of them are not particularly pleasant, but some are worse than others. Port-au-Prince compared unfavorably with many of the old walled cities of China. The terrible overcrowding undoubtedly has a good deal to do with this. Today there are some five million Haitians jammed into half the space available for only three million Dominicans next door. Furthermore, the density rises yearly, as Haiti has one of the highest birth rates in the Western Hemisphere. Ninety percent of the Haitians live in abject poverty, many apparently on the verge of starvation. The individual gross national product is just sixty-seven dollars, the lowest in all the Americas. In a long drive about the city we did not see a single dog.

The better classes also have a rough time of it. There is no phone service, even for the foreign embassies. Communication is by privately owned walkie-talkies. The roads are appalling. Six months earlier a water main had burst near the Argentine Embassy. The road was still under several feet of water. There are no zoos, no parks, and no game laws. If it can be eaten—it usually is. One of the last flocks of flamingos was exterminated by a local "sportsman," who later complained that the birds were not very good eating.

Despite all these and a host of other depressing facts, the average Haitian is a cheerful and charming person, and Lane Timmons, like most other ambassadors who have served there, is very fond of the people.

All of this notwithstanding, our objectives in Haiti were primarily to find out about surviving wildlife. The answers we got were almost as discouraging as the political and economic facts of life of the country. Ambassador Timmons has been to the pine forests, too, but has heard nothing about any horses there, wild or otherwise. So great is the pressure for meat that he doubted if any animal the size of a horse would long survive. Both his cat and his pet peafowl, he said, had been shot by poachers. George Leger, the leading lawyer of Haiti and a sportsman of note, told us that although he often visited the pine forests and camped there he had found no trace of wild horses. He did, however, confirm the fact that there are some surviving solenodons, having seen several which

54

had been caught by dogs. Of the peripatus, he was as ignorant as all of us; but being small and ostensibly inedible, it may have a better chance to survive in Haiti than Papa Doc.

The destruction of wildlife on Haiti is particularly sad—even ironic—in that the republic was a charter subscriber and ratifier of the Convention on Nature Protection and Wildlife Preservation in the Western Hemisphere of May 1, 1942. The convention, which was the first of its kind ever to be proposed on this continent, establishes a basic pattern for a scheme for parks and reserves throughout the Americas. It also calls for appropriate protective laws for threatened flora and fauna as well as favoring cooperation in scientific field studies, the protection of migratory birds and vanishing species, and the control of contraband fauna and flora that are protected by the laws of other countries. For the full text of this vitally important convention see Appendix I.

The old city of Cartagena in Colombia is full of ghosts. As the port of embarkation for much of the wealth of the Spanish empire in South America, it was one of the richest prizes in the New World. Although sacked by the French pirate Robert Baal in 1543, and by another buccaneer in 1697, Cartagena was always gallantly defended. It withstood a siege of three months in 1741 by Sir Edward Vernon at the head of a force of 27,000 men and 3,000 pieces of artillery. With him at the time was a brother of George Washington, and it was for the British general that Mount Vernon was named. The hero of the defense was the Spanish general Blas de Lezo, who had one eye, one arm, and was lame. We visited the scenes of the siege, the cathedral, and the palace of the Inquisition, where the black-robed judges of the Holy Order applied torture and fire to unbelievers.

The antiquities of Cartagena were, in fact, well documented, but the student of natural history has a harder time. There was no public zoo. Only by luck did we find a small private zoo run by an American named Dennie Sebolt, who divided his time between his establishment in Cartagena and a similar attraction in Panama City, Florida. Sebolt dealt mainly in snakes. He not only sold them to zoos and scientific organizations, but extracted and marketed the venom as well. Sebolt's interest extended to many other forms of wildlife. Consequently he was able to tell me something about the local manatees. They still exist in the Canal del Dique, an arm of the Magdalena River, which runs for fifty miles connecting Cartagena and Calamar. He believes that laws have been enacted in Bogotá to protect the manatee. Nobody, however, pays the slightest attention to them. The fishermen spear any they find and sell the meat in the local markets. The supply, now very limited, is becoming more so with each passing year.

In my previous book, *The Empty Ark*, I have written a good deal about the manatee in Brazil, and about its cousin the dugong from Ceylon and Australia, but for the benefit of new readers I will describe it. Despite its ancient designation as a mermaid which thrilled sailors long at sea, the manatee is far from beautiful. In the rather harsh words of Dr. Colin Bertram, a zoologist and fellow of St. Johns College, Cambridge, who is an authority on the manatee, "it has grey skin which is constantly sloughing; a broad tail that is usually chipped at the edges; and a back which is often covered with green algae." Hair on the body is sparse, and the muzzle is surrounded by bristles. There is one part of the female manatee, however, which is undeniably feminine and, seen through several fathoms of water, undoubtedly attractive—these are the breasts, which are nicely shaped and in no need of a brassiere.

Easy to capture because they show no fear of man, the manatee inhabits shallow water and is the only mammal in the world that feeds exclusively upon marine vegetation. Furthermore, they grow up to twelve feet long, and their flesh is excellent. The dugong lives in salt water, while the manatee is found in the brackish water of the estuaries or in fresh water. On a previous mission to Brazil, I saw several manatees in an aquarium at Manaus, halfway up the Amazon, and even held a small one in my arms.

According to Dr. Bertram, the young are conceived, born, and suckled in the water, for no manatee or dungong has the capacity of hauling itself out of the water like a seal. The sailors of old who claimed to have seen long-haired mermaids sitting on a rock were doing wishful thinking. No studies have been made of the composition of manatee milk, but it must be very nutritious because the young grow rapidly. The milk of the elephant seal, which we saw on the Falkland Island beaches, has been analyzed as fifty percent fat. This enables the calf to grow from 100 pounds at birth to four times that size in only three weeks.

In 1965 we visited Melville Island off the north coast of Australia where the aboriginal tribes still hunt dugong as their principal source of food. The missionaries there arranged for me to talk with the paramount chief, who told me that his tribe of about 200 people catch an average of five or six dugong a month and that in his lifetime—the chief is a very old man—he has not noted any important decline in the number of dugong in the surrounding waters. By Australian law, only the aborigines are allowed to hunt them. I was shown a dead male and invited to taste his flesh, which I politely declined.

The West African species of manatee is said to be able to live on water hyacinth, that lovely but navigation-choking plant that has caused such havoc in the African rivers. In the Nile, the water hyacinth makes up much of the vast swamp known as the Sud. In the newly formed Lake Kariba on the Zambezi, the weed has made it impossible for fishermen to drag their nets. The icthyologist in charge at Cariba told me that experiments with poison had got rid of the water hyacinth but had also poisoned the fish. Thus, he was wondering if it might be possible to import manatee from the estuaries of Somalia and Kenya. The problem, however, is one of breeding in captivity or semicaptivity. So far, nobody has accomplished this, but I have heard that the authorities in both British Guiana and Florida are studying the subject.

The manatee and the dugong are both of the Sirenia order, making up two of its three genera. Steller's sea cow, the third member of the order, is no longer with us. In his exciting book, *Where the Sea Breaks Its Back,* Corey Ford tells the sad story of its extinction. First described by Georg Wilhelm Steller, the German naturalist who accompanied Vitus Bering on his expedition to Alaska in 1741, this huge marine mammal was thirty feet long, slow-moving, and utterly unafraid. Starved for meat, Bering's sailors threw grappling irons into them, then hauled them bleeding and groaning ashore. The males would not leave the females and made pathetic attempts to break the ropes by imposing their bulk between the shore and their agonized mates.

Scientists estimate that there probably were not more than 2,000 sea cows in the world at the time of their discovery. By 1830, no more were reported—the sailors had simply killed and eaten them all. Despite occasional rumors of sightings since then, the world has not seen hide nor hair of these great and interesting mammals.

Steller also gave us the first description of the once scarce sea otter, a mammal that has been able to stage a limited comeback only by the lucky survival of a few individuals. Now rigidly protected, it may still be seen gamboling and playing with its pups in the smoky seas of Alaska.

Sebolt's little zoo in Cartagena also contained a number of speckled cayman, the subspecies of the local alligators that inhabits this part of the Caribbean. He told me that their belly skins brought twenty pesos for a two-foot specimen. They are still fairly common, according to Sebolt, but the pressure on them steadily mounts as the natives use the skins to make shoes, belts, and bags. Great numbers are also exported to Japan. One curiosity he showed us was a large male that had refused to eat for a solid year. It was still alive, although very thin and wan. While Colombia has laws against the killing of cayman less than three feet long, there is no one to enforce them. In Florida, where enforcement is strict, the fine for killing or taking an alligator is $500 or two years in jail.

One reptile with economic possibilities which is not in short supply is the Colombian boa constrictor. Despite a brisk demand for the skin for shoes and bags, the boa is such a prolific breeder that its future seems assured. Although Sebolt has been bitten numerous times by this poisonous snake, he walked through a pit of them with impunity. He even milked a fer-de-lance for us, its gleaming white fangs exuding pale yellow drops of lethal poison in the process.

CHAPTER IV

Howling Monkeys

Suddenly the silence of the jungle was shattered by a series of thundering roars that rose and fell like the hunting challenge of the great predators. If we had been in Africa, I would have sworn it was a pride of lions driving their evening meal, but we were half a world away on Barro Colorado Island in the middle of Gatun Lake in the Canal Zone of Panama. The awesome sounds came from a clan of howling monkeys warning neighboring clans to stay out of their territory. We had heard those monkeys in 1963 in the llanos of Venezuela. Their habitat there was the treeless flatlands where the acoustics hardly compared to those in a tropical monsoon forest such as Barro Colorado Island. Here great almendro trees, more than a hundred feet high, wild cashews, black palms, and many other jungle trees hung with a variety of creepers and vines acted as a sounding board for the primitive chorus.

My first acquaintance with howling monkeys came in Robert Ardrey's book, *African Genesis*. Ardrey gave a vivid description of the experiences of C. R. Carpenter, professor of psychology at Pennsylvania State University, while he was doing research on these same Barro Colorado monkeys. At the time of Carpenter's study, twenty-eight clans divided the 4,000 acres of the island into twenty-eight domains and lived in total hostility with their neighbors. The howling monkey defends his territory with his vocal chords instead of his teeth.

Carpenter's "Behavior and Social Relations of the Howling Monkey," published in 1934, was a scientific bombshell at the time. He proved conclusively that, despite Freud, it is not sex that holds the primate troops together but the defense of a social territory. In the howling monkey, sexual jealousy is nonexistent. No male wants a sexual priority

Howling Monkey,
Barro Colorado
Island, Canal Zone

over any female. Sex is simply a pleasant occurrence in which all males share all females. Furthermore, the clan, or troop, is always the paramount consideration for all individuals. According to Carpenter, no jealousy, neglect of young, or defiance of leadership can exist at the cost of the clan's welfare. Offspring are the joint responsibility of all adults in the troop. All males, in response to a special cry, will go to rescue any youngster fallen from a tree. The howling monkey without his clan would indeed be a "man without a country." Carpenter's findings have been well corroborated in the years since he did this work.

We had been taken by launch to Barro Colorado after having been met at the little railway station of Frijoles, thanks to Dr. Martin H. Moynihan. Dr. Moynihan is the director of the Smithsonian Tropical Research Institute, which operates this biological preserve and research station. Formed in 1914 when the Chagres River was dammed to create Gatun Lake as part of the Panama Canal, the island is about three miles long and 4,000 acres in extent, with a shore line so irregular that it runs nearly thirty miles. Although he had made our arrangements, Dr. Moynihan was then leaving on a trip to Africa, Ceylon, and India. (I gave him letters to various friends, including E. P. Gee, the Indian wildlife expert), so he could not, unfortunately, be with us on the island. However, Nicholas Smythe, a young British mammalogist and his attractive Canadian wife, Tanis, took excellent care of our party of five, which included Ambassador and Mrs. Ellis Briggs, my wife and me, and Douglas Bjorn, a foreign-service officer our embassy had kindly assigned to us during our stay in Panama.

The camp where we were quartered is situated near the top of the island. A formidable flight of 200 steps leads up to it from the waterfront, but once on top the view alone is worth the climb. The blue-green lake, ringed by lush jungles, lay spread below us, while two steamers, looking like toy boats, cruised slowly across its calm waters.

After supper that night we were provided with head lamps to enable us to see what animal life we could find in the darkness of the rain forest surrounding the camp. Before starting, however, we were well squirted with insect repellent, for the island abounds with ticks, spiders, tarantulas, and other crawling things. Snakes, although rarely seen on the island, include the deadly fer-de-lance, coral snake, green vine snake, and the boa constrictor. Fifty-four other species of reptiles also have been identified.

The island is rich in mammals,too, with sixty-five species recorded. We had hardly started up the slippery jungle trail before our headlights picked up a pair of red eyes. Later the beam settled on the head of a huge tapir. It proved to be Napoleon, a tame male on his way to the camp for his nightly feed of bread. Hunted relentlessly all over Panama, tapir meat is often sold in the markets. According to Smythe, it brings forty cents a pound. Deer meat is worth sixty cents, and paca at eighty cents is the highest of all. Poachers invade even Barro Colorado, with its preserve and research station, since there are only two guards for all the island's miles of jagged coastline which, in certain areas, is only a few hundred yards from the mainland. Moreover, the illegal meat hunters do not stop at the ground animals but shoot the red spider monkeys as well. These attractive little creatures have been almost exterminated in much of Panama.

In the black canopy of the branches we picked out other sets of eyes

Tapir, Panama

which proved to belong, respectively, to a marmosa, a small opposum, a common opposum, and *Bufo marinus*, a tree toad. In a clear little brook we saw fresh-water shrimp and, scurrying away from their drinking pool, a brace of pacas. One must be very careful on these nocturnal excursions to avoid reaching out for tree trunks, even when one stumbles. When I did so, I got a fist full of needle-sharp spines from a black palm. Even the monkeys never try to climb this tree. They wait until the fruit is ripe and falls to the ground. The fruit has a sugary coating which the animals like, and their habit of carrying it away widely disseminates the seeds. Twice we heard the retreat of peccaries, the wild pigs, which are also a constant target for the poachers. A larger cousin, the white-lipped peccary, is made of tougher stuff, for it can cut a man very badly indeed.

Later I asked about the rarity of the *rano dorado*, or "golden frog," which is restricted, I was told, to a small area in the La Valle district of northern Panama. It is in danger of extinction if the natives continue the practice of selling all they can find to tourists. The U. S. Army has helped the future of this rare frog by trapping several hundred, which are to be transported by helicopter to a remote mountain area where it is hoped a new colony can be established. Thanks to Molly Thayer, the writer, there may even be a nucleus of a colony in the National Zoological Park in Washington, D.C. Mrs. Thayer sent specimens from Panama several years ago.

Back at the camp, while selecting pictures of the wildlife of Barro Colorado taken by Smythe, I found a picture of a strange wormlike creature with a pair of antlers on its head. To my delight I discovered it was peripatus, the missing link between the earthworm and the centipede that Dr. Ivan Sanderson found in Haiti. I intend to present these pictures to the photographic library of the World Wildlife Fund at Morges, Switzerland.

With Smythe and other scientists on the island, we discussed the rarest animals of Panama, such as the spectacled bear and the bush dog. Two of the scientists had been in the jungles of Darien, the partially explored province between Panama and Colombia, but neither of them had any firsthand information on the bear in this area. However, the bears' habitat in South America in the lower mountain ranges of the San Blas range, which begins east of Colón and runs to the Colombian border, has many peaks reaching to 3,000 feet. It is not impossible that some stray individuals might be in the province of Darien.

The spectacled bear, which has a black body and yellowish head, gets its name from a white semicircle around its eyes. It is one of the survivors of the entire family of bears that have one by one vanished from the earth. In 1780, when the Atlas bear was exterminated in Morocco, the last bear in Africa ceased to exist. In our own country the California Coast grizzly had disappeared by 1908, the Klamath grizzly by 1911. Five years later, the Tejon and the Southern California grizzly both joined the dodo in Valhalla. Luckily, the spectacled bear does breed in captivity. There are now forty-three of them in twenty-six zoos. Nine of these, according to the International Zoo Yearbook, were bred in captivity. Two are in Mexico City.

The World Wildlife Fund financed a project to provide up-to-date information on the status of this rare bear. Dr. Albert W. Erickson, associate professor of zoology and curator of mammals at the Museum of Natural History of the University of Minnesota, was conducting the survey, then still in progress.

A survival of the ancient canines is the bush dog of Panama. Brown with tawny foreparts and dark hindquarters, this rare dog sometimes has pale patches or bands on its belly. Very little seems to be known about it although it is said to be found in eastern Colombia, the Guianas, eastern Peru, and northern Bolivia, as well as in Panama. It is reported to like wooded and savanna areas. The San Diego Zoo bred litters of four or five pups, and zoologists agree that it could be domesticated. Its closest relatives are the dholes, the wild dogs of India (which I wrote about in my reports from Assam), and the Cape hunting dogs of Africa. I saw several of these dogs while on a shooting trip in the lower Cape in 1961. Both Moynihan and Smythe believe the bush dog still survives but has become so rare that there is no way to trace it. Indian reports mean little, as they seldom differentiate between the feral dogs from the villages and those that live always in the jungle.

Early the next morning, armed with Dr. Alexander Wetmore's *The Birds of the Republic of Panama*, and a pair of good Leitz 10-power glasses, I went bird watching. Two hundred species (out of a total of 310 in Panama) are said to breed on the island. I was accompanied by a visiting lecturer from the National Audubon Society of America who pointed out an ant shrike, lesser kiskadee, tropical flycatcher, green honey creeper, and blue-gray tanager. Later, on my own, I spotted a large-billed hawk, which, despite its bill, is actually a small hawk. This one was sitting on the branch of a dead tree, methodically eating mouthfuls of lizard.

Dr. Wetmore begins his new two-volume book of the birds of Panama with the tinamous, a family of forest game birds that inhabit virtually all of Latin America from Mexico to Tierra del Fuego. Of the forty species, three, known as *perdices*, are found in Panama. Two dwell on Barro Colorado. Delicious eating, they are hunted over their entire range. The tinamous cannot stand such great pressure, however, and is becoming difficult to find. The birds were formerly sold in the market in Panama City but are now rarely offered. The great tinamou *(Tinamus major)* resides in the heavily forested area. Unfortunately, the progressive destruction of these lands is taking a heavy toll of its habitat. Like partridge in Vermont, the tinamous explode when flushed. If not pressed, they tend to creep away like a pheasant.

I am glad to report that the future of Barro Colorado Island is probably assured. Even if Panama eventually gains control of the Zone, it is unlikely that such a long-established reserve would be taken over. There are, however, other valuable wooded areas in the Zone which may not be able to withstand the economic onslaught. It was rumored that lumber interests in the United States were already negotiating for rights in the Zone in anticipation of the Panamanian government's sovereignty. An impressive and protective addition to Barro Colorado Island would be the shores of Gatun Lake, for it would help prevent the poachers from slipping across by canoe at night. Another important habitat in the Zone is the so-called "pipe-line area." If it were possible for the Zone authorities to proclaim both these areas sanctuaries, and if Panama agreed to keep them as such, it would be a big step for conservation. I discussed this possibility with both the Zone and Panamanian authorities. But until a basic agreement has been reached as to the future of the entire Zone, little progress can be made.

In addition to the loss of habitat due to the opening of the land to cultivation, the fauna of Panama has suffered at the hands of careless hunters. There was no limit on the number of animals or birds that might be shot and no closed season. Not only was the available game driven by dogs, but anything that looked edible or might be considered a trophy was shot. A current tourist magazine displayed a picture of a hefty female hunter with her automatic 12-gauge shotgun and a tiny mangled catlike animal known as a *tigrillo*, while her husband posed proudly with a buck deer so small that it resembled a large rabbit with vestigial horns. Both heads mounted could be worn as watch fobs.

This sad state of affairs had not gone unnoted by the Panamanian government. In 1966 the Cerro Campana National Park was established in the mountains some fifty miles west of Panama City. No funds were then available for guards, whereas it is estimated that at least six would be needed to patrol the perimeter. Because this is Panama's first national park, and is said to contain not only tapir but a variety of other animals and birds such as the rare quetzal, the raising of money to guard it, for an initial period at least, might prove a worthwhile project for the World Wildlife Fund.

To regulate hunting, the Panamanian government had appointed a board, on which Dr. Moynihan sat, to draw up a list of animals and birds which at the beginning will be totally protected for a period of one year. This board was also to make regulations governing the shooting of abundant species. Included in the protected list were the tapir, manatee, green turtle, iguana, all local species of deer, paca, all species of timamous, curassows, doves, ducks, and the quetzal.

The Guardia Nacional of Panama issued licenses to carry a gun for five dollars per year, while the Canal Zone authorities issued a similar permit for shooting in the Zone for one dollar. Shooting is allowed on about three quarters of the Zone's 553 square miles. As I noted above, there has been some discussion about proclaiming a park, to be known as the Pipe Line Reserve, in a fifty-six-square-mile area of the Zone near Gamboa. I understand that both the Panamian and the Zone authorities were in favor of the reserve. But little had been accomplished as the whole question of the future status of the Canal Zone was involved. The government of Panama has two objectives regarding the Zone. One is the transfer of effective sovereignty over the canal from the U.S.A. to Panama, and the other is to secure enough money from the operation of the canal to finance the country's land reform and other popular programs.

The two men directly responsible for our relations with Panama were our ambassador, Charles W. Adair, Jr., and the governor of the Canal Zone, Colonel H. R. Parfitt. Ambassador Briggs and I made our first official call on the ambassador. We had a long and interesting talk with him about Panama and conservation. As Briggs has a wide background knowledge of Latin America, it is a privilege for me to have him accompanying me on these calls. He has represented us with distinction in Peru, Brazil, Cuba, the Dominican Republic, and Uruguay.

Ambassador Adair gave us some good news about the manatees. It seems that the Zone authorities purchased twelve of these vegetation-consuming mammals and released them in the canal. This effort was to see how much of the water hyacinth, which regularly chokes the waterway, they would be able to eat. Eight of the school, however, managed to escape through the net and probably made their way to Peru, whence they came. The remaining four manatees took their new job seriously and were still chewing diligently for the Canal Zone authorities.

Governor Parfitt then read us some of the laws regulating shooting in the Zone. As I noted above, a license was necessary, and there were regulations governing the game—duck season lasted from December 1 until June 30—but enforcement was a function of the Zone's civilian police. It has been my experience all over the world that only wardens expressly assigned to game protection pay much attention to this job. Obviously, wildlife preservation played a very small role in the duties of the safeguarders of the peace in the Zone.

The Zone authorities did, however, maintain a small zoo. Also, a part of the training of jungle troops was to recognize wildlife, probably primarily for a source of food. Hence the subject was of some interest, at least, for the armed forces. General R. W. Porter, our military commander in the zone, invited us for cocktails at his residence at Quarry Heights, the historic hill where the military commander has lived since the days of Teddy Roosevelt. A cavalry officer who graduated from West Point in 1930, the general was fond of horses and fly fishing. He planned to retire in the Virginia mountains, where he can raise rainbow trout.

General Porter fished in the mountains of Panama near the Costa

Rican border. He told me that rainbows were introduced to the El Valle River in 1922 by an American named Green, who took the fertilized eggs up by horseback. Only a few survived the rough journey, but these prospered so well that two years later eighteen-inch fish were caught in the river. Later, other mountain streams were stocked. However, there was no supervision by the Panamanian government. As a result the market fishermen dynamited and poisoned the streams with impunity. Now the easily accessible areas have been cleaned out, and the Panamanian government has suggested that the United States restock the streams. My own opinion is that until legal safeguards have been instituted this would not be a rewarding operation.

Conservation in Panama, and eventually even in the Zone, depends on the government of Panama. Consequently I was pleased when His Excellency, Marco A. Robles, President of the Republic, received me at the Palace. Not a member of the oligarchy of land-owning families who usually rule Panama, Señor Robles was elected in 1964 and proved to be one of the few presidents to serve out his full four-year term. Since the Panamanians declared their independence from Colombia in 1903, there have been thirty presidents, only one of whom has served a full term. There is a frieze of portraits of the presidents around the handsome state reception room. Among them, I noticed, was one of a man named Jean Guardia, who had served a single day in 1941.

Also present at this conference were Ruben D. Carles, the minister of agriculture, Ambassador Adair, and Ambassador Briggs. The president opened our talks by telling us that he is very fond of shooting—in fact, he invited us to shoot dove with him any time. He is also interested in conservation. I congratulated him on the establishment of Panama's first national park, the Cerro Campana, and said I would look into the possibility of helping him to provide game guards for the park for a limited period. I also asked about the work of the game commission, which was presently in session to draft a law relative to closed seasons for rare animals and birds. The president said he had signed a decree in favor of the law. This, for all practical purposes, makes it effective now.

The minister of agriculture asked about restocking the streams in the mountains with trout. Ambassador Adair said he had heard that these streams were being dynamited. The president replied that dynamiting was against the law and was no longer practiced. Following a pregnant silence, Ambassador Adair said that in that case the restocking would be taken under advisement.

My net impression was that both the president and the minister of agriculture believe there is a tourist potential in conservation. They will, I believe, lend their support—up to a point. Panama, however, is not a rich country. When the land reform program picks up steam, it will be more difficult to get parks proclaimed. Therefore I urged the minister of agriculture to get as much land as possible set aside and entrenched by law now so that it cannot be alienated later by unscrupulous persons.

Panama signed and ratified the Convention on Nature Protection and Wildlife Preservation in the Western Hemisphere.

Two days after Ambassador Briggs and I discussed conservation with His Excellency Marco A. Robles, *El Día*, a leading newspaper of Panama City, published a full-page report on the new game laws and the animals and birds that they will protect. It was, of course, pure coincidence that the law, which had been under consideration for some months, was passed and signed while we were in Panama. However, I think it did please the president that we took so much interest in this ordinance.

Unfortunately, the commission's statute fell short of authorizing a specific body of wardens to enforce the new game laws, or, as I noted above, to guard the perimeter of the new park. Nevertheless, the president's decree was forcibly expressed and included complete protection of the manatee, tapir, quetzal, two species of timamou, and our special concern, the rana dorado, or the golden frog. The law also included a ban on the sale of live iguanas in markets. It ordered the National Guard to take action whenever they find iguanas being offered there. In fact, enforcement of all the provisions of the act was laid in the lap of the National Guard, Panama's all-purpose police-cum-army organization. Administration of the law, however, was made a function of the Ministry of Agriculture.

Conservation of wildlife by the establishment of sanctuaries and the proclamation of protective laws are, in most cases, the best measures that can be taken to withstand today's pressure on animals and birds and their habitat. Far more basic, however, is the problem of educating the people to the importance of saving their natural heritage. This is particularly necessary in the less-developed yet fast-growing nations where people are hungrier and where the desire for land is still unsatisfied.

With this thought in mind, I talked with Dr. Carlos Sucre, minister of education of the Republic of Panama, about ways to inform young people of the necessity for conservation. He said that science classes do touch on this subject, but there is no real effort to sell the idea to Panamanian youth. I also discussed this with Zone officials, as the Zone schools enroll many Panamanian as well as American children. Simple primers, liberally illustrated and printed in Spanish, English, and the most common Indian dialect would be cheap to produce and interesting to look at. Venezuela, for example, does a good job with similar booklets in its primary schools. The problem is, of course, to find someone to pay for the project. A possibility might be the group of wealthy Panamanians who have taken up the cause of the golden frog. Among these is Cecilia Heurtematte, a member of the Twenty Families who are said to rule Panama—or did until recently. An attractive, purposeful lady, Ceci not only thought up but followed through with the idea of having a replica made of the golden frog found in a pre-Columbian tomb and selling it (through the Friends of Panama Museum) to interested people in the effort to preserve these rare amphibians. A description of rana dorado could be included in the accompanying booklet, which would deal with all of the endangered animals and birds of Panama. Another possibility would be to sell our AID mission on the idea.

I also talked with Fernando Eleta, minister of foreign affairs, who is young, able, and attractive. He immediately responded to my interest in wildlife with the suggestion that Coinba, an island off the Pacific coast which is now used as a penal colony, would be a fine place to turn into a sanctuary for Panama's rarer fauna. He said it had been virtually decided to move the prisoners elsewhere anyway. Thus he thought there was a good possibility that the government might respond to a plan to use the island as a reserve.

Panama had no public zoo, and the Zone, I thought, only a single private institution. This was inaccurate; there were two zoos in the Zone, and one of them—Summit Gardens—could be expanded into a first-class institution. Situated in a charming and handsome botanical park, the zoo was old, with antique iron grilles on the cages. But the inmates were the best-looking bunch of cats, monkeys, and birds that I had seen in some years.

Robert Ardrey, in his recent book *Territorial Imperative*, tells fascinating stories about the defense of territories by birds and animals. However, he does not explain why at exactly 5:45 every evening hundreds of grackles, known locally as *telingo*, alight on the trees in front of the Panama Hilton Hotel (now the El Panama) and spend the night there. Since Panama's area is nearly 30,000 square miles, most of which is jungle, the birds must have other reasons besides finding a place to roost when they choose the Hilton. They started roosting in the Plaza of the Cathedral in downtown Panama City many years ago. Then the mayor cut down the trees. Now they have at long last found a home where they are not only tolerated but liked. The inhabitants of the Hilton, who in a very real sense are also defendants of a territorial way of life, seem to understand the winged guests.

To find who really lives in Panama one must consult that modern Baedeker, *The South American Handbook*, published in London. According to this unemotional source, Panama's population of about 1.3 million is 12 percent white, 14.5 percent Negro, 72 percent mixed, 1.5 percent others. Although Panama spends one third of its budget on education, nearly 50 percent are illiterate in the country, but in the cities less than 10 percent. Sixty percent of the children are born to unmarried mothers. Perhaps a quarter of the population live on land for which they pay no rent and which is not their own.

The La Pava Barrio, or slum, in the heart of Panama City, is such a district. Built on a hill, La Pava is populated by about 3,000 persons who have simply drifted there, put up shacks, and stayed. In an attempt to eliminate districts like La Pava, the government was actively endeavoring to sell low-cost housing on long-term credit to squatters. But at best the process was a slow one. The population is surging ever upward. Demand for land close to Panama City will create a powerful political incentive to divide many areas of the Zone, when and if Panama takes it over, and it is primarily for this reason that every effort should be made to form inviolate sanctuaries at this time.

There are about 60,000 Indians in Panama. A good number of these are known as the San Blas tribes, who inhabit the Caribbean side of the Darien Peninsula and numerous offshore islands. Panama's relations with them are tenuous. In fact, the Indians are frank to say that they do not like Panamanians. Ever since 1923, when the Indians rose and massacred some 200 Panamanian officials, the policing of the San Blas territory has been left largely to local chiefs. Hence I am afraid that the new game laws will have little effect there, for since time immemorial the animals of the jungles have been the Indians' only source of meat. According to my wife, they eat tapir, painted rabbit, and pacas when they can find them. However, ninety percent of the time their diet is fish and such vegetables as the sandy soil can produce.

Some of our pleasantest times in Panama were spent with Charles and Gay Lord. Charles is the son of Oswald and Mary Lord, who went with us to Mongolia and Siberia.

CHAPTER V

Green Turtle Refuge

Seven hundred miles northwest of St. Helena in the South Atlantic lies Ascension Island, about equidistant from the coasts of South America and Africa. In 1961 I flew there from Recife, Brazil, as part of a trip down the Atlantic Missile Range, and marveled at man's ability to find this tiny thirty-four-square-mile speck in the watery wastes of one of the world's loneliest oceans. While I stayed on the island, a missile, launched half an hour previously at Cape Canaveral (as it was then), splashed into the water exactly on schedule. Both of these feats of navigation are spectacular to the layman, but they pale beside the homing abilities of the green turtle. From thousands of miles away, these great sea turtles find their way to Ascension every February to mate and lay their eggs on their ancestral beaches. The administrator of this British island showed me the beaches as well as the old barracks of the Royal Navy, where giant turtle shells hung on the wall.

On Ascension turtles are being conserved, but on most of the world's beaches they are slaughtered and their eggs pilfered. Thanks to the Caribbean Conservation Corporation (C.C.C.) and Dr. Archie Carr of the University of Florida, a refuge has also been established at Tortuguero, a hamlet on the Caribbean coast of Costa Rica. For our visit to this refuge, my wife and I were indebted to James Oliver, director of the American Museum of Natural History in New York and a friend of Dr. Carr.

Fortunately, the green turtle has dedicated friends. The man in Costa Rica most interested in their preservation is Guillermo Cruz, an official of the British-American Tobacco Company. Billy, as he is known to his many friends in America and Costa Rica, arranged for a plane to ferry us on the last leg of the trip. Early in the morning four of us—my wife, Billy, and Joe Romanelli, a young foreign-service officer assigned me by Ambassador Raymond Telles—took off from San José for Tortuguero in a little single-engine Cessna. Tortuguero is about 100 miles due northeast from the capital. We flew low over the 4,000-foot valley of central Costa Rica, where the land was a patchwork of little plots. When we started climbing to fly over the jagged cordillera, I saw the smoke of burning clearings high on the slopes.

On the other side of the mountains the land falls away to a green blanket of rain forest laced with gleaming yellow rivers. We passed a few disused banana plantations, but these swampy lowlands are not hospitable to man, and there were few hamlets. Just an hour after take-off, we landed on a rough dirt strip between the Caribbean and the Tortuguero River, which parallels the beach. Leon Martinez, the dedicated manager of the conservation station, was on hand to welcome us. After Billy had shown us the camp, Martinez told us about the turtle operation.

From the Costa Rican government the C.C.C. leases a tract of land including twenty-two miles of beach and reaching inland about two miles. From June to October in a normal year some 18,000 giant females, weighing up to 350 pounds each, waddle onto this beach and lay three sets of eggs, numbering from 85 to 108 for each clutch.

Before 1954, when Dr. Carr became interested in saving this valuable source of food, few if any mother turtles made it back to the sea. Men slaughtered the turtles, and any eggs left unfound were often dug up by feral dogs, foxes, and iguanas. The few little turtles hatched were then a prey for the carnivorous birds. So relentless was man's hunger for the sea turtle that it disappeared from beach after beach. First it was Bermuda, then the Bahamas and Florida. In 1886 a commercial hunter named Peak caught 2,500 turtles near Sebastian, Florida. By 1895 he could find only fifty. Like the apparently endless herds of buffalo, the green turtle was vanishing from the earth.

After a trip to the Cayman Islands, where he found the track of a single turtle, Dr. Carr wrote eloquently of this vanishing species:

> The history of the turtle fishery—its burgeoning and exhaustion, the heedless killing of the females bearing eggs, the plight of the people who had no other way to live and their tenacity in following the declining schools from one remote shore to another—is as extraordinary from the standpoint of human ecology as from that of resource depletion.

To reverse this decline and save the green turtle from the fate of the dodo, Dr. Carr established the Tortuguero sanctuary and also interested the U.S. Navy in helping him to restore the green-turtle colonies on the beaches where they have been exterminated. The Navy is interested in the green turtle *(Chelonia mydas)* not because it is a source of excellent soup but because the Office of Naval Research would give a great deal to know how it navigates. How, without sextants, radio, or radar do they find their way unerringly to their home beaches? I encountered similar questions in a different form while I was ambassador to Ceylon. There a young man arrived at the embassy one day saying he would like to store twenty large boxes containing bats. It turned out he was doing a study of bat "radar" for the U.S. Navy.

During every breeding season the Navy supplies an Albatross seaplane with a crew that flies baby turtles to selected beaches in Mexico, Colombia, and the Caribbean islands where the governments have agreed to provide protection. To provide the Navy with baby turtles the C.C.C. men and their helpers dig up the eggs from the sand, hatch them, and pack them carefully in batches of several hundred in wooden boxes of brine-soaked plastic form.

75

Operation Green Turtle at Tortuguero was started just in time, for in the entire Caribbean area there is only one other beach left—Isla Pagaros, on a virtually inaccessible part of the coast of Venezuela—where the green turtle still comes to breed in any numbers. The period October, 1968, was to have been crucial for Operation Green Turtle, as the females do not return to breed until they have grown at sea for five or more years, or so it was thought then. More recently, however, the return time has been estimated at ten to twelve years. Hence the outcome of Operation Green Turtle remains open.

Although the green turtle is full of hundreds of pounds of delicious meat—live turtles in the hold kept the crews of the old sailing ships from dying of scurvy—today's poachers take only the "calapin," about five pounds of fatty matter that covers the stomach. This is shipped to Germany, where it is made into gelatin and soup. Because the twenty-two-mile sanctuary at Tortuguero is patrolled by only two wardens on horses, there is little doubt that poachers still take an occasional mother turtle.

The male green turtle does not go ashore but consummates his mating about two miles out at sea, remaining there while his wives risk life and limb to perpetuate the species on the beaches. The males can be harpooned as they wait for the females, and many are; but the sea is rough, and the job of dragging one behind a light wooden skiff is not easy.

The sea turtle is a species of very ancient lineage. Two hundred million years ago it swam in the warm oceans in just about the same shape as it exists today. Hiding behind its well-nigh impregnable shell, and able with its powerful flippers to escape the great sea predators, the sea turtle would be in fine shape except for the unreasonable acts of man.

The C.C.C. camp is a few miles from the village of Tortuguero. Billy escorted us by boat on the Tortuguero River, which runs just behind the beach. There has been talk of dredging this river so that barges could ply from the town of Limón, some seventy miles down the coast, to the border of Nicaragua, about thirty miles north. If this becomes a fact, more people will come into the area. A national park would then be of great help in protecting the turtle beaches, not only in the twenty-two-mile stretch leased by the C.C.C. but all along the coast.

In the village, a cluster of some twenty unpainted shacks, we met Sibella, the cook who takes care of the camp people and is a favorite of

Billy Cruz (right) and a Navy flier inspecting a shipment of baby green turtles.

the University of Florida students who come during the turtle breeding season to help with Operation Green Turtle. Most of the inhabitants are Mestizo Indians, and several of them spoke English. One stalwart man I talked with said he supported himself by safaris into the jungles. His bag included wild pig, turkeys, iguana, and tapir. He did not think tapirs were particularly rare and claimed he shot a good many with a .22 rifle. He also occasionally speared a manatee in the river, but added that they were increasingly hard to find. He fished in the river, the estuary, and the sea, his catch consisting of robalo, guapote, dorado, corbina, and tiburon. In addition to these sporting ventures, he planted a hectare of rice (2.4

77

acres) in 1967. As a result of the depredations of the wild ducks and pigeons, however, he harvested only eight sacks of rice as against a normal yield of about twenty-five.

The natives of Tortuguero felt a strong vested interest in the Green Turtle project, I am glad to say, and the boys competed for small prizes awarded for catching poachers.

At present the camp is completely isolated, for it lacks any means of communication with the outside world. A two-way radio linking it with San José would thus be most useful. The nominal cost of such a set would be an excellent investment for the World Wildlife Fund, as the project is clearly doing so much to save one of the world's most interesting species, one which could have a real economic potential if it existed in sufficient numbers.

The active volcanoes of Irazú and Poas dominate the pleasant highlands of Costa Rica, sometimes bringing death and destruction to the inhabitants. Today this little country lies under a far greater threat; her annual population increase of 4.3 percent is one of the highest in the world. No less than half of her 1.5 million people are under sixteen years of age. This is not only a staggering statistic for the economy of Central America's most successful democracy, but it is having the inevitable effect on the land. More and more of the forests are cut down, and higher and higher up the slopes of the cordillera creep the small farmers with their wasteful practices of burn, plant, and depart. Even the wet jungle lands, which ring the Caribbean coast, are being steadily invaded, though at a slower pace. However, two thirds of the population prefers to crowd the highlands rather than start a new life in the low country. The highlanders are almost entirely white, while the few indigenous Indians, the Negroes, and the Mestizos live in the lower altitudes.

Despite his imminent departure for a new assignment, Ambassador Telles received Ambassador Briggs and me with assurances he would do all he could to further our conservation mission. He immediately arranged appointments for us with His Excellency, Professor José Joaquín Trejos F., President of the Republic; Lic. Fernando Lara B., minister of foreign affairs; and Ing. Guilermo E. Yglésias P., minister of agriculture. I explained to the ambassador that our purpose for this meeting was twofold: one was to congratulate the president and his ministers on the formation of El Cabo and Cachi national parks; and the other was to urge him to proclaim other sanctuaries before the pressure of population becomes so great that establishment would be difficult.

A good way to find out the status of the game in a country is to talk with a hunter. I was lucky in finding a knowledgeable sportsman in Kennedy Crockett, then the counselor of our embassy and subsequently ambassador to Nicaragua. Although he does not shoot anything bigger than wildfowl and upland game birds, Crockett's experience in the bush during his years in Costa Rica enabled him to supply us with some pertinent facts. In the first place, he scotched the report of an American news magazine that Costa Rica has no game laws. There are laws governing the hunting of virtually all the game birds and animals. Furthermore, the laws include closed seasons and bag limits. It is also necessary to buy a license. However, the article's breezy statement that "no one ever heard of bag limits, game wardens don't exist, and critters are everywhere," has some basis in fact. The only wardens for the nation's 19,575 square miles of territory are a group of some 250 government officials whose primary job is the collection of local customs. There is little public dissemination of the game laws. In fact, if Crockett had not expressly asked to see copies of them, he might not have known they existed. Since he had sighted only one tapir, he believed they were becoming rare. While the duck populations seem to be holding up in the wilder regions, he said that the farmers poison them in an attempt to stop them from feeding in the rice fields. He also mentioned the dreadful toll that pesticides take of all birds and animals. Earlier I had heard a disturbing report in Washington that chemicals that cannot be used in many parts of the U.S.A. are sold in Latin America.

In Costa Rica, the semiautonomous government agency that had charge of the forests was the Instituto de Tierras y Colonization (ITCO). As its name implies, ITCO seemed to be primarily an organization to pump surplus city population back into the country. Moreover, when ITCO was formed, it took over the forest wardens of the Ministry of Agriculture.

An interesting sidelight on the Costa Rican government's handling of land was given me by David Challinor, a biologist of the Smithsonian

Institution, who pointed out that the country's policy discriminated against undeveloped land. The tax on unused land over 100 hectares ranged from one fourth of one percent to two and one half percent of its value. Exemption from the tax was provided for those lands which remained in their natural forest state and thus served conservation as a water shed, or for sustained-yield forest operations as long as the unused portion is not greater than half the total land. Challinor points out that it is difficult for the large owner to show that half his land is "productive." Instead he is more likely to fell the forest and plant pasture to avoid paying taxes on the unused land.

Through the good offices of David Challinor I got in touch with Dr. Robert Hunter, head of the Tropical Science Center, a private consulting firm of biologists working for a number of clients, including our Department of Defense, the National Science Foundation, and the Organization for Tropical Studies. The son of a missionary to China, who served in the U.S. Army in China during the Second World War, Hunter knows a great deal about Costa Rica and was most helpful to me.

On a sunny Sunday morning he drove the Briggses and us to Cartago, the former capital, to show us a dramatic example of revenge the land can take when man abuses it. Cutting through the outskirts of the old town is a desolate swath about a quarter of a mile wide and several miles long. Not a house was left standing there after the night in December, 1965, when a wall of mud began rumbling down the slopes of Irazú. The 11,500-foot active volcano has always threatened Cartago in one way or another. Since the days when man stripped its slopes of the forests that absorbed the rains, floods have created landslides of volcanic mud. Luckily for the citizens, the 1965 slide moved slowly, and no lives were lost.

Hunter next drove us to the Cachi Hydroelectric Project, where an imposing dam is backing up the Revantado River. Water for this dam depends on the adjacent forests, and so a national park has been declared in the surrounding hills. While the primary purpose of the park is to save the trees, shooting has also been forbidden in the area. During a short drive around the park, it appeared to me that there was a good deal of farming still going on in the park, but I was unable to learn of the existence of any wardens specifically assigned to protect it from hunters.

The Peace Corps, in conjunction with the Food and Agriculture Organization of the U.N., is also considering a conservation program for the country. I talked with Malcolm Young, the deputy director of the Corps, about it. Evidently the Department of Tourism of Costa Rica, another semiautonomous agency like ITCO, would like to develop parks that would attract tourists. With this thought in mind, it was suggested that Dr. Kimberly Miller, a young naturalist with FAO, select a suitable area for a park, and that the Peace Corps provide a landscape architect to plan tourist lodges, walks, etc. The major hitch in this plan seemed to be lack of money, for the Department of Tourism, like ITCO, had virtually none. What funds were available would go toward the "improvements," not toward guards for the animals.

There is, however, a very good case for tourism in Costa Rica. The climate is one of the best south of the border, the country offers everything from tropical beaches to pine forests and peaks, and the government has a long record for stability in an area where this is very much an exception. Lastly, the Costa Ricans as a whole are like Americans. Thus there is none of the anti-U.S. sniping in the newspapers which crops up so frequently in some Latin American countries.

One of the men interested in the possibilities of tourism for Costa Rica was Dr. Stephen B. Preston, director of the Organization for Tropical Studies, an institution created by a consortium of sixteen universities in the U.S.A., the University of Costa Rica, and the Smithsonian Institution of Washington. Dr. Preston, who believes that tourism is Costa Rica's most valuable unexploited asset, has been working out tentative agreements with ITCO to develop natural areas for this purpose. He told me that although Costa Rica has 400 species of trees, only twenty have been utilized. A small wood-research laboratory has been set up at the University of Costa Rica to study the forest possibilities. Dr. Preston, then on leave from the University of Michigan, heads an organization whose primary purpose is not conservation or the attraction of tourists to Costa Rica but acquring and disseminating a broad understanding of its tropical environment.

Leon A. Shertler, representative of the Ford Foundation for Central America, is also well informed on the conservation problems of Costa Rica. He informed me that the cotton farmers used so much toxic pesticide in 1967 they were unable to export to the United States all the beef fattened on the cotton plants after the bolls had been harvested. If the cattle were so badly contaminated, what must have been the effect on the birds? Like all students of the Costa Rica scene, Shertler was also alarmed by the population growth. His foundation deserves credit for having done more than all the governments in Central America together to try to check it.

As the sad day may come when zoos will be the only places where careless mankind can still see many of the earth's rare birds and animals, I always make it a point to visit them in my travels. San José has a municipal zoo called the Parque Bolívar. It is not listed in the International Zoo Year Book; nor can it be a source of much pride to the citizens. For the cages were small and dirty, the inmates listless and dejected. I counted nine species of mammals, including some families of white rabbits, twenty-six species of birds, and five species of reptiles. The director was not around.

Largely as a result of the efforts of Olaf Wessberg, a Swedish emigrant to Costa Rica, an area of 3,000 acres lying at the tip of the Nicoya Peninsula on the West Coast has been designated as the Cabo Blanco Reserve. The sanctuary, which includes a small island, was created with the purpose of protecting the forest habitat and the indigenous wildlife. Financed by a number of American conservation agencies as well as the World Wildlife Fund, the main contribution came from the Philadelphia Conservationists, Inc. Responsibility for managing the area had been taken over by the above-mentioned ITCO.

Aside from these bare facts (and the excellent ecological survey of the area prepared in 1962 by Waldemar Albertin, of the Inter-American Institute of Agricultural Studies at Turrialba, and John Milton, who is now with the Conservation Foundation in Washington, D.C.), very little seemed to be known about Cabo Blanco. The only man in San José I could locate who did have some firsthand knowledge of the area was Dr. Joseph A. Tosi, Jr., a partner in the Tropical Science Center, a private consulting firm with an excellent reputation in its field. In 1965 he and his partners, Dr. Leslie Holdridge and Dr. Robert Hunter, submitted a plan for the management of Cabo Blanco that included the building of a fence to keep out cattle, a row of mango trees to form a fire break, the hiring of wardens, and an agreement to provide periodic inspections. Their report also gave me some useful background information. It seems that the area was not vacant, but contained a number of squatters. ITCO bought out about half of them with the proceeds of a bond issue. The Philadelphia Conservationists and other conservation agencies raised the money to buy out the remainder of the squatters.

The plan of the Tropical Science Center was not accepted, however, and ITCO took over the responsibility for running the reserve. No fence or fire break was built, but a warden was retained. We know little about this minion of the law beyond the rumor that he drank and that Wessberg was not pleased with him. Consequently Wessberg, who lives at Moctezuma, a hamlet about ten kilometers from Cabo Blanco, is really the only person who can keep a constant eye on it. I wrote Wessberg and finally wired him. When I received no reply, I could only conclude that communications in this remote section of Costa Rica were slow.

In addition to the rumor about the unstable warden, I heard that the squatters were not all out of Cabo Blanco. Therefore I decided the only solution was to charter a plane and fly down to see for myself. There is no landing strip within ten miles of the reserve, and since even telegrams sometimes take days to deliver, we had no way of ordering horses to meet us. The best plan seemed to be to fly low over the area for a close inspection. I was fortunate in persuading Dr. Tosi to accompany me, as he had flown over the reserve two years before when his firm submitted the bid for running it. As a trained forester—he had his Ph.D. from Yale —he would quickly recognize signs of cultivation indicating the presence of squatters.

Dr. Tosi arranged for a charter from a young American who owns a shark-catching operation at the town of Punta Arenas and knows the area. He warned us that the trip would be rough in his single-engine plane because of down drafts over the mountains and the strong winds along the coast. Taking off from San José we flew down the Central Valley of Costa Rica. Below, Dr. Tosi pointed out to us the two remaining patches of original forest in the valley where two thirds of all Costa Rica's inhabitants live. One ran to about twenty acres, and the other to several hundred.

At Puntarenas, a straggling little town on the Gulf of Nicoya, we asked a local pilot about possible landing strips near Moctezuma, as I was still trying to get in touch with Wessberg. The pilot said all the fields in that area are risky and seldom used, but we might try to get down at Tambor, a village on the east coast of the peninsula about ten miles north of Moctezuma. We flew across the blue gulf, passing shrimp boats surrounded by myriads of gulls, and finally located Tambor. The "field" itself was harder to detect. We had to buzz the two houses and their barren pastures before we were able to make out the faint outline of a strip that ran from the sea to the base of a mountain. After a bumpy landing, we were welcomed by a thin peon on a small white horse. He wore huge spurs strapped over his bare feet and greeted us with an engaging smile. I gave him ten *colones*, the going rate for a day's work, to ride down to Moctezuma with my letter to Mr. Wessberg. In it I asked Wessberg to pay the bearer five more colones on receipt. My message requested Wessberg to meet me at the hotel in Puntarenas, where we would spend the night on our way north to Managua in Nicaragua.

From Tambor we flew down the coast to Cabo Blanco, which consists of a mountainous cape and a rocky offshore island. Dropping down low, we inspected the island first. According to the survey, the island was said to be the home of a colony of frigate birds and other marine wildfowl. All we could find, however, were two huts and some implements used for the collection of guano.

As there were no fences to mark the borders, it was not easy to tell where the main portion of the reserve started. But since 3,000 acres of it encompass the tip of the peninsula, we drew an arbitrary line and then proceeded to fly circles at minimum altitude over all of the territory from the sea to this line. We counted two cornfields, two banana plantations, and four huts, spotting several people in front of one of them. On the beach, just in front of the offshore island, we saw another hut and a canoe. As these huts were all in the jungle or second-growth areas, and as the bordering lands were under obvious cultivation with no tree cover, I think it was logical to assume that we were over the reserve all the time.

Dr. Tosi estimated that original forest now covers only about twenty-five percent of the reserve, the secondary growth slowly taking over the bare areas. He thought that the land showed signs of protection, at least from the more obvious forms of exploitation, such as burning for clearing.

However, the risk of fire wiping out the reserve was obvious from the air, as the cultivated land outside it ran right up to the borders. Without a fire break there is no way to check the flames. Although this part of Costa Rica has intense rains, which result in luxuriant vegetation, no rain at all falls for a six-month period, and the dense underbrush dries into a highly combustible hazard. As a protective measure the Tropical Science Center report suggested the planting of mango trees. Not only are these fire resistant themselves but they create such a thick cover of leaves that nothing can grow underneath them. Two parallel rows of mangos could provide fifty feet of fire break.

After leaving Cabo Blanco, I had the pilot fly us over other areas of the Nicoya Peninsula. Here Dr. Tosi pointed out other stands of virgin dry-zone forest. These turned out to be few and far between, so there is little doubt that the reserve area on the Nicoya Peninsula possesses one of the better remaining stands. Dr. Tosi said this type of forest does exist in larger concentrations in other parts of the West Coast of Costa Rica, which we were to see later.

I was interested in our World Wildlife Project report stating that the reserve contains the "very rare Black-browed Miriki, or Spider Monkey." In his study, *The Mammals of Costa Rica*, published by the American Museum of Natural History in 1946, George Godwin writes that the habitat of the spider monkey extends over a very large portion of Costa Rica, some of which is still heavily forested. The zoologists of the University of Costa Rica also did not think that the spider monkey was particularly rare. The Red Book of rare and endangered species kept up to date by the International Union for the Conservation of Nature and Natural Resources (I.U.C.N.), at Morges, Switzerland, does not list the spider monkey. In my mind, therefore, it remains an open question.

On our last day in San José, Kennedy Crockett took Ambassador Briggs and me to call on President José Trejos and his ministers. As I had visited all three of his country's conservation projects and talked with local experts in virtually all fields of natural science, I felt reasonably well informed on the subject. It was also fortunate for me that President Trejos, having been a professor of economics at the University of Costa Rica, was more interested than most chief executives in conservation. A man of considerable charm, he went out of his way to show his interest in our mission. Because Costa Rica was in a very bad economic position at the time, he was quite frank in saying that his main concern with conservation was in connection with its tourist possibilities. The President was particularly interested in the Green-Turtle Project at Tortuguero, so I took the opportunity to suggest that a national park be proclaimed there. He did not seem to know that the station only leases the twenty miles of beach where the egg operation is carried out, and asked his minister of agriculture, Guillermo Yglésias, who was also present at the conference, to look into it. We then discussed the Cabo Blanco, but when the president heard of its remoteness his enthusiasm waned a bit.

A year after my return to the United States I learned from Allston Jenkins, president of the Philadelphia Conservationists, that he made a trip to Costa Rica early in November, 1968, to look into all matters concerning the Cabo Blanco Reserve. As Mr. Jenkins was a moving figure in the financing of the reserve and has always taken a keen interest in it, I am sure that his visit did a great deal to improve the protection of this valuable wildlife sanctuary.

Later in the conference, Doubles Sanchez, the deputy foreign minister and an official of the Tourist Board of Costa Rica, asked me if it might be possible for Costa Rica to start parks at a low cost. I told him of the rondavels that have proved so successful as guest cottages in the South African parks, explaining that they can be constructed for very little money because the materials consist only of mud and thatch.

Both Ambassador Briggs and Mr. Crockett said they felt the meeting was successful, and I was of course most grateful to both for their interest and support.

I have not reported much about the birds of Costa Rica, mainly because one sees so few of them. Alvaro Collado, a wealthy coffee planter and real estate owner of San José, told me that he was shocked at the dramatic decline in the number of white-winged doves that he saw while shooting in 1967. In the past he made daily bags of fifty or more birds, but this year he had seen only a few—none of which he shot. Mourning doves were also in very short supply, a fact he attributed to the increasing use of pesticides in Central America and to the loss of habitat in the doves' breeding grounds in Texas and northern Mexico.

Costa Rica, unfortunately, is neither a signer nor a ratifier of the Convention on Nature Protection and Wildlife Preservation in the Western Hemisphere. Thirteen Latin American nations have so far signed this important convention, and five of them are in Central America.

CHAPTER VI

Trouble in Nicaragua

High in the Central Valley, on the road from San José to Puntarenas on the Gulf of Nicoya, one sees a cross section of Costa Rica's landscape and economy. The shaded coffee *fincas* of the valley give way to lush fields of sugar cane, and they in turn to the semi-arid cattle lands of the Pacific Coast. The little towns—Alajuela, Grecia, San Remón—cling to the sides of the twisting road that curls snakelike along the hillsides. On the way we stopped at a small factory where wooden oxcarts are made and then decorated with geometric designs of brilliant colors that have become an art form known beyond the country's borders. During the entire seventy-mile trip, however, from 4,000 feet above sea level all the way down to the beaches on the gulf, I saw only two birds: a vulture and a hawk.

No one can say that the Puntarenians are not up-to-date. The most conspicuous food stand on the rather grimy beach rejoices in the name of "Rancho Goldfinger." The Tiago Motel, where the Briggses, Crowes, and Levys stayed the night, is built around what looked to me like a goldfish-bowl pool of murky water filled with an assortment of children who play and shout all day and much of the night, while their benign mammas loll on the beaches gossiping. Far from being alarmed by the fact that the population of their economically beset country is increasing faster than any other in the world, the Costa Ricans seem to take a peculiar pride in fertility.

In the cool dawn of the following morning we started for the border of Nicaragua. A brace of white-wing doves that had evidently survived the pesticides rose from the side of the road and settled on a purple-flowered tree. The stretches of open land between the dusty little towns consist mostly of cattle country, with gauchos riding their thin ponies after the handsome Brahman bulls. At Liberia, the capital of Guanacasto Province, we breakfasted in a little café where to our surprise almost everyone was pleasantly drunk. As it turned out, the celebrants had ridden in from the country to enjoy a festival held the previous day. Their horses still lined the street, one hapless beast faithfully sustaining his master's virtually unconscious form. On the outskirts of town we couldn't help noticing a sign that read *"Mi vaco y yo,"* which means "My Cow and I," and advertised good milk.

Eight miles farther along the Pan American Highway we came to the border of Nicaragua, where we were met by Walter Cadette, the economic officer of our embassy in Managua, and his wife, Joan, whom Ambassador Aaron S. Brown had sent to meet Ambassador Briggs and me. Cadette had been in the middle of the recent pre-election riots there. On January 22, he was covering the political rally of the Conservative Party candidate Fernando Aguero, who was haranguing his followers and incidentally urging the Nicaraguan Army to revolt and join the Anti-Somoza movement. The 5,000-man army, however, remained staunchly loyal to General Anastasia Somoza, whose family had ruled the country for the preceding thirty-one years. Then, as the situation grew tense, someone fired. Aguero and more than a thousand of his followers fled to the nearby Gran Hotel. Cadette immediately went there to report the situation to the embassy. Some eighty-nine Americans were staying at the hotel at the time, so Aguero decided to hold them as hostages, hoping

89

that America would intervene and his side would profit. Meanwhile, the army moved up armored cars and started riddling the hotel with 37-mm. shells. Cadette was injured when part of the wall of his room collapsed.

Contrary to other reports, the actual cease-fire and truce was not arranged by the persuasions of two nuns but by the Red Cross. Though some sixty Nicaraguans were killed and hundreds wounded, not a foreigner was hit.

After the truce most of the Nicaraguan rebels were sent home or treated in the hospitals, only a handful of their leaders being sent to jail. The Americans were then allowed to leave the little inside room where they had spent a miserable night under such crowded conditions that they could not even lie down. The American citizens held by the rebels, as well as Ambassador Brown and the officers of the embassy, who made constant efforts to get them released, deserve great credit.

Tachita, as General Somoza is called, won the 1967 election by a wide majority, making him the third member of his family to run Nicaragua. His father, General Anastasio Somoza, Sr., launched the family dynasty in 1936. Despite strong-arm methods, he did a great deal to push his country into the twentieth century. He built the best road system in Central America, erected hospitals everywhere, and handled the economy so well that the currency is one of the strongest in Latin America. He also organized a social-security system and labor code that have functioned so efficiently the Communists have made very little progress in Nicaragua.

On our way to the capital we stopped at Granada, the charming old city founded by Hernández de Córdoba in 1524, and lunched at the Club Social, a high-ceilinged old building where the landowning aristocrats gather to drink and talk. Granada was three times invaded and sacked by the British and French pirates, who came up the San Juan and Escalante rivers. In 1856 the American adventurer, William Walker, took and burned much of the old city. A soldier of fortune in the grand tradition, Walker was born in Nashville, Tennessee, in 1824, graduated from college there, later studied medicine at Edinburgh and Heidelberg, and even obtained a law degree. But the bar seemed like tame stuff, so in 1853 Walker led a group of freebooters into Mexico, declaring Lower California and Sonora an independent republic. Driven out in 1855, he invaded Nicaragua with only fifty-five followers. Armed with new and efficient rifles, they succeeded in taking Granada, where Walker installed a puppet president. Later he assumed the presidency. In 1856 his government actually won recognition by the United States. The regime lasted until it was finally toppled by a coalition of Central American countries, plus Cornelius Vanderbilt, who owned a transport company that Walker had taken over. His career came to an end in 1860 when he was executed by the Honduran authorities. Walker's book, *The War in Nicaragua*, makes a fascinating story.

On the evening of our arrival at the Gran Hotel—still badly scarred from the shelling—we attended a dinner given for us by James Engle, deputy chief of mission of our embassy. The drive to his house high above Managua was a harrowing experience, as the traffic laws are observed entirely in the breach. But the less-crowded country roads present fewer hazards, and there is a lot to see in this largest of the Central American Republics. Only about ten percent of Nicaragua's 57,143 square miles is used for agriculture or for cattle. Moreover, the population density is low, with only 30 persons to the square mile as against 316.3 in El Salvador. One third of the population of 1.7 million lives in Managua and other towns. The annual rate of population increase is high at 3.2 percent, but well below that of Costa Rica. Unlike Costa Rica, where the great bulk of the population is white, three quarters of Nicaragua is populated by Mestizos, who are a result of the merging of Spaniards and Indians that started when the conquistadors sailed up from Panama in 1519.

Inhabitants of a land of volcanoes and lakes, most Nicaraguans are seldom out of sight of either. Three volcanic cones rise to more than 5,000 feet in Lake Nicaragua itself. One hundred miles long and forty-five miles wide, the lake is said to be the only place in the world where tarpon, sharks, and sawfish can be found in fresh water. I doubt this, however, as sharks are known to exist in the Amazon far above the salt-water limit. The theory is that Lake Nicaragua was part of the Pacific Ocean until a volcanic eruption closed off the entrance. In time the fish became adapted to fresh water. The fresh-water seals of Lake Baikal in Russia, which we saw on our journey across Siberia in 1965, are another example of a marine species accommodating itself to a saltless medium.

The capital, situated on Lake Managua, boasts some wildlife of its own.

In the Parque Centrale, next to the Plaza, I found a three-toed sloth asleep in a tree. From the attendant I learned that no fewer than eighteen of these sleepy creatures made the trees of the little park their habitat. They subsisted on bananas, almonds, and insects. The attendant claimed a particular fondness for an old female who sometimes fell out of her tree and had to be put back.

I subsequently inquired about the Nicaraguan grackle *(Cassidix nicaraguenis)*, a rare species said to survive in small numbers on the shores of Lake Managua. However, I never did locate any of these birds. As for the fish, the lake is now so polluted, we were told, that none have survived. There were still boat-tailed grackles *(Cassidix mexicanus)* around, but long-time residents have told us that the pesticides now being used on the cotton fields have severely curtailed their numbers.

From the officer in charge of our military advisers to the Nicaraguan Army, I learned something further about the country's wildlife situation. A hunter himself, he told me that to the best of his knowledge there were only four game wardens in all of Nicaragua, and they were employed to guard small sections of turtle-egg-laying beaches, one on the Caribbean coast, the other on the Pacific. Furthermore, he had not heard of any game laws or of any licensing requirements for firearms. Later, when I took my inquiries to the Ministry of Agriculture, I discovered that there actually are game laws—on the books at least—so I secured copies of them. Like those of Costa Rica, they exist but are virtually never enforced, for nobody was empowered to do so. The American officer said that although the country swarms with quail they are seldom hunted because the cost of a shotgun shell is beyond the means of the average farmer. He shoots both white-winged and mourning dove, and has not noticed any marked decline in their numbers. Ducks and teal are also plentiful, he said, but they are suffering from the pesticides used on the cotton fields.

Almost a mile high in the cordillera of Nicaragua lies the spectacular hacienda of Don Leo F. Salazar, a descendant of an old Spanish family who has led a long and adventurous life. His 5,000 acres, which span the Continental Divide, include original stands of mighty trees. Forests of oak, long-leaf pine, and black walnut crown the rugged peaks, while groves of cedars with Spanish moss hanging in gray festoons from their branches fill the valleys. Don Leo allows no shooting; consequently game abounds. At night we could hear the roar of a band of howling monkeys, and once we caught the guttural catlike meow of a hunting mountain lion. Don Leo told us that the puma is always accompanied at night by a little owl known as the pájaro leon, or bird of the lion, who warns him of danger by its cry. Also to be found on his property are great spotted jaguar, peccaries, the rare Central American tapir, and many species of birds including the quetzal, the sacred bird of Guatemala.

In 1926 the bandit Augusto Sandino captured Santa María de Ostuma, the Salazar family's hacienda, and burned it to the ground. Don Leo himself was taken prisoner and barely escaped with his life by paying a large ransom. Our Marines were stationed in Nicaragua at that time— they had in fact been there off and on since 1903. But under the Monroe Doctrine they could protect only the property of Americans, British, German, and other foreign nationals, and could not furnish guards for Nicaraguans. Sandino, a squat little brigand who was far from the native-son hero that the American liberal press claimed, was moved only by money, women, and liquor. He was cruel in such a nasty way that even his own 4,000-man "army" were not sorry when he was eventually done in by the *Guardia Nacional* in 1934.

Today Salazar accepts paying guests. Among them has been the ex-King of Belgium who came to dig in the Indian mounds. Below the ranch house is a burial ground where Don Leo says he has found artifacts of both the Mayans and the Incas, for it was in Nicaragua that the extreme ends of the great Central American and South American civilizations met.

A number of well-known ornithologists have also been guests at Santa María de Ostuma. Colonel McChestney of the Cornell Ornithological Laboratory made a record of the various bird songs heard in the vicinity, and Mrs. Barbara Westphal of the Miami Audubon Society took moving pictures of the quetzal *(Pharomacrus mocinno)*. The month of April, when the male quetzal has acquired his full breeding plumage, is a favorite of visiting ornithologists.

The male quetzal, a gorgeous blue-green, ruby-bellied bird with a peacock tail that it grows for entrancing its mate, builds a tunnel-shaped nest. This plumage is apparently the source of a considerable vanity, for Don Leo said he once found two dead males facing each other in one of these nests—neither would spoil his tail feathers by a retreat. Unfortunately, these handsome birds are all too easy to shoot, especially during their mating displays, when they fly in the open. As a result, they are becoming rare in the unprotected areas of Nicaragua.

About an hour's drive from Santa María de Ostuma, near the village of Jinotoga, a big lake has been created for irrigation and power. Stocked several years ago with bass, it now yields some very good catches. To try for one of these and to study the rich bird life inhabiting the lake and its marsh banks, we hired an Indian and his small son to row us around in their homemade boat. Water hyacinth, the bane of rivers and lakes from the Nile to the Amazon, somehow got started and has now grown so profusely that the local boatmen can scarcely force their heavy craft through the channel to open water. It took us an hour to cover a few hundred yards to the lake proper.

Out of the lake great trees, killed by the rising waters, stood veiled in moss. Lily-trotters raced across the matted fields of water hyacinth; a flight of green teal swooped low over our boat; coots took off like bombers making long low runs across the water, and a family of stately white egrets eyed us gravely from a bay. Nightfall comes quickly in the tropics, bringing a brief sunset of vivid color. Before the light had entirely died, a full moon appeared in the sky. But for all the grand setting, my only catch was one small minnow. "They will bite tomorrow morning at five," said the little Indian boy.

To see something of Don Leo's rancho, Irene and I took horses and rode with a pair of farm hands over the Continental Divide. The scenery was magnificent. Giant oaks and mahogany strung together with creepers and garlanded with Spanish moss made a long dim aisle. Birds, some looking like tiny animated jewels, flitted in the high branches and always we heard their songs. Twice something scurried away in the undergrowth; our gauchos said it was a sounder of peccaries, the small but often vicious wild pigs of Central and South America.

We rode for three hours without crossing Don Leo's boundaries. The hacienda would make a superb national park, and on our return I talked at length with him about this possibility. He said he would be glad to consider it seriously, especially if I could persuade General Somoza to include one of his own haciendas that adjoins that of Don Leo. Together the two estates would form a 10,000-acre park of primeval forest populated by a large head of game and birds. It would also have the great advantage of being within comfortable driving distance of the Pan American Highway and the capital. Don Leo, who knows General Somoza well, said he thought the general might well be interested in such a suggestion.

A few days before we left Nicaragua, Ambassador Briggs and I drove down from the cool heights of Santa María de Ostuma to the blistering capital city to have lunch with General Anastasio Somoza, president-elect of the republic. The object of our call, which had been arranged through the good offices of the American ambassador, Aaron Brown, was to discuss conservation—especially the formation of national parks and the proclamation of game laws.

Although his father was assassinated in 1956 and there have been numerous attempts on his own life as well as on that of his late brother, Luis, during the three decades that the Somoza family has dominated the political scene in Nicaragua, the general lived in a most unfortress-like home. It was an unpretentious modern ranch house set back from the road on a large plot that included the horse barns and other outbuildings. At the gatehouse a hefty but unarmed retainer peered at us and waved us forward. On the lawn before the house two peons languidly watered the grass while other farm laborers worked on a tractor near the barns —an altogether peaceful scene. We did note, however, that there was no shrubbery for cover within several hundred yards of the main house.

Once inside we were ushered into a sitting room whose walls were lined with books and modern paintings, along with a watercolor of the general's wife and daughter. A low table between sofas held a silver cigarette box inscribed "To Tacho, from the boys in gray," a souvenir of one of his class reunions at West Point. He graduated from our Military Academy in 1946.

The general, who greeted us warmly, proved to be a large, well-dressed, and rather heavy man with horn-rimmed glasses. Despite the strain of the election riot in which some sixty people had been killed and Americans held hostage, he did not appear unduly tired or nervous. In the ensuing discussion about our mission, General Somoza conceded that Nicaragua had no parks and agreed that establishing them would not only help to conserve his country's forests and fauna but would also prove to be a tourist attraction as well. I then reminded him of his own land adjoining the Salazar hacienda in the mountains near Matagalpa, some ninety miles north of the capital. Again I suggested that if these two holdings were proclaimed a reserve, the country would have a fine 10,000-acre game park in an area that still has original forests and a good head of game. Another advantage would be accessibility, for Matagalpa is only a two-and-a-half-hour drive from Managua by one of Nicaragua's excellent roads. The general responded by saying he would gladly consider this idea and went even further to mention that he has another property in the northeast of the country near Puerto Cabezas on the Caribbean. This, he said, might also have possibilities as a park, for it consisted of some 100,000 acres of tropical lowland forest containing species of birds and animals not found in the mountain areas.

(Nicaragua is a signatory to and has since ratified the Convention on Nature Protection and Wildlife Preservation in the Western Hemisphere, so the creation of parks would be a logical extension of this interest in conservation.)

When I brought up the matter of game laws, the general confirmed that there was in fact no enforcement of such laws as did exist on the books. He also agreed to look into this problem. As the *Guardia Nacional* would be the enforcing agency for any laws the general might proclaim, I asked about the guard's organization and capabilities. Trained originally by the U.S. Marines during our occupation from 1903 to 1933, the *Guardia Nacional* was still advised by an American military mission. Without doubt the best-trained-and-equipped unit in Central America, the guard's total complement was only 4,500 officers and men. Of these, fewer than 1,000 constituted a mobile force, the majority of the force being employed as municipal, provincial, and special police. The army was well looked after and has been intensely loyal to the Somoza family despite almost continuous efforts by the opposition parties to undermine its morale. The general told us that the cost of the unit was only seventeen percent of the national budget—less than the total spent on police by Costa Rica, which boasts of having no armed forces.

When we left the general, it was clearer than ever to us that all conservation efforts in Nicaragua would certainly depend on the stability of the political situation there. There was no question about the general's pro-American leanings. Consistently anti-Communist, the general was one of the first Latin Americans of importance to warn our State Department of Castro's real purpose. On the other hand, one of the often repeated criticisms of the Somoza family is based on their wealth, which is variously estimated at $100 million to $400 million. Somoza's father started the family fortunes by borrowing from the banks and buying land. Later, when he became president, he was not against buying a piece of the various investments which well-heeled companies, American and foreign, made in Nicaragua. At the same time as he built his personal nest egg, however, the old general did a great deal more for the poor farmers of his country than anyone had ever done before. He passed social-security laws and fair labor codes that were unique south of the border. With the help of the United States, he built the best roads in Central America. These roads have been maintained to this day and are in sharp contrast to those of Costa Rica, which for several hundred miles have been allowed to deteriorate to bumpy trails.

The present Somoza's strength lay mainly with the rural farmers and the urban laborers. Ranged almost solidly against him were the landowning aristocracy and the intellectuals. Communism, although still confined to a very small number of men, was said to be gathering adherents among the university students. Perhaps the strongest point in the general's favor was the widely held impression that there was no really strong man in the opposition parties who could take over and run the country.

CHAPTER VII

The Mighty Banana

On a chilly Sunday morning the old bells of the Cathedral of St. Michael the Archangel tolled almost continuously from dawn to midmorning. In Tegucigalpa, cupped in the mountains of central Honduras, there were few people who did not hear them. Church may be something of an event, for there is little else to do but talk politics in that remote little capital. The banana industry, life blood of the Honduran economy, centers on the faraway Caribbean ports of Tela and Puerto Cortés. Aside from the administration of the government and the activities of foreign embassies, little happens here to disturb the placid cycle of the days.

In the early sixteenth century the Spaniards, pressing overland from Guatemala City, came upon silver mines in the area and founded Tegucigalpa in 1524. The scattered Indian tribes were enslaved to work the deposits, but the returns were disappointing, so the Conquistadores turned to agriculture. The isolation of haciendas led the Spaniards to intermarriage with the natives. Consequently, very few of Honduras's population of about two million are either pure white or pure Indian. Other statistical information discloses that 70 percent of the population does not wear shoes, 60 percent are illiterate, and 60 percent are born to unmarried mothers. Although education is compulsory, less than half the children go to school.

From a wildlife standpoint Honduras has a lot to offer. Although larger than all other Central American Republics except Nicaragua, only 22.4 percent of its 43,277 square miles has so far been utilized. Nearly half the country—45 percent—is covered with forest. Vast areas, including the Mosquitia Plain in the northeast, are largely unexplored. Furthermore, the country's few hundred miles of paved roads and railways are concentrated in the northeast, making communication difficult throughout the greater part of Honduras. The horse and the oxcart are still the usual means of travel.

Despite the availability of unused land, the government has not yet established any parks. A preliminary report made for me by Richard Godfrey, head of the economic section of our embassy, stated that there was not a single Honduran law on the conservation of wildlife. However, a draft law had been submitted to the congress in 1966, on which that august body had so far failed to act as of this writing. (Unfortunately, Honduras is not a signatory to the Convention on Nature Protection and Wildlife Preservation in the Western Hemisphere.) Although conservation came within the general prerogatives of the Director General de Recursos Forestales, the official primarily concerned with forests and, incidentally, with wildlife, was Octavio A. Osoria. Subordinate to him was Ing. José Memreno. According to Godfrey's report, Osoria had "informally sought to prohibit the commercial exploitation of wildlife, particularly deer and wildcat." In addition, the Forestry Service guards had instructions to apprehend anyone caught commercially hunting and to turn them over to the "appropriate authorities." Osoria admitted, however, that his office had no legal authority to take such action. In the previous year, he said, some 20,000 deer hides were exported from Honduras. Neither Osoria nor Memreno knew of any organizations interested in conservation.

Although nothing has been done about wildlife itself, the government has set aside various tracts of land as forest reserves in recent years. According to David Challinor, a biologist who visited Honduras for the Smithsonian Institution, a decree was signed in 1963 creating a reserve on the Isla de Guanaja to protect the pine forests there. Another decree protects the mangrove forests on the east shore of Golfo de Fonseca. But there was no money for guards. Moreover, according to Challinor, even the people in the ministry were not always sure of the boundaries of the reserves.

Near Tela, however, there is a patrolled forest area adjoining Lancetilla, the tropical research station run by the United Fruit Company. A rain forest watershed running to 3,400 acres, it would be extremely valuable for biological research in Challinor's opinion. He felt that the formation of a national park there would be a major approach toward the conservation of natural forests in Central America.

Our ambassador to Honduras, Joseph J. Jova, was most helpful in getting us into the country—the border formalities, which can delay travelers for hours, took us exactly five minutes. Although he was the host to three other ambassadors—working ones at that—he had us all for dinner. His deputy chief of mission, Miss Jean Wilkowski, kindly arranged our appointments and travel during our stay.

Timber is one of Honduras's great unexploited resources. A West German consortium, we learned, was about to begin a lumbering operation in a 700,000-acre concession in the pine forests of Olancho. As much of this forested area is mountainous, the resulting erosion from the stripping of the trees may pose serious problems. More government control of lumbering would be a saving force in many countries of Latin America, with benefits for wildlife as well.

On a subject of special interest to all travelers to Honduras, including roving conservationists, the American Embassy at Tegucigalpa had produced a particularly ominous circular. It contained medical and health information. In fact, if the novice foreign-service officer and his wife saw only this circular, they might decide never to take up their first post. The health hazards of Honduras are described as formidable. Food-and-water-borne intestinal diseases are of bacterial, viral, and parasitic origin, and include typhoid, amoeba, worms of various sizes and species, infectious hepatitis, and a variety of unclassifiable, transient, and frequently

The population burgeons in Nicaragua

violent forms of dysentery. Water, unboiled and unfiltered, is a sure invitation to disaster as are local vegetables and fruits, unless properly washed in a chlorine solution. Servants not passed by a reputable physician should not be hired. Insect-borne diseases such as malaria are common. Embassy personnel are warned against the bites of scorpions, tarantulas, and less-poinsonous reptiles and bugs. Don't pat the dogs! Many of them have rabies. At the end of the circular is a forbidding list of doctors and their particular specialties. Wildlife reporters take their chances, too.

For all these reasons, finding a safe place to eat in the capital of Honduras wasn't easy. But by asking our healthier-looking acquaintances we finally located the Chico Club, a Spanish restaurant where we had cold martinis, a delicious thick soup, and tender steaks. Walking home through the chilly narrow streets at ten o'clock at night we found no one. The people of Tegucigalpa were huddling around their dim fires.

The International Zoo Year Book lists a "Jardin Zoological de Honduras" but wisely gives no details of species exhibited. On a sunny Monday morning when I asked my driver to take me there, I drew a complete blank. Subsequent investigation at the American Embassy revealed that there is indeed a park in Tegucigalpa. Its name, however, turned out to be Parque La Concordia. So we proceeded through the narrow streets where every corner is one more Honduran hazard. Will another car arrive at the same time, or will we be lucky and live another day? We made it without incident and found the Parque to be a cheerful little square dotted with large sandstone idols of the Mayan period. There was a number of pools, but the only living thing I spotted in them was a single turtle. This turtle plus a host of unconfined pigeons constituted the "exhibits." Ambassador Briggs asked the park attendant, who was raking leaves out of the turtle's bath, if there were any other parks in Tegucigalpa. He smiled and said we had seen it.

To see something of the fabulous and ancient fruit so important to the Honduran economy—the banana's history goes back to ancient times—we took advantage of the kind invitation of John M. Fox, the president of the United Fruit Company, to visit some of his company's installations on the Honduran coast of the Caribbean. I was particularly glad to make this trip as the company owns the Lancetilla research station, where a great deal of valuable work has been done on plants and trees and the habitats for the birds and animals in which we are interested.

In the cold dawn we flew down from Tegucigalpa to the little port of La Ceiba, where we changed planes for Tela, the United Fruit Company station some seventy miles up the coast. There we were met by Maurice A. Bostick, the assistant general manager of all United Fruit's operations in Latin America and head of the Honduran operations. Bostick, a big, hearty man, went out of his way to make us comfortable. He put us up at the company's comfortable guest house on the beach and arranged for us to visit Lancetilla as well as to see a working banana plantation and the boxing factory where the stems are packaged for shipment.

Federico Girbal, director of Lancetilla, took us out to the station in a "motorcar," an old automobile mounted on railway wheels, which chugged along the rails through groves of rare trees. Founded some twenty-five years ago by the company, the station now has more than 1,000 plants from all over the world growing on its 1,050 acres. There are forty different species of bamboo alone, including a fine stand of Tonkin cane, the solid bamboo that makes the best trout and salmon rods. Lancetilla may well salvage the angler's future, for Tonkin Province, where this cane is native, is in North Vietnam.

The station's experiments with African palm-oil trees have been so successful that 12,000 acres have been planted by the company. Because the trees are valuable for food and for industrial use, seeds are given free to the Honduran University and to the villagers. The botanists at Lancetilla also developed a strain of wild banana that is resistant to a disease that formerly blighted the crop and caused widespread hunger. The new strain is now grown by most Hondurans.

In addition to Lancetilla, the company has a twenty-five-year government lease on 3,500 acres of mountainous rain forest that forms the watershed of Tela. This patrolled tract is valuable not only for biological research but also as the habitat of a great number of birds and animals that are protected there as at Lancetilla. These two tracts are, in fact, the only two patrolled areas in Honduras and in themselves form the only "wildlife park" in the country. Government recognition of the importance of continuing these areas as sanctuaries, even when the lease runs out, is important for conservation in Honduras.

Bostick's assistant, Kenneth Hamilton, an able young graduate of the University of Maine, is a keen bird watcher with a particular fondness for wildfowl. He has identified seventeen species, including a pair of rare snow geese. He said the Muscovy ducks are becoming scarce because they are so easy for the natives to shoot when they roost in trees. Among the migratory ducks seen in Honduras are the green-winged teal, common pintail, common mallard, cinnamon teal, blue-winged teal, northern shoveler, American widgeon, canvasback, redhead, ring-necked duck, lesser scaup, masked duck, and ruddy duck.

Chemicals are used to spray the banana plantations, but no pesticides toxic to animal or bird life are allowed. Consequently there is no loss of bird population comparable to that in the cotton-growing districts of Central America. Burt Monroe, an ornithologist from the University of Kansas, made a check list of 573 species of birds in 1962-63. So far

Hamilton has seen more than half of this imposing total. I sent Monroe's list to Colonel Jack Vincent, compiler of the Red Data Book, Volume 2, on rare and vanishing species of birds, which is published by the International Union for the Conservation of Nature and Natural Resources at Morges, Switzerland.

Bostick, who shoots, told me that he saw more white-winged doves and teal that year than he has ever seen in his many years in Central America. It may well be that these game birds have learned to evade the lethal cotton fields and are now migrating in increasing numbers to safer pastures.

Two of the most notable men we met during our ten-day stay in Honduras were His Excellency Colonel Oswaldo López Arellano, president of the republic, and Dr. Albert S. Muller, director of the Escuela Agrícola Panamericana. This privately financed agricultural college trains boys from all Latin America to get the best out of the lands in which they live. We asked the president to proclaim national parks and asked the director for his sound advice on general conservation problems.

The president conducted the country's affairs in a pastel green castle with battlemented towers, and when we arrived—Ambassador Joseph Jova, Ambassador Ellis Briggs, and I—the guard of honor sprang to attention and saluted. A few minutes later we walked down the hall, knocked on a door and entered the spartan office of the chief of state. A man of about forty-plus with a military bearing, Colonel López combines personal charm with considerable force of character. Although he came from a poor family and never went beyond the sixth grade, he speaks excellent English and is a most engaging conversationalist. He is one of the few strong men in Latin America who have not raised their own rank to general. Though he took over the government in a military coup in 1963, he legitimized his Nationalist regime by having himself legally elected in 1965. All things being equal, he will hold office until 1971.

The president began our conversation by saying that he had received a letter about me from the Duke of Edinburgh and that he was looking forward to hearing about my mission. As Honduras has no parks or game laws, we had to start from scratch, so I began by giving him a brief résumé of the World Wildlife Fund, as well as the reasons why national parks would benefit his country both culturally and economically. I pointed out that Honduras could be a tourist mecca, for only a fifth of its land so far has been used for agriculture, while the mountains, rivers, and lakes would be ideal settings for a series of parks and natural reserves. Ambassador Briggs, always a great help at these top-level meetings, then told the president of our talks with the presidents of Nicaragua, Costa Rica, and Panama. There isn't anyone, it seems, who likes to be different from his neighbors when it concerns a matter such as conservation.

Though Honduras had our Peace Corps, neighboring Nicaragua did not. Both countries are run by military men who rule with the firm support of the army. But Colonel López's brand of control is evidently preferred by those who direct the destinies of our eager young men and women volunteers. Wherever it operates, the Peace Corps would be a useful way to transmit conservation information at the lower levels. In all of the Central American countries where the Peace Corps is at work, I have thus made it a point to see the directors.

After taking our leave of the president, we went in to see Colonel Ricardo Zuñiga Agostinos, the Minister of the Presidency. (It is often confusing to North Americans that Spanish people use their mother's name in addition to their father's. Colonel Zuñiga adds his mother's name of Agostinos, but is still referred to simply as Colonel Zuñiga.) The minister, a short, powerful man who speaks little English, runs the administrative end of the government. Some people, in fact, consider him the éminence grise of the Honduran government. In any case he was most cordial to us, immediately grasping the advantage for his country of national parks. But he told us frankly that he has had no experience in this kind of legislation, and would appreciate it if I would secure copies of the articles setting up the game parks in Panama or Costa Rica. I said I also would send him a copy of the game laws of Panama, which were published in the newspapers while we were in Panama City.

In our talks with both the president and the minister, I stressed the importance of providing guards to patrol national parks, making it plain that a park without guards, such as those now in existence in some Latin American countries, is worse than useless. In fact, such phony sanctuaries are simply an invitation to the poachers to walk in and start shooting. I also made the point that all national parks should be legally entrenched so that the land cannot be alienated later on by unscrupulous politicians.

Immediately after we finished our talk with the president and the minister, the Honduran radio and press cornered us in the lobby. Ambassador Briggs gave an eloquent talk on "Fondo Internacional Para Protección de la Fauna Indígena," an apt Spanish version of the World Wildlife Fund. The local stations carried it, and both the government and opposition papers ran stories complete with pictures of the two "Honduran officials and the three American Ambassadors." Ambassador Jova was most considerate in accompanying us during these calls, for this manifest interest in our mission made the job a great deal easier. Another member of our embassy who is interested in conservation is Max Becker, the forestry officer attached to the AID program. He introduced a program of fire prevention in Honduras that has materially cut the timber losses due to carelessness.

While Ambassador Briggs and I were engaged in these interesting but hardly adventurous calls, our wives chartered a light plane and flew to Copán, the Mayan ruins near the Guatemalan border.

A particularly fascinating aspect of the Mayan cities they visited was their meticulous dating. According to Aldous Huxley's book *Beyond the Mexique Bay*, we know the exact interval of time between the rise of a city and the departure of its inhabitants, but we can only guess at the corresponding dates in our calendar. Mayan art was mathematical. Every column, statue, frieze, stairway, and temple reveals a date or relationship to time. The seventy-five steps of the Hieroglyphic Stairway at Copán stood for the number of elapsed intercalary days. More accurate than either the Julian or Gregorian systems of the West, the Mayan calendar was off only .000069 of a day out of an entire year. This was even more amazing for a people who never invented the wheel or used domestic animals to haul loads. We cannot read their writing, but from the carvings we know that one article of their faith was that the world was supported on the backs of two giant alligators. Wildlife was a favorite theme. My

Quetzal male and
female, Nicaragua

wife and Lucy Briggs found likenesses of frogs, quetzals, jaguars, turtles,
and pelicans.

The Escuela Agrícola Panamericana is some thirty kilometes from
Tegucigalpa. The road twists and turns and after crossing a 5,000-foot
pass drops into the lovely Zamorano Valley. About a third of this valley,
5,000 acres, belongs to the college. Dr. Albert S. Muller, the director,
accommodated us in his very comfortable guest house, and, after an
excellent dinner of produce raised entirely on the place, we had a good
night's rest.

107

World Wildlife: the Last Stand

We awakened to the sound of many birds; the cooing of white-wing and ground doves, the chirping of boat-tailed grackles, and the raucous call of blue jays. Before breakfast I took a long walk and admired the trees. Almost all of the roads are lined with handsome and often exotic stands. Fig trees from Java; jacaranda in bloom, with lavender flowers that reminded me of Pretoria; flame-of-the-wood's scarlet flowers; the butter yellow blooms of the palo blanco, and the pink flowers of the Matisleguate.

Dr. Muller was justly proud of his college. As he drove us around the fields, pastures, and buildings of the college, he told us something of its history and purpose. Founded some twenty-five years ago, with an initial endowment of $3.5 million from the United Fruit Company, the college is still the only agricultural institution of learning in Latin America where the students learn by working in the fields as well as in the classroom. In 1967 there were 191 undergraduates and they had come from almost all South and Central American countries north of Bolivia. The cost to the student for the three-year, eleven-months-a-year course is a nominal $120, while the actual cost per student of about $3,000 is made up by the college. In addition to the original gift from the United Fruit Company and many subsequent grants, the college has received substantial grants from the U.S. AID program and private contributors. It still, however, operates at a loss of more than $50,000 per year, which has to be balanced by withdrawals from the endowment fund.

So popular is the college that 790 high-school graduates from all over Latin America took the entrance examinations in 1967, while only seventy-one could be accepted. Graduates are about equally divided among those who go into farming for themselves, those who work for the Alianza para el Progresso, and those who go into agricultural industry. There are said to be ninety graduates employed by the Department of Agriculture of Honduras. Close to 1,000 alumni now work in fourteen different countries south of the Texas border.

In addition to the broad fields of cotton, corn, beans, sugar cane, and vegetables, the school owns part of a mountain bearing a million dollars' worth of timber. Shooting is not allowed on the school property, so that this 5,000-acre tract, along with the Lancetilla research station and its

adjoining forests at Tela on the Caribbean are, in effect, the only protected wildlife areas in all of Honduras. Significantly, the United Fruit
Company is responsible for both of these sanctuaries.

Dr. Muller, a small man with a deceptively mild demeanor and an
engaging smile, was nearing retirement after having been director of the
college for nearly five years. Unlike many of the principals of colleges all
over the world today, he did not put up with student disobedience. If an
undergraduate did not obey the rules, he was dismissed, but so pleasant
and profitable is life at the college that very few caused trouble. Dr.
Muller has had twenty species of fungi named after him and is about to
give his name to a new species of walnut that has just been discovered
in the college forest. Thousands of species of plants from all over Latin
America can be seen in the college gardens and fields. There is an
excellent library of 11,000 volumes.

The school has had many distinguished visitors, including Richard
Nixon, Nelson Rockefeller, and all of the recent presidents and most of
the ministers of Honduras and adjoining countries. Charles Sillman,
former treasurer of Time, Inc., is a director and a frequent visitor at the
college, as is John Fox, the president of the United Fruit Company. Dr.
Archie Carr, the savior of the green turtles, used to be on the teaching
staff. Billy Cruz, who took us to the green-turtle station at Tortuguero,
Costa Rica, is a graduate of the college.

The college, which possesses a good collection of bird skins assembled
by Mrs. Archie Carr, was about to set up a display room for the birds and
animals of the region. A shipment of Kalej pheasants (a bird I used to
shoot in the north of India) had just arrived. Chinese ring-neck pheasants
might also do well in the valley. I fished in the college pond and hooked
but did not land a big bass. I also rode one of their good horses into the
hills. By using a Morgan stallion with Honduran mares, the college has
bred a bigger and more useful animal than one sees any place else in the
country.

In the late afternoon when the shadows were starting to run up the
rugged mountains while the valleys were still bright with warm white
light, Dr. Muller drove us to San Antonio de Oriente. We passed the
hacienda of Don Arturo Portín, who used to own the whole valley where

the college now is. Under a great ceiba tree his stone fountain still stands, but no more water flows there, and the gates of the old Spanish house are closed.

The village was built for the silver mines which the conquistadores worked in the seventeenth century but which finally closed for good in 1910. Since then there has been nothing to do in the village, so the men walk ten miles down to the valley every day to work, leaving their large broods of children and tired wives on the mountain.

San Antonio de Oriente is the home of the well-known Honduran artist José Antonio Velasquez. Although he makes thousands of dollars for his paintings and was elected mayor of the village, he seems to have done little for it. In the whitewashed church there was only one of his pictures. San Antonio de Oriente had no priest of its own, but one always comes for Holy Week to marry all who wish it and to confess the sins of a year. In the little graveyard is the tomb of Dr. Paul Standy, the famous botanist, who worked for six years at the college and wished to be buried among his friends in the village.

As we ate our last meal with the good Dr. Muller, we heard on the radio that martial law had been declared in Guatemala, our next stop after San Salvador.

CHAPTER VIII

San Salvador

It is a long ten-hour drive from Tegucigalpa, Honduras, to San Salvador, the capital of El Salvador and, from the standpoint of a conservationist, a sad one. We passed stark, eroded hills from whose tops the last tree had been cut by man or killed by fire, fields barren of anything but acacia bushes and cactus, and along the sides of the roads thin cattle and thinner horses trying to find a mouthful among the dusty weeds. We crossed an almost dry river bed where women were washing clothes in the few stagnant pools. The people lived in little thatched houses, very similar to the Bantu huts of East Africa. The towns—with such apt names as Perspire—drowsed in the heat. The only birds I saw were a pair of vultures sitting on a dead tree above a dying calf.

At the border we were met by Edward Curtis, the deputy chief of mission of our embassy at San Salvador, who had driven more than a hundred miles to facilitate our crossing. For even with diplomatic status this procedure can be time-consuming and is invariably conducted in crowds of struggling humanity.

In a scant thirty minutes we were cleared for entry into the smallest nation in Central America. With an area of 8,260 square miles, El Salvador is the size of Massachusetts. It is also Central America's most densely populated country. In 1965 an estimated three million people lived there, an average of 360 persons per square mile. According to the South American Handbook, the rate of population increase is a whopping 3.5 percent a year, with a life expectancy of twenty-six years. Because of its burgeoning population and limited land area, El Salvador faces an uncertain economic future, especially with a surplus of its main products— coffee and cotton.

Before our visit, I had been lucky in securing from my friend Judge Russell Train, then president of the Conservation Foundation, a study of El Salvador written in 1963 by the late William Vogt, the well-known ecologist and student of land use. According to Dr. Vogt's reports, about half of El Salvador's total land area is composed of worn-out soils to support the nation's 500,000 peasants. The country is broken by two roughly parallel volcanic ranges, between which lie warm valleys.

Two years later Dr. Vogt returned for another look at El Salvador with particular reference to birds. His report, titled *The Avifauna in a Changing Ecosystem,* is grim reading for a conservationist. On a low-altitude flight of some 150 kilometers mostly over the coastal area, he saw only three flocks of birds: two of egrets and another that he took to be ibises. Later, driving the 500 kilometers between San Miguel, El Salvador, and Guatemala City, he saw few birds except flycatchers. Even these were scarce.

He blames the sharp decline in bird population largely on an eight-fold expansion of cotton production and the consequent heavy spraying of the fields with insecticides. An interesting side effect of this spraying seems to be the increasing resistance of malaria-carrying mosquitos to DDT. This combination of lethal poisons on the fields and man's steady encroachment on the few areas of original habitat bodes ill for the birds and animals of El Salvador.

"There has probably never been a destructive force (as far as conservation goes) comparable to the Interamerican Highway," wrote Dr. Vogt

—and anyone interested in conservation who has his eyes open as he drives this 3,000-mile road from Panama to Texas would certainly agree with him. For exploitation inevitably follows accessibility. This expolitation began back in 1523 when the conquistadores invaded the country from Guatemala. Though the Pipil Indians, who possessed a civilization similar to that of the Aztecs, fought bravely, they were no match for the armored and mounted Spaniards. For the next three centuries the country remained under the rule of Madrid. Finally, on November 5, 1811, a group of Salvadoran patriots won independence.

The capital, San Salvador, was destroyed by an earthquake in 1919, with the result that the present city is one of the most modern in Central America. Broad tree-lined avenues and numerous parks with magnificent trees make this 2,237-foot-high capital a pleasure to see. I was particularly interested in the large section of middle-class housing, complete with car parks. Although the great families still dominate the economy, and 47 percent of the land is held by 4 percent of the landowners (21 percent is in tracts of 2,500 acres or more and belongs to one tenth of one percent of all landowners), a middle class is rapidly being developed which in the long run may be the bastion of democracy in El Salvador.

Referring again to Dr. Vogt's first report, I noted that there had been considerable interest at that time in the establishment of an international park where El Salvador, Guatemala, and Honduras meet. El Salvador's contribution would be 4,000 acres comprising almost the last cloud forest remaining in the country. To check on this project, I talked with Carol Deyoe, the officer in charge of Rural Development for the AID Mission, who had been to the area. He said that while there were forest guards, there was no prohibition on shooting. Whether or not the El Salvadoran tract was part of an international park or was government owned, he did not know. Asked about the possibility of there being government sponsored parks in other sections of the country, he told me that since the state actually owns very little land the chances of finding such areas in private hands would be much better.

Dr. Vogt had cited the Amigos de la Tierra (Friends of the Land) as the only private group in the country interested in conservation. This organization, which has an office in downtown San Salvador, was formed in 1947 by a group of leading coffee growers to encourage small farmers

113

in good land use. The Amigos sponsor contests in which prizes are given and also do a first-class job of promoting conservation in the press and on television.

Unfortunately, however, there did not seem to be much cooperation between the Amigos and the Ministry of Agriculture. The minister, Dr. René David Escalante Orozco, who has degrees in agronomy from the University of Puerto Rico and the Central University of Venezuela, has the reputation of being a dedicated and hard-working public servant. Yet his department cannot afford a pay scale sufficiently high to retain its best men. As a result, they almost always leave for the richer fields of private enterprise.

Roland Kelly, chief of security for the embassy, is a hunter of note and a particularly avid follower of the white-wing dove. I was pleased to hear from him that the migration in 1967—the doves fly south in October and November and north in April and May—was one of the best he could remember in his six years in El Salvador. He thought that the doves were learning to avoid cotton fields that have been sprayed with pesticides. However, he added that chemicals have had a lethal effect on the fishing in many of the estuaries of rivers that drain these same cotton-growing areas. He cited the Lempa River as one which has suffered markedly from the crop-dusting residue. To illustrate the potency of some of the chemicals used, he told us of hearing about a farmer whose favorite dog died from eating a rat. Analysis showed that the rat had recently eaten a dove which had died of poisons derived from spray!

The migrating duck population of El Salvador seemed to be suffering from a relatively new practice of draining the rice fields after the crop was harvested. In the past the flooded fields gave the ducks a good eating and resting place. Kelly said that several years ago four men would shoot twenty-five ducks apiece on an average hunting day, but now they were lucky if they got ten each. Further militating against the wildfowl population is the fact that El Salvador has no game laws, no licensing system for sporting guns, and no protected areas.

Despite its modernity, San Salvador is a city of contrasts. One wealthy man we met commuted to his downtown office by his own helicopter. But in the shack-lined ravines where the *campesinos* live, oxen drag wooden-wheeled carts over the dusty roads. It is said that fourteen families control more than half of the wealth of El Salvador. Most of them are presumed to be opposed to change. There are, however, liberal exceptions. Outstanding among these is Don Francisco de Sola, a tall Oxford-educated aristocrat who is deeply interested in the future of his countrymen. It was De Sola, along with Napoleón Viera Altamirano, editor of *El Diario de Hoy*, the country's leading paper, and others, who joined with William Vogt in organizing the Amigos de la Tierra.

We met De Sola at a dinner given by the British ambassador, Geoffrey Kirk, in honor of Lucy Briggs's birthday, and immediately took note of his keen interest in and grasp of the conservation problems of Central America. He is a director of the Escuela Agrícola Panamericana in Honduras, where we had spent three profitable days. De Sola arranged for Ambassador Briggs and me to call on Colonel Julio Adalberto Rivera, the president of the republic, and accompanied us when we went to see him. A stocky, dynamic man of forty-five, he was one of the leaders of the military group which overthrew a left-leaning Junta in 1961. His group, known as the Directorate, governed the country for two years and was then dissolved. In the peaceful and free elections of 1962, Rivera

Bush dog, Brazil and Guianas

won a five-year term, which was concluded by the election in 1967 of Colonel Fidel Sánchez Hernández. De Sola thought, in fact, that my conservation pitch to Colonel Rivera would be handed on to the next president.

Before the meeting, De Sola had briefed us on the forested area on the border of Honduras and Guatemala, a site considered suitable for El Salvador's first national park. The area, known as Monte Cristo, is owned mostly by a family named Freund. But the president said he believed that a swap could be made. The government would negotiate for the Freund holdings at Monte Cristo and recompense them with government-held land elsewhere. I urged the president to see that the charter for the park continue in perpetuity so that succeeding regimes could not alienate it. I also urged him to appoint guards and to see that regulations against shooting be enforced in the area. Because El Salvador lacks game laws, Ambassador Briggs and I explained to the president the importance of establishing them in order to retain the country's good dove shooting as well as to protect the rarer birds and animals.

According to De Sola, the original idea of a park where Honduras, Guatemala, and El Salvador meet envisioned a trinational scheme in which the borders of the park would include land from all three countries. Neither Honduras nor Guatemala was prepared to go along, however. And until our talk with the president, the concept of a park for El Salvador alone had not been considered at this level of the government.

The president asked if the World Wildlife Fund would be able to help in making a survey of the area and of fauna there. I told him that while we did not have staff scientists I would be glad to look into the possibility of having such a survey done by the AID mission of the embassy or by FAO of the United Nations. (El Salvador is a charter member of the 1942 Convention on Nature Protection and Wildlife Preservation in the Western Hemisphere.)

The president also inquired if any of the islands in the Gulf of Fonseca might make possible sanctuaries for fauna. But in checking later with men who had been there, I learned that the islands are small, barren, and practically waterless. Hence the number of game birds that could live there would be limited.

De Sola, who is a bird watcher, took us to one of his coffee *fincas* overlooking the city early one morning. It was just after dawn, and the sun had not yet risen from behind the great San Salvador volcano. Now quiet but ever a threat, this volcano once wiped out the capital. Met by his delighted pack of German short-haired pointers, we walked over some of the 200-acre *finca*, admiring De Sola's collection of more than forty species of exotic trees and plants. Often we heard the sweet clear call of the robin and saw numerous flycatchers, wrens, parakeets, and mourning and white-winged doves. We heard but did not see a motmot, a relative of the quetzal.

De Sola, like other thoughtful people in Central America, admires the research being done by the United Fruit Company at its Lancetilla Gardens in Honduras. He told us that in his opinion all the countries of Central America owe the company a great deal for this valuable botanical facility. Somewhat of a breeder of rare specimens himself, De Sola has developed a seven-eighths pure Morgan horse with which he hopes someday to win the 100-mile ride in Woodstock, Vermont. He was one of the first to import Morgan blood into El Salvador, and by crossing Morgan stallions with local mares, bred what he believes is the ideal horse for his country.

On our last night in San Salvador, the American ambassador and his wife, Mr. and Mrs. Raul H. Castro, gave a dinner for the Briggses and for my wife and me at their residence. (Earlier in our visit, it should be said, Ambassador Castro's forthrightness and effectiveness in his post had greatly impressed us.) They kindly invited Minister of Agriculture and Mrs. René Escalante Orozco. Dr. Escalante, who used to teach agriculture in Venezuela, was the man most directly concerned with land use in El Salvador. I told him of my talk with the president and of our hopes for a park at Monte Cristo.

Dr. Escalante was most enthusiastic, saying that his country should also have parks for the conservation of rare trees and plants as well as birds and animals. He told me of a tree of the genus Zapotacea which grows twenty feet in diameter and is of such hardness that carvings made from it in the Mayan days are still in existence. Although this tree can live from 200 to 300 years, there are only a few remaining in El Salvador. The minister, who attended Virginia Polytechnic Institute and speaks English fluently, invited me to tour his country with him. I only wished that time allowed it, but we were soon to move on. He was making studies of the kinds of trees and shrubs that would grow best on the volcano slopes. He was also interested in marine life and told me that there was a lake full of "soda water" where there are some unusual types of fish. I presume they are of Scotch descent.

CHAPTER IX

Guerrillas
and Game Laws

In contrast to the barrenness we left behind in Honduras, the country from San Salvador to the border of Guatemala was a pleasure to drive through. Shaded coffee *fincas* lined the road, graceful girls with water pots balanced on their dark hair promenaded under the lilac-blossomed jacaranda trees, and the symmetrical peaks of volcanos dominated the blue distance. At the border, George Phelan, the consul general at our embassy in Guatemala City, and his wife met us and assisted us through customs. Asked about the state of civil unrest in the country, Phelan told us that as of that date (March 14, 1967) the nation was only on "alert" status. This was more serious than an "emergency," but not as critical as "martial law," which had been in force up to that time. The net of this was that the Communists were still making life a bit uncertain in Guatemala. No one seemed to know where they might strike next.

At the residence of our ambassador, John Gordon Mein (who was later assassinated), the gates were closed and guarded by a Tommy-gun-toting policeman who seemed a little reluctant to let us enter. Mein had a handsome house complete with pool and garden, all of which was surrounded by a sturdy wall. These precautions made sense, for only a few weeks before we arrived the army cornered some guerrillas a few blocks away, and in the ensuing barrage of grenades and rifle bullets, plus fire from a hovering helicopter, several dissidents, a policeman, and an innocent bystander were killed. The losses might have been far greater, for the incident occurred in front of the University Sports Club, where forty-eight American school children, aged eight to fourteen, were exercising. The quick-thinking director of the school, Mrs. Julio Rolz-Bennet, herded her charges into two cement-reinforced bathrooms where they were safe from the fusillade.

But life in that mile-high city ringed by volcanos was still very pleasant and apparently prosperous, too. Our hotel, the Guatemala Biltmore, was full of earnest businessmen with large order books, and even some of the taxis were last year's Mercedes. On weekends the whole town seemed to emigrate to the nearby lakes. Thanks to the Phelans, we spent Sunday at Lake Amatitlán, an hour's drive from the capital. There we swam, admired towering Agua Volcano, whose classic cone is mirrored in the blue water, and ate delicious steaks. Across the lake is a shrine called the Chair of the Child, where the Infant Jesus was said to have appeared. Every year the Indians come in boats to see if he will reappear. I was pleased to hear that not only is the lake full of ducks but also that no shooting is allowed on it or in the nearby hills.

In nearly every country there is one man who is well known for conservation. In Guatemala it is Dr. Jorge A. Ibarra, director of the Museo Nacional de Historia Natural. Dr. Ibarra, who looks about forty but is probably a bit older, has been carrying the torch for fauna for many years. We met him first at the First World Conference on National Parks at Seattle in 1962.

During a pleasant luncheon meeting, Dr. Ibarra told me that although the United Nations World List of National Parks and Equivalent Reserves (1962) credits Guatemala with no less than eleven national parks, only Tikal and a small, recently donated private park have wardens to protect the wildlife. He also reported that, sadly, Guatemala has no game laws. He urged me to convince the president of his country of the real necessity of both game laws and wardens.

Dr. Ibarra also asked me to suggest to the president and his ministers that a series of national parks with tourist potential could well be formed in the Petén, the great empty province north-northeast of the capital. Deep in the rain forest of this densely wooded area of some 14,000 square miles lie the ruined cities of the Maya. Only one of these, Tikal, has received world attention. Dr. Ibarra says there are five more Mayan ruins which someday will attract almost as much attention. He would like these areas to be proclaimed national parks now, so that when they are developed they may enjoy the protection that Tikal has been given. The fact is that, without a tourist angle, no Central American government is going to spend money on parks for animals and birds. This we found to be the weakness in the Cabo Blanco reserve in Costa Rica. It can only be reached by horse or mule, and most tourists are not willing to travel except by plane, or by car if the roads are good. Virtually every president with whom I talked, from Panama to Guatemala, made the point that conservation must be made profitable monetarily as well as culturally.

Dr. Ibarra raised another important point in regard to the Petén. Population in Central America is increasing at such a rate that it will be doubled before the year 2000. The few undeveloped areas such as the Darien in Panama, the Caribbean coast of Costa Rica and Nicaragua, the Mosquitia Province of Honduras, and the Petén of Guatemala will be inundated with hungry, landless people whose last interest will be the preservation of fauna. Already some 20,000 Salvadoran immigrants have applied for land in Petén.

Dr. Ibarra then discussed an approaching conference on conservation subsequently held in Mexico City. Promoted by the Rockefeller Foundation and the Pan American Union, the conference not only would be a focus for conservationists from Latin America but also would make a real effort to interest the press in its proceedings. As a former newspaperman and a firm believer in the power of the press, I have been astonished by the apparent inability of most scientists to make news out of their conferences. As William Vogt of The Conservation Foundation said, "International meetings and resolutions, in themselves, have little actual effect on environments. The Interamerican Conference of the Conservation of Renewable Natural Resources of 1948 was largely worthless except to the extent that it served to educate a few—a very few—people. The usefulness as an educational tool would have been enlarged if the State Department had kept its promise to publish the proceedings in Spanish." I certainly agree with Dr. Vogt on this, but I also think that instead of relying on the State Department, a committee of the conference itself should have been organized well in advance to invite, entertain, and intrigue members of the Fourth Estate.

That adequate planning brings results is clearly indicated by the press coverage we have received on our mission to Central America. Way ahead of time I made arrangements with the United States Information Service to see that all the embassies on our itinerary received an advance release in Spanish as to what we planned to do. This notice was run by leading newspapers from Panama to Mexico, so that when we arrived persons interested in conservation were eager to see us. After our conservation talks with the various presidents, a picture was taken which included the president, the American ambassador, Ambassador Ellis Briggs, and myself. This picture was always run on the front page accompanied by an article plugging not only the importance of conservation but also the president's interest in it.

Much depends on how these releases are presented. Conservation conferences frequently use words like "Biosphere," which most people think refers to a structure at a world's fair. Even as able and provocative a writer on conservation as William Vogt titled a highly readable and newsworthy article "The Avifauna in a Changing Eco-System." What copywriter can make a headline out of this? If he did, who, aside from ornithologists, would understand it? (In fairness to Dr. Vogt, he wrote this article for a professional audience. But it is a shame he did not give it another title for the nonprofessional press.) Roy Chapman Andrews knew how to get things printed. Instead of using the scientific and utterly unpronounceable names of the dinosaurs he uncovered in the Gobi Desert in Mongolia, he made them household words all over the world by calling them "a rhino with a dredge in its mouth." The great cause of conservation can and should be made much more palatable to the working press.

Guatemala is a land of many vistas, half of which are still unspoiled. There are rain forests in the lowlands and cloud forests in the highlands, where no man lives. In these areas the birds and animals are inhabiting the same land as they did in the days of the Mayan Empire. The heartening fact is that the country's four and a half million people have so far used only about 21,000 of their 42,000-square-mile heritage. More than fifty percent of the inhabitants are Indians, speaking native languages and wearing distinctive garments. Less than five percent are Europeans, the rest being Ladinos or mixed descendants of the Spaniards who arrived from Mexico City in 1523.

Unlike some Latin American countries, the Indians of Guatemala have not been absorbed into an alien civilization. Instead, they have retained a great deal of their ancient culture. One of the best-known historians of the Indians is Mrs. O. E. Osborne, whose book on Indian weaving, titled *Indian Crafts*, is a classic work. To pay our respects to her and to see her famous collection of village costumes, we went to her home in the old section of Guatemala City. A kindly and highly intelligent lady of advanced age, Lily de Jongh Osborne showed us some of her 350-piece assortment of ancient and modern weaving. The clothes were of cotton or wool and the dyes made of vegetables. While the designs varied greatly, the motif was often of flowers or of animals representing fertility. She also showed us a modern man's coat from a village deep in the interior, with the maker's idea of what constituted proper cuffs. The cuffs, copied from those on the sleeves of the priest who came once a year, are simply an adornment—the Indian's hands project through a slit above them, and the cuffs are sewed together!

Dr. Ibarra had accompanied us to Mrs. Osborne's and was able to show

123

us which animals were represented in the old designs. The following morning we visited his museum, unique in that its primary purpose is not to house musty collections of fauna, but to teach young people which of their country's varied wildlife should be preserved. The exhibits of hawks and owls, shown with rats and mice clutched in their talons, are accompanied by signs explaining why these carnivores are friends of the farmers. Since most of the people of Guatemala live on corn and beans, rodents are deadly enemies even to children. The room was indeed full of children gazing with awe and wonder at the great harpy eagles and at the glittering, jewel-like sun birds.

To illustrate the balance of nature, Ibarra has a display of a jaguar stalking a herd of deer. A sign explains that the big cats keep down the deer population that might otherwise destroy the crops. He even makes a case for the crocodile as a useful citizen. Without this scavenger, many lakes and rivers would be continually polluted by dead cattle and other ungulates. He told me that one formerly plentiful species of crocodile, *Crocodilus moreletti*, is now rare in Petén Province because of extensive hide hunting.

As I noted earlier, there are no over-all game laws in Guatemala. A few laws, however, apply to individual species. The quetzal, for example, is legally protected because it is the national bird as well as the unit of monetary exchange. But the law, while stating that nobody can shoot or trap the bird, says nothing about selling its skin. Consequently, the Indians in the high cloud forest where the quetzal lives "manage" somehow to get these beautiful skins and sell them. Ibarra has for years been urging the government to add a clause prohibiting such sales. Another protected bird is the giant grebe of Lake Atitlán, of which I will have more to say later when we visit that lovely body of water. The manatee, listed in the Red Book of endangered species, is also on the so-called protected list. But since there are no wardens, the Indians of the Caribbean coast spear them with impunity. Several hundred pounds of meat is simply too tempting.

Unfortunately, many of these rare species are good to eat, and so the hard facts of hunger are in combat with the enforcement of game laws.

It is probable that at least three million of the country's total population (64 percent of the people have an average yearly income of only $64) have little more to eat than the staples of beans and corn. Per capita gross national product was estaimated at $314 in 1965, or less than one tenth of the figure for the United States. In addition, more than sixty percent of the population is illiterate. The life expectancy at birth is under forty, compared to nearly seventy in North America.

The equitable distribution of land is a pressing problem. A census made in 1950 revealed that seventy percent of the area suitable for cultivation was owned by two percent of the landowners. While the pressure on the land is nowhere near so severe as it is in Costa Rica and Panama, the Communists and other leftists still make propaganda out of the necessity for agrarian reform. The regime of Julio César Méndez Montenegro had passed out some government-owned land to the peasants, but had not yet expropriated any from the landowners because it wished to give "confidence to the capitalist class." The government's inability to pay for private land is another reason for the failure to take it over.

Ibarra used to be director of the country's zoo, but he differed with the authorities over the displays. He wanted, and quite rightly, I think, to publicize the indigenous birds and animals of Guatemala and keep the exotics to a minimum. Today the Parque Zoologica La Aurora has very few of the handsome native birds—Ibarra thinks there may be as many as 600 species in his country—and an equally limited number of native animals. I did, however, see a pair of suitisizils, or cabrios de monte, the tiny deer which, with the common white-tailed species, are the only members of the deer family in Guatemala. There was also a lonely tapir and a family of rather dispirited looking spider monkeys. According to Ibarra, spider monkeys are plentiful in the jungles of the Petén, while the howling monkeys are rare. Yellow fever, the bane of the closely knit monkey clans, wipes out large numbers of simians when it strikes.

Julio Cesar Méndez Montenegro, president of the Republic of Guatemala, was a busy man with some very pressing problems. Falling world prices for coffee and cotton, his country's major exports, plus the constant threat from roving guerrilla bands, gave him little time for other matters. Despite these continuous headaches, he took time from a crowded schedule to discuss conservation. He assured me that his government was sincerely interested in national parks and the protection of rare birds and animals. The conference, which took place at the palace, was also attended by the minister of foreign affairs, Emilio Arenales Catalán, who translated for the president, along with Ambassador Mein and Ambassador Briggs.

I was specifically interested in furthering Ibarra's ideas for more parks in the Petén, and the president said he would consider them. Guatemala was one of the charter signers and ratifiers of the convention on nature protection in the Western Hemisphere and I reminded the president of his country's long interest in conservation. I also told the president of my talk with his cousin, Francisco Montenegro Girón, minister of agriculture. The talk could not have been more opportune, for the minister told me that he was in the midst of framing a set of game laws to protect the rare fauna of his country. The minister also said he would be pleased if I would immediately send him a list of those birds, animals, and reptiles that my organization considered to be in danger of extinction. The list I sent him included the horned guan, agami heron, and Muscovy duck —the quetzal and giant grebe are already protected—and the tapir, brocket, margay, ocelot, howling monkey, and the Petén crocodile. (The manatee is also nominally protected.)

Although physically small, the president possessed an impressive personality and had earned the respect of his troubled country. Before entering politics he had been dean of his country's law school.

Considering his nation's dropping export income, I reminded the president that in 1966 U.S. travelers spent $70 million in countries south of the border, excluding Mexico, and that Guatemala, with her beautiful scenery, ancient ruins, and pleasant climate should be able to extract more from this bonanza. Development of national parks would be profitable from a financial as well as from a cultural standpoint. I made the point, however, that parks without guards are worse than useless. The subject was left with the understanding that I would have Ibarra prepare specific proposals for establishing and protecting some new parks.

Travel in some parts of Guatemala was risky because of the guerrillas. There was also much to be said for being cautious while trekking around the cities. But these hazards did not keep most Guatemalans, as well as visitors, from enjoying their country. We were delighted with the hospitality we received, particularly from Mrs. Franz Pieters, Irene's cousin, and many others. On a bright morning we drove to Antigua and lunched with Mrs. Charles Stillman, the wife of the former treasurer of Time, Inc., who has a lovely house whose garden frames the volcano of Agua. The former capital of Guatemala, until it was destroyed by an earthquake in 1773, Antigua was once the leading city of Central America with a population of 80,000, numerous churches, a university, a printing press, and a reputation as the home of famous painters, writers, and craftsmen.

In Guatemala, as in the other countries of Central America which we visited on this mission, the most effective wildlife conservation was on private or leased land where the owner had a personal interest in preserving the fauna and its habitat. However, there may not be continuity in these reserves, for people die and their heirs may not share their protective instincts. But worst of all, the instability of many of the governmental regimes leave the national parks at the mercy of politicians. Who can say that the survival of the rare birds and animals of Central America may not, in the long run, depend more on individuals than it does on their governments?

In our travels around Guatemala we visited some big estates—*las fincas principales*—where the owners have made the conservation of wildlife an important part of the management of their properties. The first of these was El Zapote, the beautiful *finca* of Leif Pettersen, which lies on the slopes of Fuego, a 12,000-foot volcano. A Norwegian who came to Guatemala in 1919, Pettersen and his wife, who is a talented artist, used to own 60,000 acres, but have reduced their holdings to 2,400 acres.

On 600 of these they grow most of the cinchona produced in their country. Quinine, still an important medicine in the control of malaria, is made from its bark.

Above the cinchona plantations the virgin forest climbs far up the skirts of Fuego. In this wild and steep habitat live many mammals. There are sounders of peccar, the wiry little wild pig, and white-tailed deer. Preying upon them both are the puma and the jaguar. No shooting is allowed, and the 200 employees and patrols help to discourage poachers. Pettersen has built a series of ponds which beautify his lawns and are the home of flocks of Muscovy ducks, the indigenous wildfowl rapidly becoming extinct in many areas. Each December, hundreds of cattle egrets settle on an island in one of these ponds.

Pettersen, an active and entertaining man of over seventy, with white spade beard and twinkling blue eyes, told me he is interested in acquiring a pair of suitisizils, or cabros de monte *(Mazama americana)*, the little deer of Central America which are now very rare. He felt sure that they would thrive in his protected forest.

An important contribution to the wildlife of his country has also been made by Robert Dorión, a Dartmouth-educated Guatemalan who is president of El Salto, the nation's largest sugar producer (one fourth of the entire output). Situated only an hour's drive from Guatemala City, the 10,000-acre estate provides a unique refuge for some of Guatemala's rare birds and animals.

To see the wilder parts of El Salto, Bobby Dorión provided horses for the ride to the top of the range of mountains which border the active volcano of Pacaya. The trail, lined by coffee trees, wound steadily upward, taxing our patient horses to their limit. Well did the Conquistadores say that "after God, we owe the victory to our horses," for to climb the mountains of Latin America on foot would have given pause even to the conquerors. We passed many mounds, long forgotten fortifications of the Maya, which must have made the mountain strongholds almost impregnable. Water from a mountain brook cascaded down the steep slopes, and we came upon groves of great trees that may well have been there in the days of the Spanish. Most of El Salto is said to have been originally presented to the *caballero* who prevented Sir Francis Drake from making a landing on the nearby Pacific Coast.

There are two ways to ride a horse in Central America, both methods going back to Spain in the days of the wars with the Moors. The Moorish seat, known as *"a la gineta,"* is ridden with short stirrups, while the Spanish style, *"a la brida,"* depends on long stirrups. Though I have ridden both, I prefer the latter, especially for long hours in the saddle.

We kept a sharp lookout for birds and saw quite a number. Rarest was a huge king vulture, which circled above us when we arrived at El Mirador, highest point of the ride at 3,500 feet above sea level. Through my binoculars I could make out its brilliant colors of orange, yellow, scarlet, blue, and purple. I could even see the carbuncle of orange surmounting the black bill. The king vulture is a rare bird in the Guatemalan mountains, according to Dorión. Only occasionally has he seen single individuals and never a nest. In *Birds of Tikal,* F. B. Smithe reported sighting of a nest of these great birds *(Sarcorhamphus papa)* in Panama in 1965. Its gorgeous plumage and little fear of man have resulted in its rarity. We also saw the black vulture *(Coragyps atratus),* and the turkey vulture *(Cathartes aura),* both of which are common.

Other birds included the scissor-tailed flycatcher, a woodpecker which we could not identify, a bird which Dorión said was a turquoise-browed motmot, several white-wing doves, and a pair of hawks. Beside the trail we saw the skin of a large boa, and in the damp earth near the brook, the impression of an otter's pads.

On our way back to the *casa,* or main house, Dorión showed us a former maternity hospital that was used by the *finca*'s laborers before a clinic was established lower on the slope. For a nominal sum he is willing to give or lease this building to the Organization for Tropical Studies, a consortium created by sixteen American universities and the Smithsonian Institution, which is doing important research in Central America. In San José I had talked with Dr. Stephen B. Preston, the director; hence I was pleased to hear from Dorión that Dr. Preston expressed an interest in the possibilities of such a research station at El Salto and would send a team of four scientists to look it over.

Dorión, who is keen on the Boy Scouts and is the International Representative for Guatemala, told me that his plans to give the local scouts a camp on the sugar estate include promoting a badge for excellence in conservation. A lively group of agile youngsters would be a great asset

129

for a group of scientists interested in collecting specimens from the rugged terrain of El Salto. Some of these jobs may be rather specialized, for Dorión told me he has a scientist coming to study a kind of fungus found on the feet of certain grasshoppers. Whether these hoppers limp as a result of a minute case of athlete's foot he did not know.

Near El Salto is the much smaller but equally interesting *finca* of Hugh Craggs, an Englishman who is the leading orchid grower of Guatemala. He gave us lunch at his home and showed us his greenhouses, holding some 8,000 to 9,000 orchids of 1,000 different species or hybrid varieties. Only in the mountains of Assam in India, with my friend the late E. P. Gee, have I seen such gorgeous blooms. Like Dorión, Craggs prohibits shooting on his *finca*. Craggs is also a collector of rare books, and I had a good time browsing through his library on Central America. In addition, he owns El Patio, one of the best restaurants in Guatemala City, which includes a bookstore of the old and rare. There I bought a two-volume first-edition set of the classic *Incidents of Travel in Central America, Chiapas and Yucatan* by John L. Stephens, published by Harper and Brothers in New York in 1841.

One finca that my wife visited was that of her cousin, Mrs. Franz Pieters, whose "Pangola" produces some of the best beef cattle in the country. She uses Santa Gertrudis bulls, crossing them with local Brahman cows. On her 1,100 acres she runs 1,000 head that average 1,000 pounds each. The grass on her *finca*, known as pangola grass, is in great demand for grazing land all over the country.

Later we learned of an unusual instance where interest in conservation had prompted one large landowner near Antigua to leave his estate of about 1,000 acres to the nation. Now known as the Parque Florencia, the tract—if properly guarded—will be an important addition to the preservation of native fauna. Its location near the city will insure its popularity with tourists.

Before two churches, Santo Tomás and that of the Black Christ, the witch doctor mumbled his charms, giant firecrackers exploded, an old man played his lute, boys beat drums, and a statue of a small wooden horse hung with old coins was held high for all to admire. Thus do the Quiche Indians invoke the rain gods, and in 1967 the ceremonies were

Christ over Guatemala

in deadly earnest, for a six months' drought had parched the uplands. Unless the rain came soon, the corn and bean crops, on which most of Guatemala and almost all of her two and one-half million Indians depended, would not receive their needed moisture. This drama took place at Chichicastenango, a market town almost 7,000 feet high to which some 10,000 Indians flock on Sundays and Thursdays to trade, talk, flirt, and pray.

The Indians of Guatemala live by and for the land. On the long 110-mile drive to their highlands from Guatemala City, we had many opportunities to see how they treat it. Terraces, a rather poor copy of those of the high Yemen in southern Arabia, try to protect the thin soil of steep hillsides. Corn is the main crop, and since corn takes much from the soil, fertilizer is necessary. Conrad Ter Keuile, an agronomist who works for the United Nations Food and Agriculture Organization in the Indian country, told me that the tribes are now the largest purchasers of chemical fertilizers in Guatemala. He also told me that there are taboos against cutting certain trees. Evidently the taboos are observed, for the tops of most mountains have been allowed to retain their forests so that the water is absorbed and does not ruin the hillsides by erosion. These mountain-top trees also furnish seed for the reforestation of lower areas.

In the patio of the Mayan Inn, a remarkably attractive hotel on the edge of Chichicastenango, stands a carved wooden statue of a saint. At its feet is a bird holding a bell in its mouth. Nobody could tell me what kind of bird it was supposed to be or why it was holding the bell, but undoubtedly it is ringing a silent warning to the birds of Guatemala. Although the Indians do not use methyl ethyl parathion, the deadly pesticide that has thrown a carpet of death over the lowland cotton fields, the children are all adept with slingshots—and any bird large enough to eat is fair game. As in other parts of Guatemala, game laws are either unknown or unobserved.

Soon after the clear cold dawn, I walked down one of the cobbled roads to the open country and scanned the forested hillsides for birds. I spotted an acorn woodpecker with its striking red crown patch and white wing marks in sharp contrast to its black body. I heard but couldn't see a tropical mockingbird, whose sweet call is unmistakable. High in the heavens a pair of vultures hovered.

Because there are some very rare birds in the highlands, I have always hoped to find the horned guan *(Oreophasis derbianus)*. One Pascal Ordoñez, an inhabitant of Panajachel, told Jorge Ibarra that he saw a horned guan high up in the mountains about a hundred kilometers west of Chichicastenango. Questioned as to when, he admitted that the famous sighting took place fifteen years before. The year before our visit Dr. Robert Andrle, an ornithologist, came to Guatemala to try to find the guan but did not succeed. Although about the size of a turkey, the guan is very shy, seldom leaving its steep and forested habitat. It has a red horn on top of its head, white eyes, and black feathers. There seems to be no Spanish name for the horned guan, the Indian name differing from one district to the next.

The sacred bird of the Mayas, as well as the national bird of Guatemala and the monetary unit, the quetzal is endowed with a mystique that goes far back into legend. In her amusing and enlightening book, *Birds of the Mayas,* Anne La Bastille Bowes tells the tale of how the quetzal became the king of birds. Halach-Uinic, the Great Spirit who ruled Mayaland, grew weary of the chatter and bickering of the birds and decided to organize them under king who would keep the peace. Many birds wanted to be king. Co-pol-che, the cardinal, claimed the kingship as he was all red and certainly very handsome. X-col-col-chek, the mocking bird, drew attention to his lovely voice. Cutz, the wild turkey, made the observation that he was the strongest. The only bird who kept silent was Kukul, the quetzal, who thought his chances dim, for he was poorly dressed, could not sing, and was weak as well. Then an idea occurred to him. He flew over to his friend, Xtuntun-kinil, the road runner, and a very well dressed bird indeed. He pointed out to the road runner that he did not need all those nice feathers for his job of road running—he should lend them to him. After much persuasion the road runner agreed, and the plain quetzal blossomed with a coat of blue and green and a breast of brilliant orange. So pleased was the Great Spirit that he immediately named the quetzal the King of the Birds.

As king, the quetzal was so busy that he forgot all about his promise to return the road runner's feathers. Naked and shivering, the poor road runner was about to die when some kindhearted birds gave him a few feathers each. That is why the road runner today has such an oddly

133

colored coat. It is also why he watches the roads and keeps saying plaintively, "Puhuy, puhuy," which means in Maya, "Where is he, where is he?"

Surrounded by mountains and reflecting the cones of majestic volcanoes in its azure waters, Lake Atitlán has inspired many a writer and artist. Aldous Huxley considered it more beautiful than Como, while our own countrymen have compared it favorably with the lovely lakes of the Rockies and the Sierras. Although a number of artists have painted it, their work looks to me like the fantasies of Maxfield Parrish. In fact, none of the representations seems accurate. Or perhaps in other periods the lake presented a different impression. Just before the spring rains, when the clouds hang low over the volcanic peaks and a gray mist hides the shores, the lake has a mystical quality that defies any easy definition. Even trying to find comparisons is difficult, though in some ways it reminded me of Lake Baikal in Siberia, the vast, lonely inland sea where we went to see the fresh-water seals in 1965. I have also thought of the Wulwar Lakes in northern Kashmir.

Nor does Atitlán's uniqueness rest only on its setting. Along its eighty-five-mile shore line, hiding mostly in the reed beds, survives one of the Western Hemisphere's rarest birds. Because it cannot fly and is therefore

The Giant Pied-billed Grebe

able to escape only by diving and swimming, the giant pied-billed grebe *(Podilymbus gigas)* has been reduced to a point where its future is in grave doubt unless it is afforded additional protection. That it is not extinct today is largely due to the efforts of Anne Bowes, the American ornithologist and author, who has devoted a great deal of effort to saving this rare and interesting bird.

When Mrs. Bowes made a census of the giant grebe for the Smithsonian Institution of Washington in 1960, she counted some 200 individuals. During a 1965 visit she counted only 100 specimens. To counter this dangerous trend, she started "Operation Protection Pok" (the native name for the giant grebe) and succeeded in persuading the Guatemalan government to provide a game warden to patrol part of the lake. World Wildlife Fund grants of $3,000 to aid in the protection of the grebe were also helpful but had not been expended.

In order to check on the present state of these rare birds, Ambassador Briggs and I invited Jorge Ibarra to join us at the lake for a two-day survey. As soon as he arrived, Ibarra in turn invited Manuel Crespo, manager of the local Texaco station at Panajachel and an honorary warden dedicated to the protection of the pok. We then hired a large motorboat and set out to find the grebe. Subject to violent windstorms, Atitlán was rough on the first day we explored it. Nevertheless, we skirted the coast and finally arrived at a little bay that had been sealed off by a stone breakwater. On it we saw twin signs, one announcing that the area was under the protection of the Ministry of Agriculture, the other sporting the familiar Panda of the World Wildlife Fund. Money supplied by W.W.F. had been used to build the breakwater as well as a little house from which grebes in the area could be photographed.

To our dismay we found that most of the reeds in which the grebes breed had been destroyed by fire. Crespo, who had visited the area in August of 1966 and seen a grebe in it at that time, was most upset. He said we must be sure to report this damage when we went to see the governor of the province the following day. Although we searched the little bay carefully with our glasses, we found only a pair of handsome purple gallinules and a family of coots.

Continuing around the lake, we put into the Bay of Santiago-Atitlán and tied up at the wharf of Edgar Bauer, the only full-time warden retained to protect the grebes. A young man whose main occupation is running his father's coffee *finca*, Bauer told us that he manages to patrol the lake for a part of each day, but since the outboard motor supplied to him was getting old, he does not dare get too far away. From Ibarra I learned that Bauer's salary is $60 per month plus an allowance of gasoline for the outboard, both paid by the Ministry of Agriculture. Asked about the grebes, Bauer said that he thought the population in his section of the lake was slowly increasing, as he had seen more birds this year than in the previous year. An exact census is, of course, extremely difficult for one person to make. Not only are the grebes very shy, but the reed beds where they nest are virtually impenetrable. At this point Crespo simulated the call of a grebe, and to our amazement one answered back from the reeds.

On the way home we saw our first bird, a male which Ibarra spotted swimming and diving not far from a small island at the entrance to the Bay of Santiago-Atitlán. Through my glasses I could clearly see the black mark across its bill, the distinguishing characteristic of the giant pied-billed grebe. Its body is almost twice the size of the common grebe, but the bird's stubby little wings are not capable of lifting its body into the air. I could not see the tail, which is very small.

On our second expedition we were fortunate enough to spot another giant grebe. This trip took us to the village of Santa Catarina, where we found an Indian cutting down reeds in an area which was supposedly protected. Asked by Ibarra and Crespo why he was doing it, the Indian replied that he had permission from the owner of the reed bed. This was a perfect example of how difficult it is to reach and to explain to all landowners on the lake the importance of regulating the cutting of the reeds. Thanks to the efforts of Mrs. Bowes, Crespo, and Bauer, a great number do understand that the reed crop, from which the Indians make baskets, should be harvested in such a way that at least half the reeds in each bed are left standing for the grebes' protection. The most important period is during the mating season, which begins in April, or just about the time we visited the lake. Then the grebes build floating nests of vegetation and lay four or five eggs. After hatching, the chicks are carried on their parents' backs to protect them from fish hawks and big black bass.

Introduced some years ago to provide sport fishing, the bass have thrived and multiplied to a point where ten-pound monsters can swallow a baby grebe at a single bite. To try to avenge the little grebes, I spent an entire morning trolling and casting with the most alluring hardware that Abercrombie & Fitch has to offer. Net result was four small bass that could not have snatched a large mosquito, much less a fledgling grebe.

The grebe population probably never was very large, for when Ludlow Griscom named the species in 1929, he estimated the total for the lake at only 100 pairs. In 1936, Dr. Alexander Wetmore made the same estimate. When Mrs. Bowes and her husband, C. V. Bowes, Jr., made their first survey in 1960, they put the total at the same figure of 100 pairs or 200 individual birds. Thus the drastic decline to half that total took place in the seven years after the introduction of the large-mouthed black bass.

In addition to the incursions of the bass, the grebes are said to suffer from poaching, though why anyone would want to eat a bird that exists largely on fish, frogs, water insects, and crawfish I simply cannot fathom. During the migration times when other waterfowl visit the lake in large numbers, some of the gunners undoubtedly take pot shots at the grebes purely for fun. Stealing of the eggs by the Indians was also listed as a cause of the decline.

Poaching and egg stealing are in direct defiance of Guatemalan law. In 1959, largely through the efforts of Mrs. Bowes, Jorge Ibarra, and others interested in this rare bird, Lake Atitlán was made a national waterfowl refuge. But it was not until 1965 that a program of enforcement was begun. It was then that Mrs. Bowes met with the minister of agriculture to have a game warden hired. Existing laws were also restated and stricter fines imposed on those caught disobeying them. In addition, the governor of Sololá (the department in which Atitlán lies) wrote the mayors of the twelve Indian villages surrounding the lake advising them of the protection program. Mrs. Bowes subsequently visited every village to put up posters on the walls of the town halls.

To report the two incidents of lawbreaking that we saw, Ambassador Briggs, Ibarra, Crespo, and I drove up the steep, winding road to Sololá, the capital of the department, and called upon his rotund and hospitable excellency, Julio A. Monterossa, the governor. Ushered into his office immediately, we were pleased to see a large placard on the wall urging protection of the pok. It hung in an honored position between a picture of the President of the Republic and the governor's flag of office. Ibarra then told the governor that we had already talked with both the president and the minister of agriculture about conservation in Guatemala and had specifically mentioned the grebe. The governor said he was delighted, speaking to us at great length of his interest in conservation. When advised of the illegal reed cutting and burning, he said he would take immediate steps to investigate. He respects Mrs. Bowes, and I was sorry that I could not give him a firsthand report about her, never having met her.

Mrs. Bowes, however, went to some trouble to furnish me with a letter containing full information about the project, so that I knew exactly whom to see and what to look for. She said she had heard from the minister of agriculture that $4,000 might become available from the government to continue the protection campaign. The minister had said nothing to me about this, but he did mention a conservation bill that he was about to send to congress. Mrs. Bowes also told me that Dr. Dillon Ripley, director of the Smithsonian Institution and a director of the World Wildlife Fund, had interested the *National Geographic* magazine in doing an article on the grebe.

As for the immediate problem at Atitlán, my own view is that even though Bauer and Crespo are dedicated men and do their best to patrol the lake, at least two additional full-time wardens are necessary. Bauer cannot patrol an area larger than the Bay of Santiago-Atitlán, where he lives. Crespo, being an honorary, unpaid warden, cannot afford to take much time away from his business. This means that many of the reed beds that exist intermittently along the lake's shore line are not regularly checked.

CHAPTER X

British Honduras

When Queen Victoria was told that her minister to La Paz had been insulted, she promptly summoned the royal cartographer and commanded him to take Bolivia off the map. Today the tables are turned, for the maps produced by Guatemala show Queen Elizabeth's loyal Crown Colony of British Honduras simply as a province of Guatemala called Belice. That the inhabitants prefer to see the Queen's picture on their money is evident as soon as one steps from the airplane from Guatemala City. The baggage boys refused a Guatemalan quetzal, which is the equivalent of one dollar, but later cheefully accepted a British Honduran dollar worth only seventy cents.

Few people go to this 8,866-square-mile chunk of territory on the Caribbean. There is no road to the capital of British Honduras from Guatemala, and land communication with Mexico is also uncertain. Belize (the inhabitants spell it with a *z*), has a good air strip, however,

and TACA and other lines make regular stops there between New Orleans and the Central American capitals. To see the country and discuss
conservation with Her Majesty's governor, Sir John Paul; the premier,
the Honorable George Price, and ministers of the government, Ambassador Briggs and I flew down from Guatemala City. At the airport we were
met by Robert Tepper, the American consul, an able and attractive officer
of about forty-five, who was most considerate in showing us the town,
putting us up at the Fort George Hotel, and setting up our official appointments.

Built on a mangrove swamp, Belize is a ramshackle collection of
houses. Most of them are on stilts, for when the hurricanes sweep in from
the Caribbean, the streets can be six feet under water. Some of the
buildings have wrought-iron grilles that reminded me of the old French
quarter of New Orleans, while others have painted corrugated iron roofs
that resemble elaborate Indian blankets. The people, of all shades and
colors, come from many races. Although Afro-Belizeans, or Creoles,
make up sixty percent of the population of 112,000, there are also Mayas,
Caribs, Mestizos, Mennonites, Chinese, East Indians, Lebanese, and

British Honduras: Ambassador Briggs

even a few Europeans. Most look cheerful and carefree, and the crowds thronging the dusty little streets always seem to be laughing.

Once the land belonged to the Maya, and it is estimated that 700,000 of them lived in the now ruined cities that dot the countryside of British Honduras. For some reason that we do not know, the Maya abandoned these cities at the same time they left Tikal in Guatemala and migrated to the Yucatán in Mexico. Columbus sailed across the Bay of Honduras, and Cortés may well have hacked his way through the jungles there, but it was not until 1638 that Europeans actually settled there. The first of these were shipwrecked British sailors who were followed by pirates, and later came English planters from Jamaica with their slaves. But Britain did not recognize the territory as a colony until 1862. In the interim period only the strongest men survived. Spain claimed the land under a Papal sanction and staged a series of invasions. The decisive battle, known as the "Pork and Dough Boys War" (as forest laborers were provided with fat pork and flour weekly), was fought on September 10, 1798, and the Spanish were soundly defeated.

British Honduras has been a self-governing territory since 1964. From an economic standpoint the country is in some straits. The mahogany forests, which used to be the basis of her exports, have been largely cut down, and sugar and citrus haven't entirely taken up the slack. However, another largely unexploited source of revenue for British Honduras is tourism. Inside a barrier reef stretching almost 150 miles along the coast lie some 200 sea islands replete with sandy beaches and superb bone fishing. In addition, virtually the whole 174-mile coastline from the Tío Hondo in the north to the Sarstoon in the south is laced with rivers where tarpon, snook, and black snapper abound.

One of the few entrepreneurs attracting tourists was Victor Barothy, an American from Chicago, who ran a first-class fishing camp on the Belize River a few miles outside the capital. He and his wife could take care of twenty-four guests at a time in their clean and comfortable cabins and in their three modern houseboats. They also operated a fleet of sturdy skiffs for fishing the rivers. As guests of the Barothys, Ambassador Briggs and I spent a very enjoyable day exploring the rivers, canals, and estuaries of the coast. It is a green world of mangroves and swamps intersected by meandering waterways across which dart kingfishers, herons, and frigate birds. Out by the islands we saw double-crested cormorants and gulls. When we stopped at a tiny shack to get coconuts to quench our thirst, we were pleasantly surprised to have the owner, a tall, ragged Negro, not only refuse payment but do so in excellent English.

British Honduras has game laws, but they are not observed, as we soon noted. At the mouth of one of the rivers, for example, we saw boats with nets. This practice—strictly forbidden—may ruin the sport and commercial fishing in the rivers if not stopped. There is also a law protecting the manatees, which used to throng the sluggish rivers. Nobody pays the slightest attention to it, however, and manatee meat can be bought in the local market. Although there is a legal closed season on deer, they are shot all year round. Lack of wardens plus a natural desire for meat results in wholesale flouting of the laws. Despite her vast stretches of unused land, British Honduras imports about one third of her food.

The Honorable George Price, the premier, paid Ambassador Briggs and me the great compliment of inviting us to attend a meeting of his full cabinet to discuss our views on conservation and wildlife protection. A handsome man of forty-eight who looked younger, George Price was born in Belize and educated for the priesthood. Before entering politics he was private secretary to one of his country's leading chicle producers. From 1947 to 1965 he served on the Belize City Council and twice as elected mayor of the capital. In 1963 he led a delegation to London to persuade the British to grant his country a constitution under which it could be self-governing.

Not one to stand on ceremony, the premier came to the door to meet us and led us into the cabinet room, where we shook hands with the six men and one woman who comprise its membership. Ambassador Briggs then made a graceful speech of thanks in which he touched on our travels in Central America and remarked on the opportunities for tourism which our stay in Belize had revealed. I followed with a short summary of the background and objectives of the World Wildlife Fund. The minister of natural resources told us that a commission had been set up to make a survey with a view to establishing a national park and that he would see that I got a copy of the report. Again I made the point—which can never be repeated often enough—that parks without adequate guards are useless. With this the minister agreed. During an ensuing discussion of

Belize's game laws, I told the cabinet that we had seen men netting at the mouth of a river during our boat trip the previous day. The premier interjected that this was illegal and asked the minister of justice to look into the matter immediately.

Despite her uncrowded country, British Honduras has to import about one third of her food. There is plenty of farm land available—even though one company, Belize Estates, owns a third of the country—but the average inhabitant does not like to labor in the fields. According to long-time residents, it has become uniquely disreputable to engage in agriculture so long as some kind of living can still be wrung from the forests. Lumbering is intermittent but well-paid work which the Belizians have learned to like. Farming, on the other hand, goes on all the time, with smaller rewards. As noted, most of the big mahogany has been cut, and the young trees take some seventy years to mature. Unless her population—increasing more than three percent each year—can be employed in new agricultural enterprises or new industries, the electorate may prove increasingly hard to pacify.

There is one group of people in British Honduras, however, who work very hard indeed. Mennonite communities, emigrating from Canada and the United States, have been arriving in the Crown Colony in such numbers that there are now more than 4,000 of them. Already, they have hacked out sizable farms from the upcountry jungles. One of their developments is near Roaring Creek, the site of the proposed new capital of British Honduras.

Looking around Belize's leading department store, which reminded me of those of Ceylon, I saw a Mennonite girl trying to buy a clock. She said plaintively that she had only four dollars, and the clock cost $6.50. I bought her the clock, and she told me that she knew "the Lord would provide." Quite pretty in a plain way, the girl said her name was Nancy Coblenz, she came from America and was working in a Mennonite mission school upcountry. Her dress was held together with pins, as these Mennonites do not believe in buttons.

Belize has a long list of problems, both economic and political. Whether a democratic government can flourish through the transition to full independence remains to be seen. As in all Central American states, the future of conservation and wildlife is closely linked to political stability and economic progress. Our short visit in the small country made this important connection clear to us once more.

The Convention on Nature Protection in the Western Hemisphere was never signed or ratified by the government of British Honduras—I do not know in fact if Her Majesty's government was ever asked to do so—but the new country of Belice should certainly join this good club, and I urge the next conservationist who talks with the government to bring the point up.

CHAPTER XI

North to Mexico City

From Panojochel on Lake Atitlán, 5,200 feet up in the highlands of Guatemala, to Oaxaca, in the Sierra Madre of Mexico, is a matter of about 620 miles. Driving slowly and stopping frequently, Ambassador Briggs, his wife Lucy, and Irene and I made the journey in three days. In 1840, another ambassador, John L. Stephens, President Van Buren's envoy to the Central American Republic, covered some of the same ground. His two-volume *Incidents of Travel in Central America, Chiapas and Yucatan* gives a vivid picture of the life and towns of those days. Stephens's task was far more difficult than ours, for no less than three generals claimed the presidency of a territory which is now broken up into the five nations of Central America. Consequently he spent most of his time trying not to yield his credentials to generals whose chances of running the country did not seem good.

Stephens was charmed by Quezaltenango, one of our stops en route to the Mexican border. He noted the handsomely paved streets, picturesque houses, and imposing cathedral on a stone-paved plaza with a fine fountain in the middle. He enjoyed the magnificent view of the volcano and the mountains. He commented dryly on the religious devotion of the Indians, saying that so many were baptized after their defeat by Alvarado that "the priests from sheer fatigue could no longer lift their arms to perform the ceremony." Today Quezaltenango is the second largest city in Guatemala (40,000 people) and, owing to its altitude (7,656 feet), has a pleasant, invigorating climate. Although most of the city was destroyed in 1902 when Santa María erupted, the people rebuilt it in the hope that the volcano would not blow up again. Still active, she gives the town an occasional rumbling reminder that she might turn mean any time.

We spent the night at the Virginia, a clean little motel just outside Coatepeque. The town itself, with unpaved dirty streets, is unattractive. For some reason we cannot fathom, the lower one gets in altitude the dirtier the towns appear to be. Coatepeque is only 1,580 feet above sea level. We saw few Indians there wearing their traditional gaily woven garments as do almost all the inhabitants of the mountain villages. Only the old women dressed in the traditional costumes. I couldn't help thinking there should be a conservation program aimed at saving the endangered arts as well as the endangered species before all of the Indians of Guatemala appear in cheap printed cottons.

At the Rio Suchiate we began negotiating the border. Unfortunately, the peon who kept the key to the room where we had to process our papers had had a bad night and was not anywhere to be found. The Mexican inspector, dismayed by the situation, promised to get immediate action. Two husky soldiers with large revolvers then arrived. After gravely surveying the locked door and shaking their heads several times, they inserted a kitchen knife under the sill. The door failed to yield. I suggested that they simply blow out the lock with their pistols, but they did not take to the idea. After another probe with the kitchen knife, they shrugged and retired. At this point Ambassador Briggs, who is usually the soul of patience, suggested tartly that it was a very bad idea indeed to keep two ambassadors waiting for more than one hour. The inspector

146

then took matters into his own hands and with a mighty shove burst the lock open to his office.

It was almost exactly twenty-nine years since Irene and I had last been in Mexico. That was on our honeymoon when we drove from Nuevo Laredo to Acapulco. Because General Cedillo was then in revolt against the federal government, there were no American tourists, with the result that our cabin on the cliffs above the sea cost exactly one dollar each per day. Meals were another dollar, and a fishing boat four dollars per day. Today Acapulco has become a Mexican Miami Beach, its charm gone with the wind. During Holy Week there is a plane from Mexico City every three minutes.

Chiapas, the Mexican state bordering Guatemala, appeared wild and empty to us just as it did to Stephens in his day. As we sped along the excellent Pan American Highway we passed very few people, mostly cowboys on the best-looking horses we had seen on our trip. Once for more than two hours we met no other car.

On the left the coastal plain sloped to the Pacific and on the right the rugged peaks of the Sierra Madre Occidental stood out stark against a cobalt blue sky. Though the thermometer I always carry on these trips registered 104 degrees, the wind generated from our speed kept us comfortable. The bridges over the little rivers have strange names: Puente Jesus, Puente Guisano (worm), Puente Bobo (boob). During the entire ten-hour drive from the border to Tehuantepec, I saw an iguana, a quail, a golden eagle, two cattle egrets, and a flight of parakeets. In the mountains into which we climbed later in the day, we came upon terrible fires with so much smoke in some places that we could not see the road ahead. It is this wasteful land-burning practice that drives the birds away.

The Hotel Tehuantepec is a dreary place, enhanced considerably by its adjoining restaurant, where the Indian waitresses have strikingly pretty faces. The town is famous for its Zapotec Indians, whose social organization is matriarchic. The tall, graceful women, with ribbons braided in their hair and lavishly embroidered costumes, run the show entirely. The men, who do not even dare appear in the market, work humbly in the fields. After we sat down, three biologists from the Universities of Kansas, Missouri, and Arkansas joined us for a drink. They were not, I was sorry to discover, very sanguine about the future of conservation in Central America and Mexico.

From the lowlands of the Isthmus of Tehuantepec we climbed into the mountainous state of Oaxaca, where the road twisted and turned through barren, eroded hills. We lunched at Mitla, a charming town famous for weaving, Zapotec ruins, and mescal, an authoritative drink distilled from a variety of cactus. This beverage bears the same relation to pulque, which is fermented, as good Scotch whiskey does to "Guinea red." At the Museo Frissell de Arte Zapoteco de la Universidad de las Americas, I dutifully regarded the ceramics of the ancient Indians and then saw more modern and, for my purposes, more useful objects, including *A Hunter's Guide to Mexico.*

Written by an American, Sam W. Landis, with thanks to Dr. Rodolfo Hernandez Corzo, Director General of the Game Department of the Mexican government, and to Professor José Angel Dávila, Chief of the Wildlife Conservation Department, the little book is full of interesting information. I was a bit shocked to see a picture of an ocellated turkey. Although this turkey is legitimate game in the province of Yucatan, where the hunter is allowed two cocks per year during the period of December 15 to February 28, it is extremely rare in Central America as a whole and consequently should be protected in all of Mexico.

The book includes a copy of the Mexican Game Laws, and I was pleased to see that among those species the hunting of which is permanently prohibited were the volcano rabbit, the Mexican grizzly bear, and the Mexican pronghorn antelope. Unfortunately, the list does not include the Guadalupe fur seal, Caribbean monk seal, or the West Indian manatee, mammals listed in the Red Book of the International Union for the Conservation of Nature as endangered and facing extinction. The government list does, however, include a good many species that are becoming rare in Mexico; to wit: the water opossum, woolly opossum, collared anteater, two-toed anteater, prairie dog, flying squirrel, porcupine, beaver, muskrat, black bear, badger, otter, skunk, bison, desert sheep, and deer on a number of islands.

The list of birds permanently protected are swans, all shore birds, upland plover, all songbirds, hummingbirds, hawks, owls, eagles, vultures, falcons, ospreys, pelicans, flamingos, cormorants, herons, ibis, gulls, terns, macaws, toucans, quetzals, peacocks, and last but not least, the horned guan. This does not include the following birds on the danger list of the I.U.C.N., which are: the masked bobwhite, imperial wood-pecker, slender-billed grackle, the cozumel curassow, the kestrel, rock wren, kinglet, house finch, and junco of Guadelupe Island, and McGregor's house finch of San Benito Island.

The government laws protect lizards, chameleons, and boas, but do not mention the Atlantic ridley or Morelet's crocodile, two species listed by the I.U.C.N. as extremely rare.

The brocket deer *(Mazama americana)*, although rare in Central America, is still listed as game under the current Mexican Game Laws. From February 15 to April 15 a single male may be taken. There are two species: the red brocket, found in the states of Tamaulipas, Veracruz, Tabasco, and Chiapas, and the brown brocket, found in Yucatán. Small-est of the North American deer, the brocket weighs only about forty pounds. The male has tiny straight horns, the female none. They are preyed on by jaguar, puma, and ocelot. The fawns are sometimes taken by the larger eagles.

Usually the brocket keeps to dense jungle, where it is exceedingly hard to shoot. But with hounds, especially in areas where the habitat can be surrounded, the brocket will sooner or later be flushed into view. Even so, Landis reports that the "Weatherby Award Winners," the group of big-game hunters who compete for trophies (sometimes regardless of their rarity), have so far failed to report a brocket.

The use of hounds to hunt the big cats is legal in Mexico (although they are not legal in India for leopard and tiger or in most of Africa for lion or leopard). Consequently, the dwindling population of jaguar, jag-uarundi, puma, ocelot, margay, and bobcat are mostly taken with the aid of packs of local hounds.

Wolves and coyotes can be shot at any time and in any number in Baja California, Sonora, Chihuahua, Coahuila, Nuevo León, and Tamaulipas. There is a picture in Landis's book of the Burnham brothers with a day's bag of some twenty-five coyotes. These intrepid hunters wear camou-flaged clothing, conceal themselves, and lure the unfortunate wolves and coyotes into range with a patent call. In sheep or cattle country there is of course good reason to keep down these predators, but this necessary protective measure hardly belongs under the heading of "sport."

There are few more pleasant places to have one's shoes shined than the Plaza of Oaxaca. Purple-blossomed jacarandas shade the flower-bordered walks, and señoritas in pairs stroll past. Time slips by, and the clear bells of the cathedral remind one that it is the hour to go to the arcade of the Hotel Marqués del Valle and order an ice-cold mescal before lunch. The plaza must have looked very much the same forty-three years ago when D. H. Lawrence lived in Oaxaca and wrote *Mornings in Mexico* and *The Plumed Serpent.* Of a similar morning he said:

> There is a smell of carnations and the resinous smell of ocote wood, and a smell of coffee, and faint smell of leaves, and of morning, and even of Mexico. Because when all is said and done, Mexico has a faint, physical scent of her own, as each human being has. And this is a curious inexplicable scent, in which there are resin and perspiration and sunburned earth and urine among other things.

Countless centuries before Lawrence wrote his striking characterization of Mexico, the civilization of the aboriginal peoples rested on maize, or corn, and the cycle of clearing the land by fire, planting, exhausting the soil, then moving on. In the old days this process, while wasteful, did not injure the soil permanently. The little holes made by pointed sticks for the seeds were too small to create erosion, so the land retained most of its humus. With the coming of the white man and his new methods of agriculture, however, the soil came under increasing pressures. Spanish plows ripped the topsoil; Spanish axes denuded the forests. The Maya and the Aztecs never cut the timber on the steep mountains because they knew it held the precious water. Creation of the great haciendas—Cortés owned 25,000 square miles personally—forced the Indians to use marginal lands. As a result, the ruinous new cultivation crept higher and higher on the mountains.

The effect on Mexico's wildlife can well be imagined. Forest habitats became bare hillsides; the birds and animals that once thrived there vanished. Even today with improved methods of tilling and the use of fertilizers on worn land, the habitat is being whittled away. The lowlands are still overgrazed and the forests are still being cut. We saw some fine forests on our long drive through the mountains of southern Mexico, but much more frequently the view consisted of bare and denuded peaks and occasionally a lonely cactus.

Before leaving on this mission, I wrote Dr. A. Starker Leopold at the University of California and asked him to send me his classic work, *Wildlife of Mexico*, published in 1959. This rewarding book deals fully and clearly with the present status of birds and animals of Mexico, concisely summarizing the urgent need for conservation. Dr. Leopold wrote:

> For centuries it has been the custom to clear the mountain slopes, plant to corn until the topsoil has washed away, and then abandon them for new clearings higher on the mountain. It would be difficult to change this custom even if the population were stable. Unfortunately, it is not stable but is increasing at a dangerous rate (3.5% per year). This means that demands upon the land were more severe each year. Wildlife is affected not only by habitat deterioration, but by direct use as well. As a rule, Mexican game is taken at any time and in any quantity that can be had, game laws notwithstanding. The problems of population underlie all the woes of game conservation in Mexico.
>
> Today Mexico has some 44 million people living on 760,335 square miles, or nearly 500,000,000 acres, but 85% of these acres lie within arid or semi-arid zones. It has been estimated that on more than 60% of the tillable land, crops are obtained less than one year in two. The result is often malnutrition and according to government statistics about 15% of the Mexican population is suffering from hunger ranging as high as 21% calorie deficiency.

William Vogt, whom I have previously cited, also fears for the Mexican forests: "The poverty-stricken *campesinos*, hungry for a corn patch, firewood, charcoal, or a bit of salable building material, destroy timber nearly everywhere it is accessible." He estimated in 1963 that there were only about 400 forest guards for the entire country, many of them without any means of transportation but shank's mare.

The state of Oaxaca, in whose sunwashed capital we stayed, consists of 36,370 square miles and has a population of about two million people, many of whom are Indians of the Zapotec and Mixtec tribes. Inveterate hunters, these Indians scour their sparsely settled terrain for almost anything edible. Inquiries revealed that the following game are taken whenever the opportunity arises: paca, agouti, peccary, and deer, as well as a variety of smaller animals and birds. Further local inquiries revealed that the game laws are virtually unknown to most of the back-country Indians. Even those who have heard of them pay little if any attention to them. Such enforcement as exists seems to be in the hands of the forest wardens who, unfortunately, have a good many other things to do.

Cortés described the Valley of Oaxaca as the most beautiful he had seen in Mexico. If he could return today he would be shocked. Few trees now crown the barren hills that cup the town, and the blighting hand of erosion has cut deep gullies in them. Alexander von Humboldt described the Valley of Mexico in 1803 as enhanced on its northern rim by superb forests of pine and oak. What has happened since is sadly recounted by Leopold:

> Subsequently the forests were completely removed from the hills, and agricultural crops were grown until the soil would no longer support them. When the topsoil was gone, the land was planted to maguey, the sturdy Agave which can grow even in parched subsoil.

Years of maguey culture finally reduced the land to bare and impervious hardpan, and cultivation was abandoned. Since then burros and goats have grazed the scant xerophytic vegetation until no recovery of natural flora is possible. Game is nonexistent.

The Mexican government has made numerous efforts to do something about conservation of wildlife. Although the first protective legislation was passed in 1894, no provision was made for reinforcement. In 1940, governmental organizations for forestry and game were set up. But unlike the United States, where the Federal Government has jurisdiction over migratory wildfowl and the states handle local game, the Mexican government has declared all game to be the "property of the nation." Regulations issued by the secretary of agriculture apply to hunting all over the nation.

Another divergence from our way of doing things applies to the licensing of hunters. In order to purchase a license, a Mexican must belong to a recognized hunting club which presumably will certify to his peaceful ambitions. The actual gun permit must previously be obtained from the Ministry of Defense and the number of the gun permit entered on the license.

In his book, Leopold notes that only 160,000 pesos ($13,000) was allotted to the wildlife program in 1954 despite the fact that the 13,680 licenses sold that year produced 481,854 pesos for the Mexican treasury. Even a magician cannot run a conservation program for game on $13,-000.

Between Oaxaca and Cuernavaca the super Pan American Highway runs for 300 miles through some of the most desolate country we saw in Mexico. In the distance the jagged mountains recede in a series of rows. They are particularly lovely in the early morning when they are tinted with rose and in the evening when they are deep purple. But as one approaches, they reveal themselves as barren, eroded hills where only giant cactus and the more hardy acacias can possibly survive. Scrawny goats and a few patient burros pick a meager sustenance from the parched ground, while high overhead vultures sail the wind currents in an empty blue sky. Several times we passed new plantations where the government was attempting to reforest the ravaged hillsides, but the saplings looked stunted and thirsty, and goats had already browsed away the lower leaves.

In the midst of this desolation we suddenly came upon a vast cathedral and the adjoining ruins of what must have been a monastery. Rising from the brown landscape without a hamlet, much less a town to sustain it, the lofty stone church might have been set down in the wilderness by a giant hand. Climbing the worn stone steps we found ourselves in the interior of one of the largest churches we saw in Mexico. Far up by the altar were arranged a few benches for worshipers, and candles guttered nearby, but not a soul was in the church.

Certainly built in the days when it stood in the midst of a rich farming community, the church is a tragic reminder of what man has done to the

153

land. The great stands of pine and oak that held the water have long ago been cut, and the countryside is almost uninhabited. For miles before and after the church we saw no human habitation at all.

At sunset we arrived at Cuernavaca, where we stayed at the home of Arthur Train, grandson of the writer of the same name who enlivened the pages of the old *Saturday Evening Post* with his stories of Mr. Tutt. This Arthur Train, in addition to exporting weaving and ceramics, has an interesting job connected with the production of "the pill."

Train is in charge of buying the roots of the dioscorea plant from which the pill is manufactured. This valuable plant grows wild all over the world in humid country, but only the Indians and the botanists can recognize it and find it easily. Train makes many trips in the states of Veracruz, Tabasco, and Chiapas to arrange for its collection. He not only speaks fluent Spanish but also has a smattering of the various Indian tongues as well. He buys the root from seven different tribes. The Indians, however, gather the roots only when their own agricultural duties are slack, and use the root themselves for medicinal purposes unconnected with birth control.

Ironically, the sale of the pill in Mexico is perfectly legal—one can buy it in any drugstore without a prescription—but the government has not so far endorsed any birth-control legislation, probably for fear of the reaction of the right-wing branch of the Church. In the meantime the population is increasing at the dangerous level of 3.5 percent per annum.

Only a minute percentage of Mexico's population can afford to hunt for sport. According to Dr. Starker Leopold, three persons per 10,000 population take out licenses as against 912 per 10,000 in the United States. However, this small group of sportsmen includes some famous shots. Among them is Julio Estrada, the premier hunter of Mexico, who was judged one of the ten best hunters in the world in 1963 by an international committee of experts.

To talk to Estrada about conservation and see his famous collection of 250 trophies, I phoned him at his Cuernavaca home and was promptly invited to call at the Villa Safari. Estrada, a stocky, well-preserved man of seventy-five, met us at the door and ushered us into a series of lofty rooms where walls were adorned with heads from almost all the big-game lands of the world. African lions, Indian tigers, Latin American jaguars all vied for attention.

We had a good deal to talk about. Estrada has shot in Mysore in South India, and in South-West Africa, two of the lesser-known hunting areas where I have also taken big game. His bag in the former included two fine male Indian bison (gaur or seladang). Most of the heads were mounted by Roland Ward of London and Louis Jonas of New York. I did not see a poor trophy in the entire collection. Like most good sportsmen, Estrada is keenly interested in conservation. Not a single trophy could I find that was on the danger list of the International Union for the Conservation of Nature.

Asked about conservation in Mexico, Estrada said frankly that the effort is too late and too little. He and other well-known sportsmen have done what they can to persuade the government to spend more on enforcement of game laws, but without much success. Only a minute fraction of the population pays any attention to the laws anyway. Hence it would take a really formidable body of dedicated wardens to make a dent on the illegal killing. Nor does the average *campesino* consider himself a poacher. Because he and his family are hungry for protein, he traps, nets, shoots, or even poisons all the meat he can find.

Estrada mentioned the case of the bighorn sheep *(Ovis canadesis),* which used to range over most of the deserts of northern Mexico but is now restricted to a few scattered herds in Coahuila, Chihuahua, Sonora, and Baja California. Even museum collectors have a hard time getting permits to shoot specimens. Yet with the connivance of local authorities, arrangements can be made to shoot these rare sheep for pleasure alone. The pronghorn antelope *(Antilocapra americana),* is also in very short supply. Originally found all over northern Mexico as far south as the grassland extended, it now lingers only in small pockets.

In *Wildlife of Mexico,* Dr. Starker Leopold tells of a great hunt held in Hidalgo in 1540 for the first Spanish viceroy, Antonio de Mendoza. Before it was over, the Indians had killed 600 deer and antelope. Even as late as 1777, Fray Juan Aguston Morfi saw antelope near Durango city. After 1800, the decline of the species was rapid. An account written a century later noted that "the pronghorn is already a rare animal in the region of the southwest, where it ranged in thousands twenty-five years ago."

The great cats also are growing scarce. Estrada, who keeps in touch with many of the better-known Mexican sportsmen, says that the jaguar have now been decimated to a point where they can be found only in the dense jungles along the Gulf of Mexico and the rain forests of Chiapas. Although several hunters to whom I talked about jaguar say that they range many miles every night, Leopold cites an old guide who was sure that the big cats lived in small territories, which they guarded jealously. The guide, J. F. Ferreira of San Ignacio, Sinaloa, had killed some sixty jaguar and undoubtedly knew a lot about them. In Guatemala I had been given a jaguar call, consisting of a hollow gourd over one end of which was stretched calfskin. A few strands of horsehair were run through a hole in the drum face and allowed to dangle down. By pulling the horsehair the gourd produces a staccato grunt that sounds very much like a jaguar. Hunters use this to provoke a male jaguar, who charges up in the belief that another male is invading his territory.

There are few more pleasant places to live than Cuernavaca. Good servants get little more than one dollar per day and their keep; the sun shines virtually all the time, and when it does not, the inhabitants like the change; Mexico City, with its cultural and other advantages, is only an hour away on excellent roads; and last but not least, taxi fares are low.

Ambassador Briggs's Dartmouth classmate, Daniel Slawson, lives all year round in Cuernavaca and frequently entertained the Crowes as well as the Briggses. His garden is a fine place to study the birds of Mexico. While drifting in his pool I noted a thrush, boat-tailed grackle, several hummingbirds, a wild canary, an Inca dove, and a parakeet. These and many other visitors flit about his jacaranda and tulip trees and dart among the flowers of the hibiscus and poinsettia.

Anti-American sentiment, of which one hears a great deal in the States, was never apparent to us in Mexico, or in any of the other countries that we visited. In fact, these warnings about the supersensitivity of the Central Americans came mostly from people who have only a casual knowledge of the countries and the people who live in them. Latinos told us that there is a good deal more friction between Guatemalans and Mexicans than there is between Mexicans and the so-called gringos. When I went alone to a bullfight in Mexico City, the Mexicans sitting near me went out of their way to offer me beer, explain the fine points of the show, and generally appear hospitable. They did this despite the fact that a row behind us an American woman, after making loud and insulting remarks about bullfighting in general and this one in particular, proceeded to be ill.

CHAPTER XII

Rabbits and Grizzlies

Within plain and dramatic sight of Mexico City's five million inhabitants rise the volcanic peaks of Popocatepetl (17,887 feet), and Ixtacihuatl (17,343 feet). But barely a handful of the citizens of this great city know that on the higher slopes of these snow-capped cones, just below where the tree line ends, there survives one of the world's rarest rabbits. Known in Spanish as *zacatuche* or *teporingo,* the little volcano rabbit *(Romerolagus diazi)* is a dark brown miniature bunny with very short ears and no tail at all. It exists today in very limited numbers at the 9,000- to 11,000-foot altitude in the sparse pine forests where there is a heavy ground cover of *zacaton* grass.

The decline and possible eventual extinction of these rare rabbits is not due to their appeal to man's gustatory desires. One of their favorite foods is a kind of mint with a strong smell that permeates the rabbit's flesh, making it virtually inedible. Both Starker Leopold and Norman Pelham

Wright, an Englishman who wrote the useful booklet *A Guide to Mexican Animals*, think that its decline is due largely to "sportsmen" from Mexico City who shoot it for target practice. Dr. Bernardo Villa, a zoologist of the University of Mexico, once saw a band of city hunters with twenty-seven volcano rabbits that they said they intended to feed to their dogs. Even the Indians who cultivate the high slopes and never have enough protein do not often bother these little rabbits.

The volcano rabbit has been protected by law for some years. The killing continues, however, with too few wardens to bring a stop to it. I talked with a member of a leading Mexico City gun club who admitted shooting rabbits whenever he saw them, in the belief they were pests. After my long—and I do not hesitate to say eloquent—defense of them, he promised not only to refrain from taking aim at another of the little animals himself, but also to tell his friends in the club not to help exterminate one of his country's rarest and far from most unappealing forms of wildlife.

So scarce have the volcano rabbits become that recently a team of zoologists from the United States spent nearly a week on Popocatepetl before they were able to collect a pair of specimens. If the 7,500-foot altitude of Mexico City did not leave me breathless most of the time, I would venture onto the volcanos and see for myself how many of these little rabbits could be found.

To learn more about the rabbits and other endangered animals and birds of Mexico, I spent the morning with Dr. Enrique Beltrán, one of the leading conservationists of Mexico. I had letters to him from Dr. Ira Gabrielson, president of the American Appeal of the World Wildlife Fund, and from William Phelps, Jr., of Caracas, the well-known ornithologist. An energetic and hospitable man of sixty-four, Dr. Beltrán had served for six years as under secretary of agriculture. Trained as a zoologist at the University of Mexico and later at Columbia in New York, where he took his Ph.D., Dr. Beltrán's interest in wildlife was a logical progression from his work on malaria. For he saw that in parts of rural Mexico a man either died from disease or he died from hunger. As a consequence, Dr. Beltrán decided to study the valuable life-giving protein supply available in many forms of wildlife. In 1940 he was appointed to his first post in the Division of Natural Resources. In 1958 he was made Undersecretary. So successful was his tour of duty in this important post, which has the responsibility for all the forests and wildlife of Mexico's 760,000 square miles, that virtually all of his major appointees were retained by his successor.

Asked about the volcano rabbit, Dr. Beltrán said that the area it now lives in—the two volcanos plus a few lower peaks in the Ajusco Range south of Mexico City—is partly a national park. The land on both volcanos above 9,000 feet is legally protected, and it is forbidden to carry guns there. Some of the forests below this level have been rented to private companies for timber cutting, so areas are at least patrolled as a protection against fires. In addition to these limited safeguards, the government has stationed some wardens there. Dr. Beltrán thinks that little shooting goes on but that the local natives undoubtedly poach and eat the rabbits despite their unpleasant taste.

Asked about the broad question of national parks, Dr. Beltrán said he agreed with me that parks without guards are worse than none and went on to point out that of the forty-five national parks listed for Mexico in the World List of National Parks and Equivalent Reserves (published by the United Nations Economic and Social Council in 1962), about half do not even belong to the government. He explained that they have the title of "park" only because some president of Mexico established them by decree, all that is necessary to proclaim a park. One "park" consists entirely of the city of Tlaxcala in the state of that name; another includes the city of Monterrey. The purpose, of course, in proclaiming these urban centers was not to save the wildlife but to protect old buildings.

Up to 1949 there were no game wardens per se in Mexico. What enforcement existed was done by the forest rangers in their spare time. By 1965 a small staff of twenty-five game wardens was set up. In addition, the 1,000 forest rangers were given some training in wildlife conservation as well as in their main job of looking after the trees.

Because all trees are under federal authority, one must have a permit to cut them even on private property. But, according to Dr. Beltrán, a myth has grown up in his country that it is all right to cut a single tree for firewood. During his tour of duty as undersecretary, Dr. Beltrán tried to explode this myth by explaining to the government and to the rural peoples that forests can be harvested just as crops are harvested. By careful selection of the proper trees for cutting, leaving the smaller trees to mature, the forests of Mexico can become much more useful to the people than they have been to date.

To carry on his good work in the fields of forestry and conservation, Dr. Beltrán established the Instituto Mexicano de Recursos Naturales Renovables. A privately financed organization, which was originally funded by equal gifts from Randolph C. Pack of Darien, Connecticut, and from wealth Mexicans, the Instituto is now largely dependent on local contributions, with some help from North American foundations, such as the Conservation Foundation and those which provide funds for special projects.

In making my appointments with Dr. Beltrán and others in the Mexican conservation picture, I was helped a great deal by members of the American Embassy. The ambassador, Fulton Freeman, could not have been more hospitable. He gave a dinner for Ambassador Briggs and me and started the wheels in motion to get me an appointment with Licenciado Gustavo Díaz Ordaz, President of Mexico.

Ambassador Freeman's minister counselor, Henry Dearborn, also went out of his way to entertain us and provide the many conveniences that a big, well-run American Embassy has at its disposal. John Scholl, the senior agricultural attaché, arranged my appointment with Professor Juan Gil Preciado, the secretary of agriculture, and gave me a concise briefing on the complex land situation in Mexico. Richard S. Croker, the regional fisheries officer, was helpful in setting up a meeting with Dr. Rodolfo Hernandez Corzo, the chief of the Department of Conservation and Propagation of Fauna, who corresponds to the head of the Fish and Wildlife Service in the United States.

One of Croker's jobs is to investigate cases of Americans whom the Mexican authorities have caught hunting illegally. There have been many cases of rich Americans arrested for shooting even more than the country's generous bag limits permit. While I was in his office, he heard a report of a pair of Stateside hunters who were picked up in Baja California, where they had shot a brace of the rare bighorn sheep without licenses either for their guns or for themselves. Another case, which I did not learn about from Croker or for that matter from anyone in the embassy, was more serious. According to my source, a close relative of one of our best-known senators, with strong Presidential aspirations, flew his plane deep into Mexico without a shadow of permission from the Mexican aviation authorities. He and his party then proceeded to shoot a jaguar without hunting licenses and were intercepted as they attempted to fly back to the States. Unfortunately, such was the importance of this "sportsman's" contacts that he got off scot-free. Such episodes do not endear us to the Mexican conservation authorities.

Close liaison has existed for a long time between the Mexican game wardens and their North American equivalents, especially along the Rio Grande border country. A careful list is kept of those visiting hunters who have been arrested for slaughtering vast numbers of white-wing dove and waterfowl on the Mexican side of the river. As a result, these illegal abattoirs have become risky to try.

Discussions that began years ago were still going on between the Mexican and United States governments with a view to forming international parks on the border between the two nations. Possible sites include the Sonoran Desert, the Big Bend of the Rio Grande, the Amisted Reservoir, and several others.

Animals meant a great deal to the men who ruled Mexico before the coming of the Spaniards. The Aztecs believed that Tezcatlipoca, the god of darkness and evildoers, appeared at night in the form of a vast jaguar whose spots were represented by stars. Tlaloc, the god of rain, was often represented as wearing a mask which combined the heads of a jaguar and a serpent. The Aztec calendar named days after the deer, rabbit, dog, monkey, and jaguar.

That these gods still stir the loyalty of some Mexican people was clearly demonstrated when the government decided to move a stone monolith of Tlaloc from the village of Coatlinchán, about thirty miles from Mexico City, to the National Museum of Anthropology in the capital's Chapultepec Park. The minute the government's plans were announced the villagers made it plain that they were not going to let their rain god go. Before the giant jacks were able to remove the 185-ton god from the ravine where it had lain on its back for centuries, 1,800 troops had to be called up so the transfer could take place.

As the villagers predicted, the god did not like being moved, for just as the twenty-wheeled, specially made flatcar on which Tlaloc was ensconced arrived at the museum, lightning bracketed the skies and a deluge of rain fell. Students from the University of Mexico, dressed in what they thought were Aztec costumes, had a field day, while the local Communists advised all the sundry to forsake the Catholic Church and return to the gods of their ancestors.

A little-known fact of this incident was that the government subsequently had to promise to build the villagers an irrigation canal and a fountain for their plaza. This was only logical, for without Tlaloc the village might have become a desert. Since Tlaloc has been sitting at the entrance to the museum, the rains in Mexico City have been much heavier than usual. On one particularly wet day, which resulted in floods, a banner appeared across the base of his statue saying, "Tlaloc Go Home."

The man who told me about Tlaloc was Dr. John S. Neiderhauser. A representative of the Rockefeller Foundation in Mexico and Latin America for many years, he had charge of a far-flung effort to get the Latinos to eat potatoes. Dr. Neiderhauser told me that on a per-acre basis potatoes have more protein, more carbohydrates, and more vitamins than corn, the basic food of the masses from the Rio Grande to Panama. Potatoes will grow almost any place, even above 5,000 feet, and would greatly enhance the meager diet of the upland peoples. Statistically put, potatoes could be grown in 25 percent of the area where 75 percent of Mexico's population lives. It is just possible that this addition to their diet might make them a bit less apt to poach the volcano rabbit and other rare forms of wildlife.

Another scientist working for the good of the wildlife of Mexico was Dr. Robert S. Sharman, an officer of the U. S. Department of Agriculture attached to the embassy. During lulls in an afternoon of bullfighting, to which he and his nice wife had kindly invited me, he told me about "the Battle of the Screwworm," one of the most fascinating stories I heard on this mission. The screwworm is a particularly nasty insect that eats the living flesh of cattle, horses, and most warm-blooded creatures of the wilds as well. Settling on the open cuts that ungulates always acquire on the ranges, the female worm lays her eggs. These soon develop into larvae that feed on the raw flesh. The resulting wounds can cause a lingering death. At the pupa stage the screwworms drop to the ground, where they mature into flies before taking off to infect new hosts.

The solution to this scourge came when Dr. E. F. Knipling, an entomologist of the Department of Agriculture, hit by chance on the startling fact that the screwworm could be sterilized. He figured that if screwworms were made incapable of reproducing and then released over the infected areas they would mate with the indigenous screwworms—but there would be no offspring. The female screwworm mates only once, while the males, like most others in the world, are polygamous.

Since the female *Cochliomyia hominovorax* can fly as far as 180 miles from her birthplace, a remote area had to be found to conduct the experiments. With the cooperation of the Dutch government, the island of Curaçao in the West Indies was chosen. Flies made sterile by X-ray treatments were then released on the 170-square-mile island, whose population of goats was heavily infested with screwworms. The experiment was highly successful. Cobalt—found to be cheaper than X-ray—was subsequently used to sterilize great numbers of flies. The field of operations was later transferred to the southwest section of the United States, where the losses for cattlemen ran to twenty million dollars a year. The next step was to move to the Southwest, where the losses ran to as high as $100 million a year.

As a result of the eradication of the screwworm in Texas, the deer population was said to have risen twenty-five percent. Eventually, the Department of Agriculture hopes to extend its operations to the Isthmus of Tehuantepec, so that all of the wildlife, as well as the livestock of Mexico above that point, will benefit.

Today, the Department of Agriculture sterilizes 120 million flies a week for dumping over infected areas along the Mexican border. The ranchers on both sides of the line send in containers of sample flies. As soon as fertile screwworms turn up, the planes dose the area with sterile hordes. The department has made a vivid and exciting movie short of this operation, which Sharman kindly ran for me at the embassy.

Sharman's main job, however, is as Co-director of the Mexico-United States Commission for the Prevention of Foot-and-Mouth Disease. Although the entire area from Panama to the northern border of Canada is now clear of this dread plague, it is so easily introduced that a constant watch must be kept. Between 1947 and 1954, it was necessary to kill a million head of cattle in Mexico alone to wipe out the disease. Sharman fears that when the Pan American Highway is extended through the Darien Province of Panama to Colombia, where there are infected cattle, the disease may again appear in Central America. Sharman was instrumental in persuading the Pan American authorities to move several herds of cattle that were in Darien. If the resulting gap is maintained, the chances of the disease's spreading north will be reduced. Foot-and-mouth is also a disease of deer, so Sharman's campaign has saved thousands of those ungulates as well.

Zoos should specialize in the fauna of the country in which they are located, but few of Latin America's do. Although Mexico City has two large zoos, neither has much to offer in the way of indigenous animals or birds. When we found Dr. Cabrera, the Director of the Parque Zoológico de Chapultepéc, he was engaged in trying to save a Wapiti doe whose calf had died inside her. While he loaded the tranquilizing gun, we had a short chat about the Mexican fauna. He said that his only Central American tapirs had burned to death when a fire consumed their house. His collection of cats was large, but I could not find a specimen of the margay. One of the rare birds I did see was the ocellated turkey. I looked among the bears for a Mexican grizzly, but no success. Interestingly enough, I noted that a pair of polar bears, along with a pair of brown bears, and, believe it or not, a pair of Indian sloth bears were all living together in apparent communal contentment.

Mexico City has the distinction of having had the first zoo in the Americas. According to Prescott, the Emperor Momtezuma II had a private zoo in the sixteenth century. Today, the Chapultepéc Zoo alone has some 3,000 animals of 300 species. Among its most unusual exhibits was that of a tiger and a dog living in the same cage. Having been nursed by the same mother, they had apparently never gotten over their childhood association.

Although crocodiles, including the rare Morelet's *(Crocodilus moreletti),* are supposedly protected under the fishing laws, I found a shop in Mexico City where it was possible to purchase any number of handbags and other articles guaranteed to be made of crocodile. There were also bags faced with jaguar skin, although it is forbidden to sell the skins of any of the cats for commercial purposes.

Not all of Mexico's rare wildlife lives on land. Along her golden Pacific beaches and off the endless mangrove swamps on the Caribbean swim some very scarce and important species of mammals and reptiles. The mermaid-like manatee still drifts in the estuaries of Veracruz, Tabasco, Yucatán, and Quintana Roo; the great sea turtles still come ashore to lay their eggs on both coasts; the seals, sea lions, and elephant seals haul themselves out to glisten in the sun on the rocky offshore islands; and the fast-declining crocodiles struggle to survive in the remote rivers.

Governmental responsibility for all of these marine creatures rested with Dr. Luis Cifuentes, director of fisheries, a branch of the Department of Industry and Commerce. To ascertain their status and find out what is being done to guard them from extinction, I went with Richard S. Croker to call on Dr. Cifuentes at his office. He soon gathered together all of his experts on these diverse species, and we sat down in the conference room to discuss them.

We started with the Atlantic ridley *(Lepidochelys kempi)*, a rare sea turtle that breeds only on a stretch of beach north of Tampico about twenty miles long. Twenty years ago, when the beach was first found, it was estimated that 40,000 female ridleys came ashore to lay their eggs there. In 1966 when the Mexican government first established a guard on the beach (four marines with rifles) the count was 3,500 females. A fascinating aspect of this egg-laying is that although the arrival date may vary from April to June, all the ladies swarm ashore together when the day comes. These invasions, known as *arribadas,* occur three times per breeding season, but the turtles never twice pick the same section of beach. While the laying ridleys and their eggs are now protected by law, calipee, the irreplacable ingredient of green-turtle soup, has become so expensive that the poachers will take great risks to get it. I was assured that the Mexican government intends to continue to protect the breeding grounds of this rare, interesting, and economically valuable turtle.

Questioned about the much more common green turtle *(Chelonia mydas),* Dr. Cifuentes said that his division is also doing its best to protect the laying beaches for these turtles. His entire enforcement staff, however, consists of only 105 men for all Mexican waters, so this is not an easy task. He also runs a turtle research station at Isla Mujeres off Yucatán somewhat on the lines of the Tortuguero operation conducted by Dr. Archie Carr in Costa Rica, an operation of which he spoke highly.

To save the remaining manatees, and nobody really knows how many there are remaining as they are very hard to locate in the murky waters, Dr. Cifuentes was working on a project to set up a manatee sanctuary at Laguna de Las Ilusiones in Tabasco. So gentle and unafraid are these great 300-pound mammals that they can be speared with ease. Thus their flesh, while oily, becomes a welcome and readily obtained addition to the diet of the protein-hungry natives of the Caribbean coast. Manatees do not occur on the Pacific coast of Mexico or in the interior. Several years ago five manatees were captured and taken inland to Lake Chapala. One was killed by a fisherman who thought it was a dangerous monster, but the rest are probably still patiently eating their way through miles of water hyacinth.

A sanctuary for crocodiles was also under consideration by Dr. Cifuentes. It would be located at Laguna Verde in Veracruz and would include the rare Morelet's crocodile as well as the common Mexican species. James H. Powell, Jr., who wrote an interesting article on Morelet's crocodile for the *Journal* of the International Union for the Conservation of Nature, believes that it is now very rare indeed. In 1965, when he went to Yucatán expressly to ascertain its status, he found that it was being shot for its belly skin. In a fresh-water swamp southwest of the Rio Lagartos his guide told him that a few could still be found. He went on to boast of how he and a companion had recently shot three big ones (about eight feet), for which they received 900 pesos ($72.00), a large sum for a Mexican peasant. He added that it was easy to sell skins in Mérida, the capital of Yucatán, where even small skins brought 100 pesos.

Powell reported that he saw fifteen Morelet's crocodiles in the Parque del Centenario at Mérida, among which was a large blind female. In 1963, when she was first captured, she made a nest in the sand and laid eggs which she brooded for two months. While guarding the nest she was attacked by students who wished to steal her eggs. Unable to budge her (she was seven feet long), they blinded her by thrusting the long pointed stick into her eyes. The eggs hatched, but the administration of the

Parque immediately pickled the babies in formaldehyde. To see that at least a nucleus of these rare saurians were saved, Powell bought five small crocs for twenty dollars from the owner of the Paisán y Venado restaurant in Mérida. After a great deal of trouble over an export permit, he was finally able to deliver them safely to The Grant Park Zoo in Atlanta, Georgia.

Off the coast of Baja California lies Guadalupe Island, where the Guadalupe fur seal is legally protected by the Mexican government. Dr. Cifuentes told me, however, that he does not have a warden on the island and is afraid that occasional poachers visit it. According to the Red Book of the I.U.C.N., the population as of 1965 was 600 individuals, and I was unable to obtain a more recent census.

The saga of the Guadalupe fur seal is a sad one. Peter Mathiessen, the novelist, wrote of a man named William Clover who sold a pair of these rare seals to the San Diego Zoo in 1928. In a subsequent argument over payment he vowed to exterminate the Guadalupe fur seal. Dashing out to the island, he killed sixty—all he could find—then died in a Panama bar while trying to peddle the skins. Far from hurting the San Diego Zoo, he made its pair even more valuable.

The seal was then listed as extinct until 1949, when a lone bull seal was seen on the San Nicolás Islands. Six years went by without a sighting until in 1954 the momentous news was broadcast that fourteen seals had been found living in a cave on Guadalupe Island.

Seals are not the only rare species found on Guadalupe Island. My friend Colonel Jack Vincent, editor of the Red Book of rare and endangered birds, wished me to ascertain the status of the Guadalupe kestrel, kinglet, house finch, and junco. I passed his request along to Dr. Enrique Beltrán, who promised to send Colonel Vincent a report on these rare birds. I also asked Dr. Beltrán to send data on the Socorro Island wren and thrasher and on the San Benito house finch and the rufous-sided towhee. I learned that the masked bobwhite, now pretty much localized in Sonora, is receiving protection and is no longer in danger of extinction. Neither Dr. Beltrán nor Rodolfo Hernandez Corzo, the director general of Fauna Silvestre, had heard about the Mexican ivory-billed woodpecker for some years. It may well be extinct.

In addition to the Guadalupe fur seal, which inhabits the Pacific Coast of Mexico, there is just an outside chance that a very rare seal—the Caribbean monk seal *(Monachus tropicalis)*—may still haunt the remote shores of Yucatán and Quintana Roo. The fishery people have no record of it, but the Red Book of the I.U.C.N. reports that a few monk seals have been sighted by shrimp captains, who believe that they migrate yearly between British Honduras and the Yucatán coast of Mexico. Dr. Archie Carr, the turtle expert, said that in 1964 a monk seal was reliably reported off the coast of the above-mentioned Isla Mujeres. The reason for the decline and near extinction can be laid squarely on men, who, since Columbus first saw them in 1492, have been slaughtering the seals for their hides, meat, and oil just as rapidly as possible.

Luckily there are two other species of this rare seal. Some 1,500 of the Hawaiian variety are still extant and are protected by that state. On the other hand, the Mediterranean monk seal, estimated to number about 500, lacks any sanctuary at all. Remarkably sluggish as well as unafraid of man, the brown-and-gray monk seal is the world's only tropical seal. For the Caribbean species, the end seems very near.

Deep-sea sport fishing also comes under the Division of Fisheries, whose offices are increasingly worried over the dramatic decline in big game fish in Mexican waters, mainly because of commercial fishing by Japanese trawlers. Dr. Ernest Chávez, a leading pediatrician and president of the Sailfish and Tarpon Club of Mexico, told me that the Japanese fishermen had taken 100,000 sailfish and 40,000 marlin from the Pacific Coast of Mexico in the preceding year. The result of this pressure can well be imagined. Dr. Chávez estimates that the sport-fishing boats from Lower California to Acapulco are boating a third less fish than they formerly did.

The Japanese trawlers use five-mile-long treated silk lines hung with thousands of baited hooks and buoyed by glass bubbles. The catches are collected for immediate processing in the trawlers. Mexico has a twelve-mile limit within which no foreign fisherman is allowed to operate, but the Japanese sometimes violate it, and the local fishermen have retaliated by cutting the lines and breaking the glass bubbles. There are evidently no Mexican gunboats on the Pacific Coast.

Sport fishing on the Caribbean Coast has suffered for other reasons, too. Illegal dynamiting, harpooning, and netting by Mexicans has so drastically reduced the tarpon that it is no longer worth while to fish out of Veracruz.

High in the Sierra Madre Occidental on the border of the states of Sonora and Chihuahua there may or may not survive Mexico's largest and finest animal—*Ursus horribilis*, the grizzly bear. For five years, no reports of these great bears that weigh up to 650 pounds have been received by the Mexican Conservation Department. Nor have the field agents of the U.S. Department of Agriculture who also travel through this remote area heard of any. But so wild and rugged is much of the country lying within the triangle delineated by the town of Montezuma in Sonora, and the towns of Madera and Nuevo Casas Grandes in Chihuahua, that a few lonely stragglers may still roam the arid uplands.

Although the grizzlies live mainly on nuts, fruit, honey, insects, ground squirrels, or other small rodents, they will occasionally kill livestock. It is primarily for this rare transgression that, even though legally protected, they have been hunted mercilessly by the ranchers. Their last known stand in a part of the Sierra Madre known as the Sierra del Nido, in Chihuahua, is owned by big cattle ranchers.

The last grizzly reported by a reputable source was in the form of a skin of a full-grown bear that George L. Mudd, a livestock inspector for the Department of Agriculture, saw hanging in a restaurant in a little town in Chihuahua in the spring of 1965. He did not know who killed it, but the skin was fresh. Previous to that there had been scattered reports of grizzlies, though few could be verified. The most recent detailed information comes from Starker Leopold's good book, *Wildlife in Mexico*, published in 1959. At that time he strongly urged special government protection for the Mexican grizzly. He also recommended that a field survey be made to ascertain how many of these great bears there were in the country.

That the grizzlies were still extant in the Sierra del Nido twelve years ago is apparent from Leopold's reports. In 1955 he examined the skin of a magnificent male killed by Isias T. García in the Cañon de Madéra on the east slope of the Sierra del Nido. The bear measured six feet six inches from nose to tail and weighed 705 pounds. Two years later García killed a female. In June of the same year Leopold and a field party of the Museum of Vertebrate Zoology saw tracks of ten bears while camped for ten days in the Sierra del Nido. Judging by their size, some of the tracks were certainly left by grizzlies. The party's twenty-eight-year-old guide stated that he had seen only thirteen grizzlies in his lifetime.

I had a long talk about the grizzlies and what might be done about them with Dr. Rodolfo Hernandez Corzo, the official in charge of wildlife for the Department of Agriculture. An able and efficient public servant with a dedicated interest in his job and in conservation in general, Hernandez spoke highly of Dr. Gabrielson, the then president of World Wildlife Fund, and of the help the Fund has given him on his white-wing dove project. He was pessimistic, however, about the grizzlies. Somewhat sadly he told me that he has only ninety game wardens for all of Mexico. This breaks down to one for every 8,444 square miles of the nation. In many parts of the country these game wardens are aided on a part-time basis by the 800 forest wardens. Even so, the chances of providing anything like adequate protection for the grizzlies is out of the question.

We agreed that if the money can possibly be found the first thing to do would be to make a survey of the Sierra del Nido to see if there are in fact any grizzlies left. If any are found and more funds can be obtained for special wardens, it just might be possible to save this noble species from extinction.

Hernandez, who did postgraduate work in zoology at Stanford University and in medicine at Northwestern, is fighting an uphill battle to popularize conservation both in the Department of Agriculture and among the public at large. He pointed out with considerable eloquence that wildlife means much more to Mexico than most people realize. Because animals and birds are an important food source for the *campesinos*, wildlife should be carefully conserved and cropped. He made the point that hunting for sport could be greatly increased if the supply of game were enlarged. Morover, those who do not shoot might well come just to see the wildlife. In Africa, for example, most people now hunt with cameras. Last but not least, he stressed the spiritual value of game and the great loss to the nation if it allows this priceless heritage to vanish from the earth.

Hernandez praised the cooperation now existing between the Mexican and American game wardens, saying it has resulted in a decrease in illegal hunting in his country. This liaison is particularly important to Mexico, for Hernandez can only afford to keep ten wardens on the border, while we have many times that number.

Speaking of the Mexican White-Wing Dove Project toward which World Wildlife Fund has contributed in the past, he said that the Mexican team which consisted of three men with one Jeep and one pickup, was in need of another vehicle. Cost? About $3,500. The team studies the doves' nesting habits and enforces the laws governing the shooting of them. Occasionally one hears dreadful stories of hunters who used to think nothing of knocking off a hundred or more doves in a morning. But thanks to the energy of this team and the other Mexican wardens, reports such as this are becoming very rare indeed.

But the only game in Mexico that Hernandez can be absolutely sure of protecting is that confined to two islands in the Gulf of California. Tiburón, an island of 500 square miles, has a fine population of mule deer *(Odocoileus hemionus)*. These big deer—they are considerably larger than our white-tailed deer—consist of two principal types, those of Baja California and those of the somewhat larger desert mule deer of Sonora and the interior of Mexico. The Boone and Crockett Club lists a specimen from Chihuahua that measured twenty-six and one-half inches around the outside curve of one antler. Tiburón also includes the collared peccary *(Pecari tajacu)*. Known as the *Javelina*, it is a highly adaptable little pig which, despite being persistently hunted all year round, manages to survive in good numbers. To discourage poachers, eight guards are stationed on the island.

The other island sanctuary is Rasa, a one-square-mile dot near Tiburón in the Gulf of California. A haven for sea birds, it is the nesting ground of gulls and terns.

As of 1967, Hernandez had no control over the sea mammals, such as the manatee and the seals. Nor had he anything to do with turtles, crocodiles, and sport fishing. Under a new law that may be introduced in the Mexican Congress, he would have jurisdiction for them in the same respect that his opposite number of North America has control over fish and wildlife. In the meantime, the Ministry of Industry and Commerce handles marine mammals, fish, and reptiles.

In addition to consulting with Hernandez, I was able to check the status of the grizzlies with Dr. Robert S. Sharman. In his office, Sharman showed me on a huge map of Mexico just where the grizzly skin had been seen two years ago and where, in his opinion, it might be possible to set up a park for any bears that may remain. He thought that Three River Section of Chihuahua would be a good place. The area would include about 250 square miles, all of which is owned by some large cattle ranchers who might, it was thought, be persuaded to go along with such a conservation scheme.

While I was in his office, Sharman phoned his regional officer who covers the Chihuahua-Sonora border country and asked him to make a careful check concerning any rumor of recent sign of grizzly.

During an interesting evening at the home of Dr. Beltrán, the conservationist, to which he also invited Hernandez and Dr. Alfredo Barrera, the director of the Museum of Natural History, we talked at length about the grizzly. Certainly these three men ought to be the best-informed group in Mexico about wildlife there. Consequently I was saddened to hear that the chances of a few grizzlies remaining in the country were not presumed to be very good.

On our last day in Mexico City, I called on Professor Juan Gil Preciado, secretary of agriculture. A man of considerable personal charm and undoubted ability, the secretary arranged for his undersecretary for forests and wildlife, Lic. Noë Palomares, to be present in addition to Dr. Hernandez, who translated.

Starting with a short résumé of the World Wildlife Fund and its objectives, I soon switched to the good job being done by Dr. Hernandez and his staff to safeguard the wildlife of Mexico and congratulated the secretary on the strong liaison existing today between the Mexican enforcement officers and those on our side of the border. I also touched on the joint efforts being made by both governments to study and preserve the white-wing Dove.

The secretary had evidently read the account in the morning newspapers of my keen interest in the Mexican grizzly, for he kindly offered to make me a guest of his government at some future date for a trip into the area where the grizzlies may still be found. If possible, I would like to make this trip with Dr. Hernandez and Dr. Sharman of our Department of Agriculture. In the meantime, both the Mexican authorities and our agricultural officers will keep a sharp lookout for signs.

I had hoped to be able to discuss the case of the Mexican grizzly as well as that of other endangered species with His Excellency Gustavo Díaz Ordaz, the President. But during most of the time I was in Mexico City, he was at the Punta Del Este Summit Meeting of Latin American Presidents. During the few days we overlapped, he was tied up with pressing business. Both our ambassador, Fulton Freeman, and the British ambassador, Sir Nicolas J. A. Cheetham K.C.M.C., did their best to make an appointment for me in the time available, but without success.

Mexico is a signer and ratifier of the Convention for Nature Protection and as such has a particularly important part to play in conservation. Much larger than the Central American nations, and one of the most important in all of Latin America, her handling of her own wildlife problems will be watched.

The trip that was ending in Mexico took almost three months. We had visited seven sovereign nations, and the two dependent territories of British Honduras and the Canal Zone. We had talked with six presidents and the governors of the two territories as well as many of their ministers and a host of men interested in conservation both in and out of governments. We had covered nearly 5,000 miles by car and on numerous occasions flew or rode horseback to areas not accessible by road.

The job of selling conservation in Central America and Mexico is not an easy one. In these nations, like those of South America which we visited in 1964, large segments of the population are hungry and illiterate. Game laws and national parks mean little to people who really want meat. No one realizes this more than the local politicians, so that with very few exceptions the excellent laws on the books are simply not enforced. People vote, but animals and birds do not.

Despite these obstacles, virtually every country we visited has a core of dedicated men who are doing their very best to save the wildlife. Some of them are in private life, others in the government. In only a few cases, however, are they in a position to influence the men who actually run their governments. Hence we were repeatedly told that the greatest help we could give them was to tell the various presidents and ministers about what was being done elsewhere and what could be done about conservation in their countries. As these conferences with the top men were invariably well covered in the local press, the resulting publicity not only encouraged the conservationists but in many cases put the presidents and ministers on record as favoring definite action to save wildlife.

While we made a constant effort to persuade the heads of the nations we visited to proclaim national parks, and congratulated others on their existing reserves, we also made it clear over and over again that parks without wardens are worse than useless. Repeatedly overlooked is the fact that they are an invitation to poachers. The sad truth is that many of the so-called parks listed by the United Nations are simply marks on a map. Others, like the park which includes only the Mexican city of Monterrey, could support no wildlife anyway. To have any value as refuges parks must have guards. But since the wildlife departments of most Latin American countries have only a handful of such men for their entire nation, there is no way to provide patrols for the parks. In a few cases, where the parks contain especially rare and endangered birds and animals, I feel it would be worthwhile for the World Wildlife Fund to consider aid for a limited period, provided that the government of the country where the park is located agrees to carry on this protection at a later date.

But the unfortunate fact is that unless there is a foreign conservation agency willing and able to continue financial aid, as in the case of Barro Colorado Island in the Canal Zone, and the Green Turtle Operation at Tortuguero on Costa Rica's Caribbean coast. The chances of survival for the rarer species are not very good. There are, of course, exceptions. The Mexican government has done a fine job protecting wildlife on some of her offshore islands. By and large, however, the efficient reserves are privately conceived and nurtured.

A prime example is what the United Fruit Company has done to protect rare birds and animals at its Lancetilla Gardens on the Caribbean coast of Honduras and in the adjoining forest area that the company rents for research purposes. The agriculture school in the Zamorano Valley of Honduras, which was originally financed by the company, is also an important refuge for the local wildlife. Leo F. Salazar's hacienda on the continental divide of Nicaragua provides a refuge for the rare quetzal, as well as more common birds under local pressure from hunters. The efforts of Robert Dorión and others to establish wildlife reserves on their estates has contributed greatly to conservation in Guatemala. Don Francisco de Sola, virtually a one-man conservation department for El Salvador, is also one of the very few men interested in the cause who also has easy access to those in authority in his country. The work of Dr. Leslie Holdridge, Dr. Robert Hunter, and Dr. Joseph A. Tosi of San Jose in setting up forest reserves in Costa Rica is also highly laudable.

On the other hand, working steadily against the conservation endeavors of governments and individuals in Central America and Mexico is the enormous increase in population, ranging from three and one-half percent per year in Mexico to over four percent in Costa Rica—among the world's highest. Unless drastically reduced, the birth rates will eventually force the cultivation of virtually all the remaining unused land—most of which is unsuitable for crops—between the Colombian border and Texas. Even in Mexico, where some agricultural yields have been greatly improved during the past decade, half the population must labor in the fields to feed the other half. (It is interesting to note that in the United States one farmer feeds thirty-two people, or, expressed another way, five percent of our population not only produces enough to feed the rest of the country but also to export millions of tons of foodstuffs to the rest of the world.)

Because the time may not be too far away when rare birds and animals of Latin America can be found only in private and public zoos, a great deal more effort should be made now to see that these institutions have good representative collections of their indigenous fauna. In visiting most of the zoos between Panama City and Mexico City, we were disappointed to see how few exhibits there are of local birds and animals. The Mexico City Zoo, one of the largest in Latin America, did not even have the Central American tapir.

PART 3

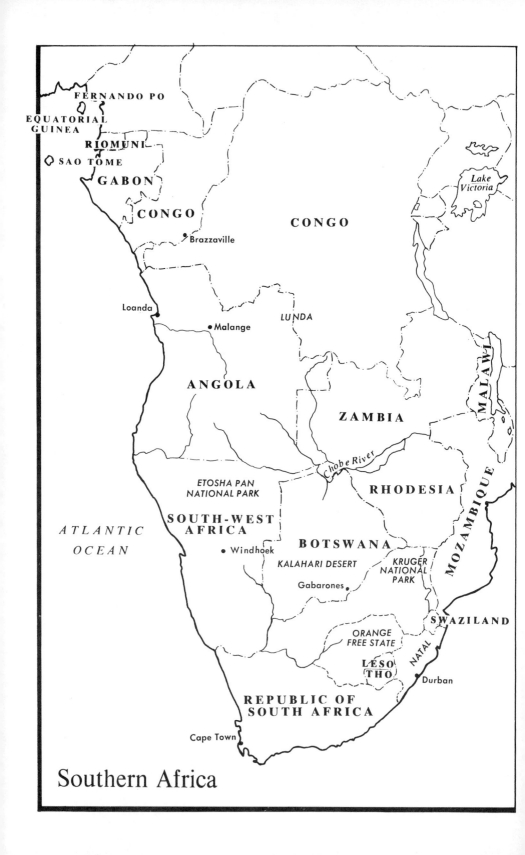

Southern Africa

CHAPTER XIII

Gorillas and Frogs

Far down the West African coast, where the Bight of Biafra simmers in the perpetual heat of the equator, lies Equatorial Guinea, which until 1969 formed Spain's southernmost remnant of empire. The little nation consists of the island of Fernando Po, a hundred miles off the coast of the Republic of Cameroon, and the mainland territory of Río Muni, bordered on the north by Cameroon and on the east and south by the Republic of Gabon. Getting there is not easy. Once a week a propeller-driven plane makes the weary thirteen-hour flight from Madrid to the town of Santa Isabel on the island. We flew across the Sahara in bright moonlight and in the dawn passed over Lagos, Nigeria, and out into the blue Bight of Biafra until we picked up the cloud-hung mountains of Fernando Po. Thanks to His Excellency Victor Suanzes, commissioner general of the then colony, an official car and chauffeur were placed at our disposal and rooms reserved at the Bahia Hotel, the island's best.

I could not find the house where Sir Richard Burton was British consul in 1861, but the old cannon of the fort are the same ones that guarded the harbor in his day, and the tempo of life on the island probably remains unchanged, with cocoa still the main crop. Undoubtedly the women of the Bubi tribe are among the handsomest on the Guinea coast. Behind the coastal plain the mountains rise to almost 10,000 feet, and lakes sparkle in the craters of extinct volcanoes. Living in dense forests of oil palm, mahogany, ebony, and oak are monkeys, civet cats, and small antelope. Pythons inhabit the dank valleys while highly poisonous green tree snakes lurk in the jungles.

Discovered by Portuguese navigator Fernando Po toward the close of the fifteen century, the island was ceded to Spain in 1778. In 1827, however, Spain, anxious to suppress the slave trade, allowed the British to administer the island and base at Santa Isabel the squadron of frigates which harried the musky-odored ships of the slavers. In 1844 Spain reclaimed the island but hired a British governor to administer it. Finally in 1858, Spain appointed her own governor, who promptly expelled the Baptist missionaries and, just to be fair, chucked out the Jesuits also.

With time hanging on his hands as British consul, Burton made frequent trips to the mainland. He was particularly fascinated by the neighboring country of Dahomey, which had the most sinister reputation on the Guinea coast. There he visited King Gezo, who sported an army of husky Amazons. Officers were chosen for the size of their bottoms, and Burton said they maneuvered their formidable female warriors with the "precision of a flock of sheep." All the lady soldiers were official wives of the king, and if caught in adultery were executed. But, according to Burton, some 150 were pregnant, a feat beyond the king's waning powers.

Today only four foreign powers are represented on Fernando Po: the consulates of Cameroon, Portugal, Nigeria, and Belgium. The success attending the rebellion of the small state of Biafra is hard to explain, but the Nigerian consul here does his best. Of more interest to the people of Fernando Po than the Nigerian war, however, was the constitutional election of 1968. Spain, perhaps the only European power that has had no trouble with her African dependencies, granted Guinea independence. This was not as easy as it seems, for the simple reason that

Fernando Po is relatively prosperous, and the 200,000 inhabitants of the Río Muni are much less so. Basically, the indigenous Bubis and Ports (the coastal population of Fernando Po, which is either mixed or descended from former slaves), did not think that they should be part of a government dominated by Río Muni. Spain, however, was endeavoring to keep Guinea from fragmenting, and since the economy of both parts of the country depends largely on trade with Madrid, the Spanish negotiators succeeded.

Fernando Po, with 61,000 human inhabitants, is the home of two rare subspecies of colobus monkey, a black and a red variety. Unfortunately, the monkeys, as well as the little indigenous antelope, are classed as game. Consequently both are shot by Europeans and natives. A favorite pastime of the local sportsmen and members of the island's hunting association is to hunt on the slopes of Pica de Santa Isabel, whose 9,350-foot altitude and dense jungle covering affords a wildlife habitat near the capital. Nominally, the area is a wildlife reserve, with a law on the books protecting the rare colobus, but the law is scarcely observed. Luckily, there is a crater in the extinct volcano of San Joaquin on the other end

Military Music on the Island of Fernando Po

of the island where wildlife flourishes—mainly because the difficulty of climbing down into it is just too much for the hunters. Later, in Río Muni, I urged the commissioner general to consider making sanctuaries of both these areas.

To try to see some of the local fauna, we drove along the coastal road to San Carlos to a black beach reminiscent of those of Tahiti, then proceeded inland high into the mountains. The island—twenty miles wide by forty-four miles long—possesses only a single road, which climbs to the interior. On the tableland at 5,000 feet lies the tiny hamlet of Moka. Moka boasts a closed mansion where the commissioner general stays during his periodic tours of the island, a church, and a garrison of white Spanish soldiers. There is also a small village inhabited by the indigenous Bubis. The travel folder says that the Bubis wear few clothes, but the one girl I found worth photographing was not only fully clothed but said in plain English, "I do not wish photography." Definitely we were East of Eden. Checkpoints evidently come into force in the evening, for we were stopped twice by Spanish soldiers on the way back to Santa Isabel. This might or might not have had something to do with local agitation over the ensuing elections. We saw a few birds and a herd of domestic cows, but of wildlife—nothing.

It takes less than an hour to fly from Fernando Po to Bata, the capital at Río Muni, but Spain's former toehold in southern Africa is considerably more primitive and nonproductive than the island. Although some 190,000 Fang tribesmen and 5,000 whites inhabit the territory—some 10,040 square miles—it costs Madrid eight million dollars a year to keep the economy going. Twenty-five percent of this is a subsidy for coffee and ten percent for cocoa. Both products are taken by Spain at well above the world market price. Furthermore, Equatorial Guinea's one natural asset, timber, is being exploited at a rate that will eventually denude the country of all its valuable trees. Hardwood in the tropics requires many decades to grow to maturity, but only a few hours to cut. Most of the ebony and a great deal of the easily available mahogany is gone. I was told that at least twenty percent of all the exportable timber in Río Muni has been cut, and there is no effort whatsoever to replant.

Fortunately, the tempo of lumbering will decline as the Spaniards leave the country. Most of it is done by whites, and since independence there has been an exodus of Spanish plantation owners and businessmen. Up to the time we left Río Muni in March, 1968, Spain had had no real trouble there. Memories of the Congo were still fresh, however, and the Fangs, unlike the docile Bubis of Fernando Po, can work up quite a head of steam on occasion. The name for the white man in the native language is "Etho," which can be literally translated as "man who kills without reason." Derived from the old slave days when Portugal owned Río Muni, the name has stuck and has an unpleasant connotation.

From casual observation, however, there was little surface tension among Bata's 25,000 people. The city was clean, and when nuts fell from the trees along the broad streets a squad of prisoners, wearing large signs across their chests with the word GAMBERRO (thief), ambled up and swept them away with witches' brooms. The schools, restaurants, and other public places had been integrated for years, but the whites continued to eat at some restaurants and the Fangs at others. Intermarriage between the races, which occurs quite often in other parts of erstwhile colonial Africa, did not seem to have been as popular in Río Muni. The Catholic Church was a power in the land, and the then president was a former catechist.

There were three American families in Río Muni: two missionary families, and that of Dr. Clyde Jones, head of the Río Muni Project for the Delta Regional Primate Research Center of Tulane University at Covington, Louisiana. Through Dr. Paul Zahl, Senior Natural Scientist of the *National Geographic* magazine, who made the trip to Río Muni to photograph and write for the *Geographic*, I was put in touch with Dr. Arthur J. Riopelle, director of the primate center, who had also been to Río Muni. Dr. Riopelle then recommended me to Dr. Jones at Bata. Thus it was that after a considerable correspondence I decided for two excellent reasons to include the colony in our West African mission. First of all, Río Muni is the habitat of the world's largest frog and, secondly, of the increasingly rare lowland gorilla. There are also two rare birds, the black pheasant and a species of honey guide which is seldom seen because it lives in the high canopy of the jungle. In the sluggish Río Muni and other rivers still lurk manatee, the mermaidlike creature whose dwindling fortunes I have been writing about from other parts of the world for the past five years.

A gorilla in the nest, Rio Muni

According to Dr. Jones, the main reason for the decline in the lowland gorilla population in Río Muni is the loss of habitat by timbering. Shy and timid, the gorillas cannot endure the noise of lumbering and are forced farther and farther back into the jungles or into areas where natives hunt them for food. For other primates, such as the chimpanzee and the mangabey, the loss of tree habitat is even more serious. Spending their lives swinging along the aerial terraces, they cannot exist without big trees. The second reason for the decline of the gorilla is poaching. The Fangs not only delight in eating them but believe implicitly that the flesh of the big primates has strong aphrodisiac qualities. They particularly relish the hands and the cheeks. Whether or not this taste is derived from the days when they consumed their enemies is open to speculation. It has, however, been more than half a century since the Fangs actively practiced cannibalism.

A third reason for the decline of the gorillas is the illegal export to the world zoos, young gorillas being worth $4,000 in Europe or America. Though the law says that only twelve may be exported per year, many times that number are actually smuggled out. I was told, for example, that in Atlanta fourteen lowland gorillas were recently purchased from a dealer. Of course, these gorillas also exist in Cameroon, Gabon, and Cabinda; but the majority of those sent overseas come from Río Muni. I was also told that a scientist working for the New York Zoological Society several years ago was unable to find any gorillas in the Cameroon and didn't see his first one until he came to Río Muni.

Dr. Jones, who had spent more than a year in the colony, said he thought there were fewer than 5,000 gorillas still living in Río Muni, with the rate of decline on the rise. Like everyone else, he could not predict just what effect independence would have on them. Under the Spanish, the licensing of firearms has been strictly controlled, so that in 1966 there were only 1,500 rifles or shotguns in the colony. The licensing authority was a hunting association which, while thoroughly integrated like everything else in Río Muni, was under the actual control of the Europeans. Dr. Jones added that although there are two game parks, both provided with guards, the guards are so ineffective that it is not worth while for a scientist to set up a study project there even for the gorillas on the protected list.

Life for Dr. Jones and his wife and two young children was not easy. There was no adequate school, so his wife taught the little boy and girl by the Calvert system. Malaria is endemic, and unless one takes great care one is sure to contract it. Mrs. Jones was just recovering from a bout of malignant tertian fever when we arrived. Other pernicious diseases rampant in Río Muni are fileria, which causes elephantiasis of the feet; dengue fever; amoebic dysentery; and sleeping sickness. Despite this, Jones, who is a young and enthusiastic scientist, liked his work and liked Río Muni. He is one of the dedicated men who work in the less attractive places of the world so that we can learn more about nature. He received his doctorate at the University of New Mexico and was only thirty-two at the time we visited him.

Associated with Dr. Jones was Jorge Sabater Pi, one of the curators of the Barcelona Zoo, who spent part of each year in Río Muni collecting animals for his institution. A lean Catalonian, Sabater has a deep interest in wildlife—especially in gorillas. He has spent twenty years in the colony collecting and taming some seventy of the big primates. The lowland gorilla (the male grows to about 400 pounds) is roughly half the size of the mountain gorilla, which I saw at Kivu in the Congo. It was Sabater who purchased the famous white gorilla from the Fang tribesman who had shot his mother when she raided his banana tree. The only albino known to science, *Nfumu Ngi*, or white gorilla in the Fang language, was tamed and sent to the Barcelona Zoo, where he is now on display. Dr. Ripelle's article, titled "Snowflake—the World's First White Gorilla," appeared in the March, 1967, issue of the *Geographic*, with a picture of Snowflake on the cover. With clear blue eyes, pink skin and polar-bear-color hair, little *Nfumu Ngi* is indeed a rarity. To most of the Fangs, *Nfumu's* color was quite understandable. They believed that the male gorillas rape black women and that *Nfumu's* mother must have been a white woman.

Not only is this story ridiculous but, according to Sabater, the gorillas are seldom driven to attack their human persecutors. Although they are distributed over approximately one half the total area of Río Muni, with a density of one animal per two square miles, the instances of attack have been few and far between. During a ten-year period in which Sabater traced down many reports of these attacks, in all cases but one the attacker had been badly wounded by the Fangs. The mature males are quite capable of charging, however, if the family includes young. Such an incident occurred in 1964 when two Fangs, Manuel Nsue and Jesus Abeso, crossed the Benito River in a dugout canoe and entered the jungle to hunt monkeys. Manuel carried only a machete, and Jesus an old single-barrel 12-gauge shotgun with a few No. 3 shells and one-ball cartridges. At a turn in the trail Nsue, who was ahead of his partner, suddenly encountered a family of gorillas, which included one adult male, two females, and one young. The male gave a piercing scream and charged Nsue, knocking him down and biting him savagely in the legs and hands. Abeso, hearing the cry of his friend, rushed up and shot the gorilla with a ball cartridge. The gorilla, though mortally wounded, tried to charge again, but dropped before he reached Nsue, who was still lying bloody and nearly unconscious on the ground. It was subsequently necessary to amputate many of his fingers. Sabater says this was a very unusual case—in fact, the only authentic record he has of an unprovoked charge by a gorilla.

Contrary to reports, there is no special park in Río Muni for gorillas. Two game reserves that did include gorillas as well as other species of game were established by the Spanish. Since the advent of the autonomous government, however, there has been a sharp increase in poaching. On a recent visit to one of them, Dr. Jones heard shots fired. The guards were either asleep or had been bribed. One of these reserves was established especially for sitatungas—antelopes. Nevertheless, according to Sabater, it is now virtually impossible to find this rare ungulate in the area set aside for it. Because gorillas move around a lot, a park established for their habitat must be large in order to be effective. It would also be necessary to prohibit lumbering and building of access roads. Lastly, a well-paid and highly motivated group of guards would be a necessity. Since the chances that any of these conditions would be fulfilled did not, at this writing, look favorable, the long-term future of the lowland gorilla in Río Muni is dubious.

After a sumptuous lunch with Señor Sabater and his wife, we were shown some of their tame gorillas. Two small ones live at their home, and their children handle them like kittens. Sabater told me that unless the gorilla babies are taken from the Fangs soon after capture, they always die of malnutrition. On a diet of milk and high-protein foods they do well and soon gain weight.

Gorillas were largely a mystery to Europeans before 1850. It was only

Jorge Sabater Pi, Irene Crowe, His Excellency Simeon Ngomo Ndumu, Civil Governor of Rio Muni

in 1861 that Paul du Chaillu published his well-known *Explorations and Adventures in Equatorial Africa.* Richard Burton knew Chaillu and defended him when Chaillu's reports on the great apes were not believed in Europe. Río Muni then belonged to Portugal. Spain took control only about sixty years ago as the result of a swap whereby Spain traded some land she owned in Brazil to the Portuguese in exchange.

Since then, Spain has done a great deal to offer education and improved living conditions to the Fangs. Today, only about ten percent of them are illiterate. An effort has also been made to give them hospitals and roads and to build model villages.

Victor Suanzes, the commissioner general and then very much No. 1 man of Spanish Guinea, impressed me. A veteran of some thirty years in the colony, he rose from a lieutenant in the colonial army to the highest post General Franco could give him in Equatorial Africa. His manner with the Fangs was relaxed, and it was easy to see that he was popular with them.

During the feasting after the official opening of a model village, I had a chance to talk to the commissioner general about the necessity of further protecting the colobus monkeys at Fernando Po and the gorillas and other rare animals of Río Muni. He responded frankly that there is little than can be done about conservation until it is decided just what kind of government will evolve in the future and who will run it. I also made a pitch with the civil governor. It was this same civil governor to whom both Harold Coolidge of the International Commission on National Parks, and the late Dr. Fairfield Osborn, president of the New York Zoological Society wrote (in 1965), offering to provide salaries and uniforms for park guards. The governor, perhaps realizing that the so-called game parks were not worth supporting, simply failed to reply.

Perhaps one rare creature in Río Muni that will not be affected much by the prospect of political independence is the giant frog. Long ago it learned that its legs are enjoyed not only by the Fangs but also by the Bayele Pygmies. As a result, the frog developed an ability to escape capture that is usually successful against all but the most planned offensive. The Bayele hunters, subsisting on the small bush elephant and the little red buffalo, as well as birds and fish, particularly relish the big frogs and lay elaborate schemes for their capture. The world's largest frog, with the scientific name *Conraua goliath,* it is the biggest of the 250-odd species of frogs known to science. It is also found in Cameroon and is called by the Fangs of both nations *"niamoa,"* or mother's son, because the size of its hindquarters reminds them of a boy child. Growing to the astonishing weight of more than seven pounds, the frog is capable of leaps that would have won millions on any Mississippi River boat in Mark Twain's day.

To see the frogs in their native haunts, Irene and I drove with Sabater and Jones to the river Mbia, thirty-odd miles north of Bata. After leaving the Land-Rover, we took a winding jungle trail down to the river. Huge, straight trees called *Terminale superba* rose out of the dense underbrush, and a hornbill, looking like a relic from a lost world, whirled down the path in front of us. Once we saw the droppings of bush elephant. Sabater said there are many herds along the river. Even though half the size of the East African species, they can run a man through with their sharp two-foot tusks.

The river was very low and the frogs extra watchful. Although we saw two, neither stopped long enough to be photographed. The instant they saw us approach over the rocks they made mighty springs and disappeared beneath the swirling water. They are found only in the fast water of the falls and rapids, where they sit in the spray and snap at their diet of scorpions, smaller frogs, and a myriad of insects. According to Sabater, captive frogs have been known to feed only on white mice. They lack vocal cords and cannot croak, but they can hear very well indeed.

While the frogs have a better chance of survival than most of the wildlife in Río Muni, an increase in guns may affect them. If the new government does away with the hunting association and grants licenses wholesale to the natives, the poaching will certainly increase. The hunting association is also the licensing authority for the export of animals. If this is put in the hands of unscrupulous men, the wildlife of Guinea will suffer even more.

In summary, I feel that the World Wildlife Fund should not at this time consider any projects in Río Muni. If the new government proves to be stable, however, the fate of the lowland gorillas, the chimpanzees, and the other scarce primates of the country should certainly be of concern to all conservationists.

CHAPTER XIV

Last Refuge
of the Giant Sable

Nearly 500 years ago the Portuguese navigator Jose de Santarem discovered the twin islands of São Tomé and Principe in the Gulf of Guinea. The world has seen many changes since December 21, 1470, but the islands still fly the flag of Portugal and in all probability will continue to do so during the foreseeable future.

Although São Tomé is only 202 miles from the humid port of Bata in Spanish Río Muni on the west coast of Africa, traveling from Bata to the island is not possible by normal means. No airline or steamship line connects the two, and even cables usually must be routed through Madrid and Lisbon. The only way one can make the journey without swimming is by charter. TAP, the Portuguese line which serves her African provinces, provided me with a swift and comfortable De Havilland Heron, and we made the run in one hour and twenty minutes. At the São Tomé airport we were met by the chief of cabinet of the governor of São

Tomé and by the director of the islands' Department of Tourism and driven to the Hotel St. Jeronimo on Ana Chaves Bay. We then paid our official call on His Excellency, Lieutenant Colonel António da Silva Sabastião A forty-eight-year-old career administrator who served in Angola for twenty years, the governor faces some formidable economic and social problems. The present population of some 65,000 is growing at the alarming rate of three and one-half percent per year. Moreover, the area of São Tomé is only 330 square miles, that of Principe a mere 42.

Cocoa, followed by coffee, coconuts and bananas, is still the mainstay of the economy. However, there is a possibility that oil may be found under the golden beaches of the volcanic islands. Tourism is always a hope, too. Certainly São Tomé rates as one of the most beautiful islands Irene and I have ever seen of all those we have visited in various parts of the world. Although bisected by the equator, the island seemed much cooler than either Fernando Po or Río Muni, which are several degrees farther north. In the interior it rises to an altitude of 3,000 feet.

At sunset we drove to the old forts of São Jeronimo and São Sebastian, which guarded the harbor in the days when São Tomé was the most important slave depot on the West Coast of Africa. With the island as a base, the Portuguese set up trading posts along the Congo and Guinea coasts. Their agents traded directly with the powerful kings of Benin and other African potentates, who secured the slaves in wars or sometimes sold their own people. Slavery was finally stamped out, primarily by British warships, but not before several million blacks had been exported to the new world. All the major maritime nations of Europe and the United States took part in the trade.

Today the population of São Tomé is a mixture of the descendants of slaves, exiles from Portugal, Jews, traders, and people from the Cape Verde islands. Because there was no indigenous population when the Portuguese settled in 1480, the only language spoken has always been Portuguese. Schools have been built, and the bright boys and girls given an opportunity to obtain higher education in Lisbon and Coimbra. The success of the island medical services in stamping out malaria and deficiency diseases has inevitably resulted in the population explosion.

According to Antonio el Bastos, the director of tourism, there are no

His Excellency
Lieutenant Colonel
Antonio Silva
Sabastiao Governor
of São Tomé, and the
author

Fishermen, São Tomé

indigenous animals on São Tomé. The wild pigs, which are hunted in the mountains, are the descendants of the domestic ones. There are, however, great numbers of birds. Among these may still survive the São Tomé grosbeak *(Neospiza concolor)*, whose native name is *enjolo*. The ornithologist Snow, who searched for it on the island in 1950, said its decline was due to the clearing of the indigenous forests in order to plant coffee. However, there are still areas of the mountainous island that have not lent themselves to cultivation. In these areas the grosbeak may yet survive. Unfortunately, Bastos did not know of a local ornithologist who could be helpful to me. Nevertheless, we took a long drive through the mountains to inquire among locals about *enjolo*, but without success.

There is also said to be a rare bird on the island of Principe. To track down this species of ibis *(Bostrychia olivacea)* an expedition of ornithologists financed by Oxford University went out to the island in 1948. They returned without finding a trace of it. Identical ibises occur on the Guinea coast, and the São Tomé grosbeak is also thought to exist on the mainland.

It is interesting to note that while the bird populations of the islands off Africa have suffered—the best-known example is certainly the dodo of Mauritius—there are few references by ornithologists to the demise of bird species on the continent. Dr. James C. Greenway in his authoritative *Extinct and Vanishing Birds of the World,* published by the American Committee for Wildlife Protection in 1967, states that for all practical purposes neither South America nor Africa has lost any known species in the past 280 years. On islands it is a different story, for there is no escape.

In 1966 a law was passed prohibiting the shooting of parrots and certain other talking and singing birds on São Tomé. This was fortunate as the natural habitat of all birds has been reduced to a point where forest remains on only about one fourth of the island. The introduction of cats, rats, and monkeys has also been hard on the birds. There is now a bounty of two escudos per kill on monkeys, however, because they raise havoc with the cocoa plantations.

In the company of Bastos and Bragos Farreira, director of public works, we took a long drive in the governor's car to Santa Catarina, the tiny fishing village on the west coast of the island where the hard road ends. There we watched the fishermen setting their huge net by means of a hollowed-out canoe. The diet of the São Toméans must be good, for I have seldom seen such powerful human specimens. They reported that there are small fish inshore, while marlin, dolphin, mackerel, tarpon, and other big-game fish are found farther out. Bastos looked pleased at this news and said he hoped one day to get the government to buy a "sportif boat, ten meters long, with chairs of combat" on board.

During the trip we stopped to inspect a maternity ward and a village school. Asked if any effort is being made by the government to try to halt the population explosion, Bastos admitted that there was not and made a sign of the cross, which could mean only that the Church was against birth control. He sighed and said on São Tomé they must expect a "hurricane in demography."

On our last evening in São Tomé we were invited to the governor's residence high in the hills. There I had a chance to give him particulars about the rare grosbeak and ibis and to urge him to add their names to the list of protected birds. In actual fact, however, the natives of Sao Tomé possess few shotguns, so it is extremely doubtful they would waste a shell on any small bird when the same charge might net them a pig.

It is difficult to assess the true state of affairs in any country from a few days' observation, but certain obvious guidelines are indicative. For example, the car and chauffeur we used on the island were the governor's own, and people seeing it either came to attention or saluted; but these gestures were in no instance subservient ones. The citizens of São Tomé smiled when they recognized the car, a reaction very different from that which one sees on the streets of some of Africa's newer nations. Whether this was due to a high regard for the governor, who has been on the island for four years, or for the regime, I had no way of knowing.

It was seven years since I had visited Luanda, the capital of Angola, Portugal's richest and most important African province. As we dropped down for a landing, I was amazed to see the building that had taken place during the interim. Luanda had doubled her population to almost a half million and changed her skyline from a modest one with only a few tall buildings to a replica of some of the cities of South Africa. At the field we were met by the representative of His Excellency, Lieutenant Colonel

Camilo Rebocho Vaz, Governor General of Angola; Harvey Summ, the American consul general; and Michael Chapman, the Luanda representative of an American firm that handles public relations for a number of important Portuguese businesses.

The infiltration of Angola by dissident elements, which began with the rebellion in the North in 1961, still persists, but the Portuguese have been able to contain them. The rebellion, in fact, is confined to the boondocks, and there has been no trouble in any of the cities or towns. In the meantime, the economy is booming, and the oil wells of Cabinda will soon be supplying the Portuguese empire with all she needs of this vital necessity.

Angola is the home of one of the world's most rare and handsome animals—the giant sable antelope. It was primarily to visit the reserves where these magnificent ungulates are protected that we went to the province. Michael Chapman saw to it that arrangements were made for us at the reserves. On the day before we started, we talked with Dr. Malacris, the officer in charge of game for the Angolan government. He kindly phoned the chief game warden at Malange to provide two Land-Rovers to take us into the parks.

We left Luanda early in Michael's car and drove across the flat Angolan plain, green after the rains. At Massangano we turned off the main road and drove to the old town where the Portuguese made their heroic stand when the Dutch captured Luanda in 1641. For seven years the settlers held out at the fortress they constructed amid the swamps of the Cuanza River, 120 miles north of Luanda. Today the old cannon still guard the walls, mute testimony to the will of Portugal to hold her African possessions. In the chapel is the grave of Paulo Dias de Novais, the founder of Luanda.

The long dusty miles slid past, and by midafternoon we arrived at Malange, 270 miles from our starting point. Malange is the nearest town to the two reserves where the giant sable are protected. We put up at the same hotel where I had stayed in July, 1961, when the rebellion broke out in the neighboring Congo. During the crisis I sent my attaché plane to save the white missionaries, and as a result never did get to see the sables. This time we hoped for better luck, although the chief wardens of both the adjacent parks told us that we could not have come at a more

195

difficult time. José Antonio Alves, the warden of the Luanda Reserve, said that the access road was waist deep in water, making passage impossible. The smaller Cangandala Reserve, however, is on higher ground. Warden Marques de Andrada promised he would make every effort to show us sable there the following morning.

I was delighted to hear that the wardens estimated the giant-sable population at about 2,400 head—400 at Cangandala and 2,000 at Luanda. As I had been told in 1961 that the herd was estimated to number not more than 800 head, this was a great increase. They added that there was virtually no poaching because of the heavy fines imposed. The only factor hindering this antelope population increase is the normal one of attrition by lion, leopard, wild dog, hyena, and jackal. De Andrada patrols the 386-mile Cangandala Reserve with the help of only four black assistants, while Alves has a white assistant and six blacks to run the 4,632-square mile Luanda Reserve. Since 1957 the giant sable antelope in both reserves has been absolutely protected. Not even the excuse of collecting for a museum can get one a permit to shoot one.

To get an early start on our quarry, we rose in the predawn darkness, jumped into two Land-Rovers, and drove at speeds that hovered around sixty miles per hour over rutted dirt roads. Owls fluttered in front of the headlights, and by dawn we were in the reserve, by seven at the ranger's headquarters about forty miles from Malange. There we had breakfast, collected several assistants and a rifle, and headed for the bush. The country consisted mainly of mapane forests and open plains. The rains had been unusually light, but still the grass was several feet high. Thus the only chance we would have to see sable antelope would be to spot them standing in the open.

As we progressed, the road became increasingly soggy. Finally we hit a spot where all four wheels sank to the hubcaps. While the wardens and the boys cut lunber to jack the wheels, Irene settled hserself comfortably in a tree with the poems of e. e. cummings, and I found a high anthill from which I could scan the horizon in all directions. Suddenly, about a hundred yards away, I saw something moving. Centering my 10-power Leitz glasses on the spot, I saw two giant sable bulls slowly entering the forest. Although the body of the giant sable is only a little bigger than that of the ordinary sable, the horns are much larger. Sweeping backward

196

from its head like a pair of scimitars, they are spectacular even at a distance.

It was our only sighting. Six more times the Land-Rover sank into the soft red-clay trail, and we finally had to call it a day. By the time we got back to the Angola Hotel at Malange, twelve hours had elapsed since we started. The time to be sure of getting around the reserves is during the dry season—July, August, and September being the best. Then the grass is dead from the drought; even the hardy mapane trees have lost most of their leaves.

Only two Angola birds are listed in the Red Book of the International Union for the Conservation of Nature. These species are the Luanda swift *(Apus toulsoni)* and Swierstra's francolin *(francolinus swierstrai)*. The swift, however, may not be in any danger of extinction, for, according to ornithologists, swifts are neither easy to collect nor to observe. The bird is said to be found along the coast from Cabinda south to Lobito Bay. Dr. Alexander Duarte, head of the Department of Biology of Angola, told me he had seen some and consequently did not think they were scarce. The francolin, on the other hand, is an inhabitant of the montane evergreen forest, which of late years has been greatly reduced by lumbering. Dr. Duarte had no information on the francolin, nor had the director of the Luanda Museum.

The giant sable antelope's scientific name is *Hippotragus niger variani* in honor of H. F. Varian, an Englishman who went to Africa in 1907 to help build the famous Benguela Railway from the Angolan port of Lobito to the copper mines of Rhodesia, 1,300 miles inland. While engaged in this work he became interested in the game and found that the Angola Boers, who had come by oxcart from South-West Africa after the Boer War, were shooting the giant sable to an extent where they would soon become extinct.

Varian interceded, approaching the governor of the district between the Quanza and Luanda rivers, where the sable lived. He persuaded the governor to have these grand animals declared "royal game," so that it was necessary to have a special permit to shoot them. As a result, this was given only for the collection of museum specimens. Varian himself shot the giant sable antelopes that are now in the British and Chicago museums. He was later made an honorary life member of the American

Giant Sable in Luanda Reserve, Angola

Museum of Natural History, one of the few Englishmen to be awarded this distinction. Varian also had the Angolan dik-dik named after him. Hence he gave his name to both the longest and the shortest horns in Africa. The record giant sable horn measured sixty-five inches, the record dik-dik's, one and three-fourths inches. In 1953 he published a fascinating account of his life under the title, *Some African Milestones*. Now over eighty-eight and reported to have married recently, Varian is living in England.

Another hunter and naturalist long associated with the giant sable is José Fenykovi, a Hungarian engineer who lives in Madrid and who for many years maintained a hunting lodge in Angola. At the start of this trip, Irene and I spent several days in Madrid, where Mr. Fenykovi and his wife were most hospitable to us. His picture of a giant sable at the close range of twenty feet is the most dramatic I have ever seen. It was Fenykovi, incidentally, who shot and later presented to the Smithsonian Institution the world's largest elephant.

A great deal has been done to increase the game reserves in Angola since my two previous visits, seven and eight years ago. There are now eight reserves throughout many parts of the country. There are also four shooting blocks in the Southwest. The gorilla, giant sable, rhino, chimpanzee, giraffe, and the manatee, which are seen frequently in the Quanza and other rivers, are the only animals that have year-round protection, I was told. Game found in Angola includes elephant, hippo, red and black buffalo, kudu, sitatunga, impala, sable, roan, dik-dik, pig, wart hog, and virtually all of the predators such as lion, leopard, cheetah, jackal, hyena (including the scarce brown species), and wild dog. Crocodiles still haunt the rivers, but the skin trade has decimated them as it has all through Africa.

I promised Dr. Clyde Jones and Sabater Pi, who were working on the lowland gorillas of Río Muni, to inquire if the Portuguese have any information on the gorillas of Cabinda, the southernmost habitat of these primates. Dr. Duarte told me, however, that he had only one man in the whole province working on animals and one on birds, and that nothing has so far been done about scientific studies of the gorillas of Cabinda.

Jose Fenykvi with giant sable he shot for Luanda Museum

Cabinda is a humid slice of jungle wedged between Congo Brazzaville and Congo Kinshasa on the coast north of Angola. Although known to the Portuguese explorers since the fifteenth century, Cabinda did not become part of Angola until 1885, when the paramount chief of the territory decided that he would rather be part of Portugal than of either the French or Belgian Congo. On February 1 of that year he signed a treaty with Guilhermo Augusto de Brito Capelo. This treaty was ratified by the Treaty of Berlin, which set the borders of European spheres of influence in Africa.

Except for timber, the little enclave of some 3,000 square miles was of small value to Portugal until the Gulf Oil Corporation made one of its most sensational oil discoveries there in 1966. As a result, the importance of Cabinda to the power structure in southern Africa has grown, and guerrilla bands operate from Dolisie in Congo-Brazzaville. So far, however, the Portuguese force of some 5,000 regulars has had no trouble containing the 600 terrorists who operate there. Sad to say, the area where the guerrillas are most active is in the Maiombi forest, the same one inhabited by the lowland gorillas, and if there is anything a gorilla dislikes it is gunfire. So the fate of the animals in Angola depends, in the last analysis, on the stability of the government, just as it does elsewhere.

CHAPTER XV

South-West Africa

Until comparatively recently, South-West Africa was about as well known to most people as the other side of the moon. Of late years, however, the vast territory that covers some 318,000 square miles has been getting a good deal of attention in the United Nations and the International Court of Justice at the Hague. The world press has been devoting millions of words to the territory and its 600,000 inhabitants because of long wrangles over its status going back to 1884, when the German Chancellor Bismarck annexed it. South-West remained part of the Kaiser's African empire until 1915, when an expeditionary force from South Africa defeated the German armed forces and took over the territory for the Allies. After the League of Nations was formed, it proclaimed South-West a Class C mandate with Great Britain as the mandatory power. Britain promptly gave it to the Union of South Africa, which was not only the nearest member of her empire but whose soldiers did the work in defeating the Germans. After the Second World War, the colonial empires started to fragment into independent nations, and pressure in the U.N. increased for the recognition of any group of people who might remotely qualify for self-rule. The empires of Britain, France, and Belgium subsequently melted until only South Africa, Portugal, and Rhodesia retained lands in Africa which the United Nations thought should be independent.

To try to force South Africa to grant self-rule to the 500,000 nonwhites in South-West, an action was brought by Liberia and Ethiopia at the Hague Court. But in 1966 the court announced that neither Ethiopia nor Liberia had the proper standing for them to have their charges against South Africa adjudicated. In other words, the judges voted that the International Court of Justice did not have jurisdiction. For all practical purposes, South Africa had won the case.

South Africa's jubilation over the ruling of the World Court has not been dampened by subsequent moves of the United Nations, and no one expects her policy toward South-West Africa to be in any way affected by future decisions of the world body. Thus for all practical purposes South-West is now the fifth province of the Republic of South Africa. Aside from the stamps that are still distinctive, the laws, currency, and political representation are all similar to those of the four original provinces of South Africa. Members from South-West sit in the republic's parliament in Cape Town, and the highest court of appeal is the Supreme Court at Bloemfontein in the Orange Free State.

It had been seven years since I saw Windhoek. When we flew there from Luanda in Angola, I was amazed by the changes that had taken place. Handsome new government buildings as well as private construction had dramatically altered the skyline of the little German town I remembered. An effort had been made, however, to save the old landmarks. I recognized the Tintempalast, the Ink Palace from where the Germans ruled the colony. The principal street still bears the name of the German Kaiser, another is named after Hermann Goring's father, who was a respectable colonial administrator, while the beer gardens of the various hotels still serve the best beer in Africa. On a tour of the city, given us by my good friends Jack and Olga Levinson, we were shown a number of new business establishments, including the Anglo-American group, famous for its gold and diamond mining. There was a great deal of visible evidence that the citizens of Windhoek have confidence in their future.

Our main objective in going to South-West Africa was to see its fine game parks. Thanks to my old friend Wentzel du Plessis, the administrator, or governor, of South-West, we were given access to every facility. Bernabe de la Bat, the director of Nature Conservation and Tourism for South Africa, arranged a series of trips for us, personally driving us to the Etosha Pan National Park, whose 38,000 square miles probably make it the largest wildlife reserve in Africa. In contrast, the island of Ceylon, which has only 25,000 square miles, is the home of more than twelve million people, while the broad lands of the Pan are populated only by a variety of game.

Setting out early from Windhoek, we drove through a countryside green with the winter rains. Even the camel's-thorn trees, whose far from tender branches have given me a number of uncomfortable experiences, were tufted with buds. The grass, which would be yellow and sere in another few months, was rank and high. We also passed the Omatako Mountains (the name in the Herero language means "bottom," a most descriptive term for their shape). Ostrich galloped beside the road, while a brace of marabou storks flew up from some unsavory meal. On the telephone lines, lilac-breasted rollers sat in sedate pairs, and a fleet of guinea fowl picked their way along in a disciplined line. A ground squirrel regarded us from atop an anthill, whose peculiar-looking points always face toward the north.

De la Bat, thirty-eight at the time of our mission, has progressed to the top of his profession since he guided me around the Pan in 1961. A graduate marine biologist who found his real interest in the bush, he runs one of the best wildlife organizations that I have seen in Africa. In 1961 his budget was about $100,000 and his staff consisted of thirteen men. In the meantime his budget had increased to $1,600,000 and he had seventy white assistants and 300 blacks.

By noon we had covered the 278 miles to the Pan and arrived at Okaukuejo, the main camp of the reserve, where we were given a delicious lunch by C. J. V. Rocher, the chief nature conservator of Etosha Pan. The camp was empty, for we came during off season for tourists.

When open it offers 200 beds in attractive guest houses and rondavels. There are two other camps in the reserve, with a fourth in the planning stage.

In the late afternoon we took the Land-Rover for a first look at the varied wildlife of Etosha Pan. On the Pan itself, a vast forty-by-eighty-mile stretch of salt and clay, nothing grows. The remainder of the land was carpeted with grass and thorn trees. Here we found a contented family consisting of a huge black-maned lion, a lioness with two cubs, and two other full-grown lionesses. The mother, uneasy at our presence, made a false charge when we got too near her cubs, but fortunately the family had fed—with their extended bellies, they simply could not be bothered to move. Finally, they all settled down, allowing us to take all the pictures we wanted at fifty feet.

When the park's four rangers gathered with us for drinks in the evening, we learned something of their profession. They showed some excellent slides illustrating the delicate operation of temporarily immobilizing elephant, rhino, oryx, zebra, and lion by means of drug-tipped darts shot from guns, pistols, and crossbows. In addition to using the process for moving animals from one place to another, the park's veterinary surgeon, Dr. Haymie Ebedes, uses it to patch up wounded lions.

One of the most interesting men we met was Peter Stark, a bearded giant who used to be a poacher and is now the park's No. 1 catcher of these unlawful gentlemen. The son of an eminent lawyer of South-West, he liked the bush so much that he became overseer of a farm near the reserve where he spent much of his spare time in illegal hunting. He shot seventy-five lions before he saw the light and joined De la Bat's staff. The first year on the job he caught 182 poachers and has averaged fifty a year since. Stark, who goes out on horseback patrol for weeks at a time with four mounted Bushmen as assistants, speaks the strange clicking tongue of the Heikum Bushman and the Herero language as well. He told me that the poachers come in during the night on their lean little horses to run the game—mostly giraffe and eland—with packs of dogs. When the game is tired or comes to bay, they spear it or shoot it with arrows.

He told me of one close call with a Bushman poacher whom he caught red-handed. When Stark tried to arrest him, the Bushman started shooting his poisoned arrows. One of them nicked Stark in the hand. Another pierced his shirt but was deflected by the pipe which he kept in his shirt pocket, but Stark fell. The Bushman, thinking he had killed him, shouted, "I have got you, you bastard!" and ran away. A week later the Bushman walked into the police post and said, with some satisfaction, that he had killed a white man. Stark admired the courage of his attacker, with the result that the judge gave the Bushman only a nominal sentence.

Under the poaching laws, whites and blacks are treated exactly alike. In 1967 six whites and forty blacks were caught and given fines or sentences by the magistrates. Two white men caught shooting a rhino were fined $2,000 each. In addition, their car and rifles were confiscated. The only exception to these rigid laws, which are much stiffer than those in most countries of Africa, or for that matter in America, concern native poachers who have killed only for food. These are released with a warning. In most cases, however, Ovampo and Herero poachers kill to sell the meat—wasting most of it in the process.

Stark's Bushman trackers were used on one occasion to track criminals. Five murderers, serving life sentences at Windhoek, escaped from jail, stole guns, and worked their way north to the game reserve, where the police lost their trail on the hardpan. The Bushmen picked up the track, and several hours later the police came upon the fugitives, who immediately opened fire. The police returned the hail of bullets, but Stark neither fired his own gun nor took cover. He simply stood by the Land-Rover and watched the battle. When a bullet hit the mudguard he was leaning against, he merely changed position. He said that after all the criminals had either been wounded or had surrendered, he found he had lost any taste for having to take part in this kind of affray.

In bed that night we heard the deep coughing roar of lions, the wild laughter of hyena, and the howl of jackal, all seemingly within a short distance of the wire fence around the camp.

In the morning we drove to Etosha Pan itself and photographed its shimmering white expanse as a single file of wildebeest trekked to the green pastures twenty miles across the Pan.

Etosha Pan was discovered in 1851 by Karl Andersson, the famous explorer and naturalist, and Sir Francis Galton—two highly distinctive characters. Galton used to dress in red hunting coat, jack boots, and a hunting cap when mounted on his riding ox. In those days, the country-

Eland and zebra, Etosha Pan, South West Africa

Young lions, Etosha Pan, South West Africa

side was in turmoil due to the depredations of Jonker Africaner, the Nama Chief. Galton suddenly appeared at the chief's kraal, so astounding the old brigand that he called off his raids for a while. Andersson, who was the first European to discover the Okavango River, made two expeditions into South-West Africa and Bechuanaland between 1850 and 1854. He wrote several fascinating books about his travels and observations, among them *Lake Ngami: Explorations and Discoveries During Four Years' Wanderings in the Wilds of South West Africa* (London, 1856), of which I have a first edition.

Sailing up to Walvis Bay from the Cape on a chartered schooner, Andersson and Galton landed in a veritable desert of sand with no fresh water available. So unused to white men were the Bushmen and natives of the area that when they saw Galton's wagon with a broken wheel they reported to him that his "pack-ox had a broken leg and as it had no grass near it, it might soon die." With lions everywhere, the Europeans lost horses, mules, and cattle. Commenting on the local cuisine, Andersson said that the natives made a hole in an ostrich egg, introduced salt, shook

Banded zebra, Etosha Pan, South West Africa

it up, and placed it in the coals to cook. He also noted that the natives, who smoked hemp, tipped their arrows with a poison made from Euphorbia candelabrum. Andersson also took down careful accounts of the birds and subsequently had a bird named after him. He died in 1867 on a trip to the Cunene River.

Not far from Okaukuejo are the graves of the Rietfontein encampment of the Angola Boers, those intrepid travelers who trekked all the way from the Transvaal to Humpata in the highlands of Angola. They stayed at Rietfontein for a period in 1876, suffering terribly from thirst and malaria. When I drove to the Cunene across the Kaokoveld in 1960, we found other graves of the Boers at Swartboois Drift on the river, pathetic markers to girls who died in childbirth at sixteen or old men who never saw the promised land of Angola. The Portuguese gave the trekkers land, where they stayed until 1928, when the government of South-West repatriated most of them. Inveterate hunters, they lived by the rifle, thus largely exterminating the game in the Humpata district. The trek took

Number Oryx, Etosha Pan, South West Africa

Tagged Lion
South West Africa

several years and covered nearly 2,000 miles. Part of it was across the Kalahari Desert, one of the world's harshest.

Near Rietfontein we came to a waterhole where the park authorities had built a concrete bunker from which scientists could observe animals coming to drink. A group of these learned men were watching the hole one afternoon when a cow elephant and her calf arrived. The calf evidently picked up their scent on the ground because it carefully picked up some earth from beneath their footprints and carried it dutifully to its mother. After a quick sniff, the cow started on a reconnaissance of the area, located the bunker, introduced her trunk into it and blew a terrific blast. The scientists concluded their operations as soon as she withdrew.

We spent the next day and night at Halali camp, where Zakkie Eloff, the artist, is the ranger in charge. The son of the secretary of Paul Kruger, President of the Transvaal Republic during the Boer War, Eloff is married to one of his former art students, and they both produce excellent pictures of wild game. Life at Halali is not without its excitement. One day, for example, a leopard invaded Eloff's garden. When he tried to chase it

209

Bat-eared Fox, Etosha Pan, South West Africa   (PHOTO C. RICHARDS)

away, it took a pass at him with its paw, scratching him deeply across the face. It then raced through the open door into the house, where Eloff's wife and young children were. Tearing after the leopard, Eloff finally cornered it under a bed and took a shot at it through the springs. The first shot ended in only a tinkle of breaking china, but the second killed the leopard.

To keep the game from invading the farms along the southern border of the park, a 287-mile-long fence, eight and a half feet high, has been constructed. The seventeen strands of heavy wire deter almost all animals except the elephant; the old pilot bulls, seeking new grazing for the herds, simply push it down. Then they guide the herd through the gap and all hell breaks loose on the farms. Because the elephant calves cannot climb five-foot fences, the bulls push these down too. Furthermore, the walls of the dams prevent the calves from drinking, so the bulls break down the dams to the right height for the three-foot youngsters. Finally, Stark is summoned. His job is then to drive the herds back through the

Puff-Adder, Etosha Pan, South West Africa   (PHOTO C. RICHARDS)

Puff-Adder, Etosha Pan, South West Africa   (PHOTO C. RICHARDS)

Crimson Breasted Shrike, Etosha Pan, South West Africa (PHOTO C. RICHARDS)

Brown Hyena, South West Africa (PHOTO C. RICHARDS)

Etosha Pan, South West Africa

Lion in his prime, Etosha Pan, South West Africa

gaps, a feat of horsemanship that requires considerable skill.

Lions, leopards, and cheetah also come through the elephant gaps to feed on the farmer's cattle. He responds by shooting, poisoning, or trapping the predators. Trapping is becoming the most fashionable because the park pays for any of the big cats that are caught and returned.

Artists thrive in the park service, and we purchased three pictures by Lynn Tinley, wife of ecologist Kenneth Tinley, half a dozen of Eloff's, and two of Fritz Krampe's. This German artist, whose work is now very popular in South-West, was killed by an elephant in India. He was completely fearless to the point of being reckless where elephants were concerned. He once chased a herd of elephants while on horseback, just for the thrill of being among the wild animals he loved.

On the third day of our visit to Etosha Pan we drove to Namutoni, the historic German fort, which has been turned into a first-class camp. On the way, we passed an old wildebeest bull wearing a broad orange collar with which he had been decorated by the park biologists to track game migrations. More than 170 animals of all species either have been provided with collars or marked in the ears. Only by this method can De la Bat determine exactly where the herds go for their winter and summer

South West Africa

Game on Etosha Pan, South West Africa

grazing. The time will come, he thinks, when he will know where to find the great majority of the 100,000 animals in the park at any given time.

Namutoni is remembered because of what happened in the dawn on January 28, 1904, when the German garrison of five soldiers and two sergeants saw an army of 500 Ovampos charging toward its walls. By racing from loophole to loophole and firing from each one in turn, the defenders managed to kill 150 Ovampos and hold the fort all day. Under cover of night they escaped on foot. This was during the Herero War, the only time that the Hereros were able to persuade the Ovampos to rise against the Germans. After the battle of Namutoni, the Ovampos retired to their homeland in the north and took no further part in the fighting.

The Hereros, by their own opinion as well as that of many observers, are the aristocrats of South-West. Handsome, tall Hamitic people, they despise the Bantu tribes around them. In the old days they held most of the Namas, Damaras, and many Ovampos in slavery. The Herero word for Damara is translated as "offal." Although no one knows exactly where they came from, they are believed to have originated near the lakes of the northeast, arriving in South-West only a few hundred years ago, with their large herds of cattle.

215

Fort Namutoni, Etosha Pan, South West Africa

In 1904, when 60,000 of the 80,000 Hereros revolted against the Germans, General von Trotha was forced to use several divisions to put down the uprising. After the war was over, only 20,000 escaped to Bechuanaland. It was said that Herero women subsequently refused to have babies so that none of their children would grow up under the Germans. The 40,000 Hereros still in South-West remain something of a problem to the government today. They refuse, for the most part, to do any type of manual labor as they dislike physical effort. On one of my trips to South-West I called on old Hosea Kutako, the Herero chief, who greatly impressed me. Through an interpreter, he told me that two of the things he held against the white man were the loss of Herero homelands (even though his people had seized these from the Damaras) and the loss of the subject peoples; in other words, the Damara serfs who used to serve the Herero. I admired his courage. He told me of Maherero, father of the Herero nation, and of the sacred fire that was always kept lighted by the wife of the chief. In the late 1800's, Rhenish missionaries showed the Herero women how to stitch the long, graceful dresses that they still wear today.

In the late afternoon we drove from the gates of Namutoni in the Land-Rover to see the game. The rains had filled many of the shallow

216

pans, and a multitude of birds was enjoying the flood. A pair of Egyptian geese with a family of six goslings sailed across the blue-green water. Little black-and-white grebes and doves appeared, and two baby avocets huddled on an island. Ducks were represented by a Cape shoveler and a brace of red-billed teal.

Inland from the pan we came on a great flock of quelea, the little weaver birds that are the scourge of the Ovampo farmers but the delight of the Bushmen. The former blast them with fire, while the latter eat them by the dozen. Great migrations of queleas, ten miles long, appear like locusts, devouring the farmer's seed crops. Because it was the mating season, the male birds were frantically constructing the hanging nests in which they hoped their mates would lay eggs. If the female quelea is not pleased with the results, she tears down the nest and tells her husband to start a new one. A number of hawks, attracted by the quelea, soared above the trees. I also saw the slim green form of a tree snake glide toward a nest.

In an open plain we suddenly came on a pair of lions: a big black-maned male and his sleek lioness. They had been breeding and were not pleased by our arrival. Maneuvering the Land-Rover slowly, Rocher took us within forty feet of the pair before the male sprang and charged to within ten feet of the car. After getting some excellent pictures, we decided not to press our luck any further and departed.

Later, in a forest of acacia and leadwood, we found a tiny dik-dik standing near the trail, with a slender mongoose beside it. I caught them both in the same photograph. Soon afterward a pair of kudu bulls posed for us. De la Bat then spotted a yellow-footed tree squirrel up on a branch. At sunset, a family of giraffe appeared, giving us a fine portrait against the fading light. By a water hole we found a strange assortment of bachelors: an ancient wildebeest, a thin old kudu, and a springbok. Just like old men in their clubs, the aging males, rejected by the younger masters of the hinds, band together for mutual comfort and defense.

There were also many greater bustards around. These larger birds are the totem of the Ovampos; therefore they are never killed or eaten by them. The tiny green praying mantis is the totem of certain other Bushmen tribes, who hold it in holy dread. Namaqua doves and a crimson-breasted shrike sat on a tree near the road, so I was able to photograph this handsome butcher bird, which impales insects on thorns, then daintily eats its victims. We saw glossary starlings, anteating bee-eaters, European bee-eaters, and fork-tailed drongos as well.

Awaiting us back at the fort was one of the few surviving Strandloopers, most primitive of all the peoples of the South-West. The Strandloopers live in the skeleton coast far up in the Kaokoveld, where they used to subsist on dead whales, seals, and fish. When I visited Kaokoveld in 1960 I saw perhaps the last purebred of the tribe, a very old man indeed. The boy at the fort was only half Strandlooper, his mother having been a Nama. He still spoke the curious clicking language of the Hottentots and had lived all his life at Seafontein in the Kaokoveld before coming to Namutoni. He said his people always used bows and arrows and bartered with the Germans for the iron for the tips. He said there are only five Strandloopers left at Seafontein, and none of them are purebloods.

Another of the workers in the camp was a member of the Bastard Community, half-castes who emigrated from the Cape in 1870 and carved out a territory for themselves under the captaincy of Hermanus Van Wyk. I visited Rehoboth, the capital of their community, in 1959, and had several long talks with old Johannes Buekes, their captain. He wanted his people to have more say in their affairs but admitted that if it were not for the white man's law few of the Bastards would have any land remaining. The law does not allow them to sell their land to a white man, and for a people who are easily confused by liquor and have a strong desire for it, the Bastards would soon have been stripped of their livelihood. Incidentally, the Bastards have strict laws themselves and dislike intermarriage with the Namas or any of the other nonwhite tribes of South-West. They are even against the Cape Coloureds, demanding that they be restricted from entering South-West. The Bastards fought for the Germans in the Herero War but for the British in World War I. In 1923 the community was given a large degree of independence but proved unable to cope with it, and it was revoked by the government. Not only are the Bastards proud of their name, but they regard themselves as superior to the Coloureds of the Cape, even though they are both the result of miscegenation.

More than half of the land of South-West Africa is now allocated for nonwhite homelands. There are areas where whites are not allowed to

218

Hartman's Mountain Zebra, Namib Desert, South West Africa

own land. In fact, millions of dollars have been spent by the government to buy up white farms so that the land could be given to the Damaras, Hereros, Namas, Okavangos, Coloureds, Rehoboth Bastards, Bushmen, Tswanas, and inhabitants of the Kaokoveld and East Caprivi territories. Furthermore, legislation will soon be approved to give the Ovampos a great deal of self-government along the lines now granted to the Transkei Native Authority in the republic.

The second-largest game reserve in South-West is the Namib Desert Park, a 5,064-square-mile waste of majestic sand dunes, rocky mountains and arid plains, which lies on the Atlantic coast west of Windhoek. It is, in fact, part of a vast stretch of similar country running all the way from Angola to the Orange River. With Rodney Baxter, the senior nature conservation officer of the park (and for that matter of all other pro-claimed game areas of South-West except the Etosha Pan), Irene and I and Baxter's wife made a three-day tour of the Namib. Leaving the mile-high town of Windhoek early, we started down toward the coast. As we drove along the excellent blacktop road, the country changed from the lush green of the rain-fed highlands to sparse desert plants and then to ever-barren sand dunes.

This is the home of Hartmann's mountain zebra, a relatively rare zebra that can be distinguished from the more common Burchell's zebra because it lacks pale brown stripes between its black stripes but does possess a distinctive gridiron pattern on its rump. Baxter estimates there are about 10,000 mountain zebra in the park. Whether the mountain zebra isn't actually the same animal as the Cape mountain zebra is open to question. Certainly both look very much alike to me. Both are massive animals about the size of Grévy's zebra of East Africa.

We passed the dim outlines of jagged ranges which Baxter identified as the Erongo and Pondok mountains. Rich in rock paintings, they are about to be declared national monuments. Nobody knows when the delicate pictures were made, but it is thought the artists may have died some 5,000 years ago. In the Twyfelfontein Mountains there are rock engravings of equal antiquity. Baxter was concerned about how to keep tourists from carving their own names over these examples of ancient art.

Dim in the distance we sighted another range, the Husab Mountains,

Dr. Koch in the
Namib Desert, South
West Africa

Springbok, Namib Desert, South West Africa   (PHOTO R. W. BAXTER)

from whose lonely valleys had come a fascinating report. H. Bachran, a German prospector, who spent many years in the more remote areas of the Namib Desert, told Baxter that he had seen a herd of zebra with stripes only in front. This raised a momentous question: Could they be the quagga, the species which for a hundred years the scientific world has considered extinct? Of course, the herd might be zebroids, the offspring of zebras and mules. But since these cannot breed themselves, it is unlikely that there would be many of them in one place. The Husab Mountains cover an area of about 100 square miles that has never been surveyed. It is just possible that the quagga, which was thought to have vanished from southern Africa with the Cape lion and the bluebuck, may have held out in the hidden valleys. Baxter is looking forward to the day when he can make a thorough investigation on horse and on foot. Flying over the area proves little, as the mountains do not allow close observation. In any case, all zebras look alike from a hundred yards.

Baxter also has charge of the game in the Kaokoveld, the 20,000-square-mile rectangle of arid bush country that adjoins Angola. When I traveled there in 1960, I saw several large herds of black-faced impala. Consequently I was glad to hear that this rare ungulate is still numerous along the Cunene River. The Kaokoveld is also the habitat of the black rhino, whose population Baxter estimated at between 150 and 200 head. On my trip through the area we saw numerous tracks but few rhinos.

Although Hartmann's zebra, the black-faced impala, the black rhino, the giraffe, and the Cape buffalo (found also on the Cunene in limited numbers) are all fully protected by law, none of the great predators are protected. It is legal for the farmers to shoot, poison, or trap lions, leopards, and cheetah if they destroy their cattle and sheep. According to Baxter, the leopards and cheetah are not yet in short supply despite the laws, but the lions are growing increasingly rare outside the parks. The cheetah is fast and wary; the leopard is a night killer. The lion, however, is often fearless and waits for the hunter.

At noon we arrived at the little German seaside town of Swakopmund, which had just celebrated its seventy-fifth anniversary. The old hotels with names such as Furst, Bismarck, and Hansa still stand, as does a very fancy greenish-colored edifice that once housed dusky ladies of pleasure. The Germans, particularly the army, came without wives in the early days, and it was to meet this lack that the building was constructed. A brace of lions surmounted the cornice, while cupids were arranged over the doorway. Apparently the house has had less glamorous tenants since the last Germans were defeated in 1915.

John Mathews, head of the Division of Fisheries of South-West Africa, told us that the rich fishing grounds off the coast are always crowded with foreign trawlers. Japanese, Spanish, Israeli, and Italian ships, along with those of South Africa, compose the western fleet, while the Bulgarians and the Russians represent the Communists. The latter frequently invade South Africa's twelve-mile limit. Hence it may be necessary to station a gunboat on the coast to keep them in legal waters. Mathews is also in charge of the seals that swarm at Cape Cross, where Diago Cam, the Portuguese explorer, raised a stone pillar in honor of his kind. The inscription under it says:

"Since the creation of the world 6,684 years have passed, and since the birth of Christ 1,484 years, and so the illustrious Don Johannes has ordered this pillar to be erected by Jacobus Canus, his Knight."

Some 8,000 seals a year are harvested here at Cape Cross and another 35,000 at Lüderitz Bay, down the coast. Guano is also a source of wealth, but sealskins and fertilizer are only a minute part of the riches of South-West. The economy rests on mining, agriculture, and fishing, all of which return handsome profits. At the mouth of the Orange River is one of the world's great diamond fields. Some of the stones actually lie right on the surface, making it necessary to patrol the beaches with aircraft and dogs.

Twenty miles north of Swakopmund lies Walvis Bay, which is not part of South-West at all but a 314-square-mile enclave belonging to South Africa. The fishing industry is centered there, and I was amazed to hear how profitable it is. Dividends of forty percent a year are not uncommon. Nor is this return based on exploitation of the nonwhite fisherman. The colored and Ovampo workers get exactly the same pay as whites, many averaging an annual income of better than $5,000. At Walvis Bay I was interviewed by the publisher of the Namib *Times,* said to be the world's only trilingual daily newspaper. It is printed in Afrikaans, English, and German.

Fishing is about the only sport I can occasionally indulge in during these wildlife missions. So when Baxter and Mathews suggested a half day's surf casting, I quickly agreed. From Walvis Bay we took a tortuous trail across twenty miles of beach to Sandwich Bay. The slightest deviation from the route could have delayed us for hours in the soft, shifting sands. The beaches of South-West have some of the world's highest dunes. We passed several that rose to more than 500 feet. Sandwich Bay used to be a harbor, one of the only two such natural shelters in South-West, but silting long ago closed the entrance. Today there is only a big lagoon inhabited by a multitude of waterfowl. We saw flamingos, pelicans, cormorants, gannets, and black-backed gulls sitting in the shallow water, while farther out we recognized red-billed, yellow-billed, and Hottentot teal, Egyptian geese, Maccoa ducks, and southern pochards.

The Cape salmon were biting that day, and we landed a twenty-pounder and some smaller fish. No relation to the salmon of Europe or

America, the Cape salmon looks to me more like one of our sea bass.

From the coast we drove inland across the Namib Desert to Gobabeb, site of the Namib Desert Research Station. Headed by the famous entomologist Dr. Charles Koch, it is the only such institution south of the Sahara. Dr. Koch, an entertaining Austrian of about sixty, received us hospitably and immediately began telling us about the Namib and his work there. Perhaps the oldest desert in the world, the Namib contains ranges of ocher-red sand dunes as well as more conventional desert terrain. In the dunes Dr. Koch and his colleagues have found a fascinating universe of insects, reptiles—and even one small mammal. There is no vegetation. The insects of the dunes have learned to exist entirely on wind-blown organic matter. It virtually never rains in this part of the Namib, so the creatures that inhabit the dunes have had to develop the ability to extract moisture from the fog. Dr. Koch compares life in the dunes to that of life in the sea. He said that temperatures in the sand vary as they do in water. Three feet down, the thermometer registers a steady 70 degrees, while on the surface it may reach 107, or fall during the night to chilly levels.

The one mammal found in dune land is the eyeless golden mole, a very rare little fellow with a handsome yellow coat. Dr. Koch's study of this mole offers an excellent chance for the World Wildlife Fund to assist a research program of real value in the preservation of a little-known species. Discovered in 1966, the sightless animal has attracted a great deal of attention in the scientific world. A grant of $3,000 or so would make a big difference in the good doctor's ability to continue his work.

Dr. Koch, an international authority on beetles, showed us a series of watercolors of his insect pets which will appear as illustrations in a book. Also found in the Namib dunes of South-West is the only white member of the beetle species in the world. Apparently it lives quite comfortably in close association with a black beetle of similar size. Through living in the sand for countless eons, most of the beetles have, like the mole, lost their eyes. The mole catches its prey, chiefly insects and beetles, on the surface, then submerges like a crocodile to eat in the sand. Though the golden mole rejoices in the scientific name of *Eremitaepa granti namibensis*, it is only a few inches long.

Dr. Koch told me that Dr. Harold Coolidge, one of the founders of the

World Wildlife Fund, was of great help to him in raising funds during the early days of the research station. Today, the station gets financial support from both the government of South-West and the Transvaal Museum. But, like all such institutions, it is always in need of funds. I cannot think of a more useful effort than to help Dr. Koch and his dedicated helpers who live deep in the desert with nothing but the shifting dunes around them.

The life in the Namib Desert consists mainly of game, birds, and a few isolated dune dwellers. Where the Kuiseb River Valley runs into this arid stretch of land we stopped for a time to talk with the chief of the Topnaar Hottentots, leader of a scattered people who live along the valley. Tall men and women with puckered yellow faces, peppercorn hair and, in the women, outsized behinds, the Topnaars came originally from the Cape but have lived in South-West for many centuries. When the British explorer Sir James Edward Alexander visited the Walvis Bay area in 1837, he described them as the tallest and best built of the Namquas. But when Agnes Winifred Hoernle, the South African ethnologist, studied the tribe in 1923, she considered them the most "miserable remnant" of the peoples of South-West. In 1966, T. Jenkins and Charles Kimberlin Brain, the zoologist, published a report on this dying community, which put the population at only 130. The old chief, who obviously had Herero as well as other crosses in his ancestry, told us sadly that his people live where they do because of permission granted long ago by Queen Victoria. The Hottentots keep dogs, however, and dogs are not allowed in any game park.

The Namib is the extreme southern limit of *Welwitschia bainesii*, the longest-lived plant in the world. A strange desert shrub which puts out long octopus-like leaves, it usually lives for centuries. Carbon tests have indicated that the plant may well last as long as 2,000 years. It occurs in a belt about twenty-five miles from the Kaokoveld south. There are both male and female plants; fertilization is performed by beetles.

Among the admirers of the Namib is Hans Kriess, a leading businessman of Swakopmund, who spends all the time he can spare taking remarkable movies of the life of the desert. He showed us vivid pictures of the sidewinder, a brilliantly colored dune snake whose bite is highly poisonous. The sequence depicted the snake's ability to wriggle down into the sand so that only its diamond-shaped head, which blends perfectly with the yellow-gold sand, remains visible. Then the film showed the capture of a lizard, which the sidewinder promptly swallowed by unhinging its lower jaw.

Another of Kriess's fascinating wildlife pictures concerned a tame female baboon who lives with and guards the goats on a farm near the edge of the desert. In the morning the baboon (named Allah) lets the goats from their corral, fetches the lambs from a separate corral, and puts each one under its proper ewe. She then leads the herds to graze and at sunset brings them home. Allah is assisted by a dog, but does not have any human help. She has been twice bred by a wild baboon, but she never allows her babies to interfere with her work with the goats and sheep. Remarkably intelligent, she bends down the branches so that the goats can graze on the leaves. When she needs a pick-me-up, she takes a swig of goat's milk from any handy udder. She also debugs the goats. What's more, she's wise enough not to try to remove ticks, which would leave an infection because the heads often remain in the host.

In a hidden valley deep in the desert we saw more than a hundred Hartmann's zebra, a herd of twenty springbok, a score of oryx, and a fleet of ostrich. The animals were extremely wary; perhaps poachers had been after them.

In addition to the game parks, wildlife conservation in South-West Africa is lucky to have the support of the great majority of the farmers on whose vast tracts (often running to 50,000 acres) sizable stocks of game are preserved. My good friend Edgar Vaatz has such a farm, where he raises cattle, karakul sheep, and game at the same time. The Vaatz farms, which take a whole day to cover by Land-Rover, harbor gemsbok, kudu, cheetah, and leopard. Both these predators prey on the sheep, but instead of shooting them, Vaatz has the animals trapped and sent to the game parks. Cheetahs, which are rare in most parts of Africa, are plentiful on his lands.

On our last evening in Windhoek, we were invited to the administrator's house for dinner, and I was told, much to my surprise and pleasure, that I had been made the first foreign Honorary Game Warden of South-West Africa. From that time on I could wear the uniform and participate in wildlife conservation on one of the world's last frontiers.

CHAPTER XVI

Kalahari Desert and
Chobe River

In 1961 when I last visited Botswana, or the British High Commission Territory of Bechuanaland as it was then called, the drought, which was to burn the land for five terrible years, was just beginning. From the Chobe River in the far north to the lands of the Bangwaketse in the south, and from the Tuli Block on the east to the border of South-West Africa, the rains failed over most of the territory's 275,000 square miles. Tens of thousands of cattle died along with hundreds of thousands of game animals. Life was harder for the little Bushmen of the Kalahari Desert as well as for the other half million inhabitants of the territory. Not until 1966 did the rains fall again. In that same year the British terminated the protectorate, and the Republic of Botswana joined the family of nations.

Not the least of the problems to be faced was that of the greatly reduced game resources. Not only had the grazing animals and the predators suffered from the drought, but there were no effective game laws for tribesmen. Unrestricted killing had contributed toward the depletion of certain species. True, there were several reserves where the game was nominally protected. But when Major Patrick Bromfield, the game officer, retired in 1966 he had only a small staff and inadequate funds. The picture was dark when Laurence Tennant, former chief game warden of Uganda, accepted a newly created Food and Agriculture Organization-sponsored post of chief game warden. Since then, real progress has been made in conservation. It was to see this that I accepted the kind invitation of Sir Seretse Khama, the President, to visit his country in behalf of World Wildlife Fund.

Mafeking, the old capital of Bechuanaland, where Colonel Baden-Powell withstood his famous and probably quite unnecessary siege, was actually outside the borders of the territory. When independence came, the capital was moved to Gaberones, a dusty little railway depot on the edge of the Kalahari only a few miles from the border of the Transvaal in the Republic of South Africa. Since then, however, a great deal of building has taken place. Today the capital boasts many fine new government buildings, a modern hotel, a hospital, and schools. Relations are good between the town's 20,000 Bechuana tribesmen and the 2,000 Europeans, mostly government advisers and United Nations technicians. Botswana claims with considerable accuracy that this happy state of affairs extends to all of the country's half-million inhabitants. The United States maintains an embassy there, although the staff consists of only two officers and a secretary. Charles Fletcher, the principal officer, had the title of Chargé d'Affaires, an arrangement that accords Bostswana the prestige of senior diplomatic recognition without saddling the State Department with the cost of an ambassador and the logistical support he would have to have. An ambassador, like a general, simply cannot function without troops. The Peace Corps is represented in Botswana by some sixty young men and women who roam the country pursuing their diverse endeavors.

My first official call was on the president, Sir Seretse, whom I had met seven years earlier in Serowe, the tribal capital of the Bamangwato, the most numerous people of the eight major tribes that compose the population. As hereditary head of the Bamangwato, Sir Seretse was in strong standing with about forty percent of the people of his country. From this

228

Author, Chief Lethslothere of the Batawana and
Laurence Tennant, Chief Game Warden of Botswana

power base he built his national position until he headed the Botswana
Democratic Party, controlling eighty percent of the country's popular
support. Tennant accompanied me on the call, and we talked of the
importance of game parks as tourist attractions as well as the possibility
of securing help toward that end from the World Wildlife Fund. Because
the president took a real interest in conservation, he appreciated the
numerous problems Tennant faced.

We also touched on the bigger issues of Botswana's relations with her
neighbors. Surrounded on all sides by white-dominated governments, Sir
Seretse maintained viable contact with South Africa, while his ministers
cooperated closely with the republic in dealing with mutual problems
such as cattle disease and game conservation. Although Botswana did
not recognize the Smith regime in Rhodesia, the only railway in the
country belongs to the Rhodesian government, so there is contact at the
lower levels. Botswana maintains diplomatic relations with Zambia and
other new nations to the north. She also recognizes the Republic of China
—there is even one of Generalissimo Chiang's ambassadors in Gaberones. Britain, which gives Botswana approximately half of the annual

229

cost of running her government (about fifteen million dollars a year), recognizes Red China, a circumstance bound to make things a bit difficult at times for Her Majesty's High Commissioner, as well as for the envoy from Taiwan.

In the president's air-conditioned office was a bronze statue of Khama, Sir Seretse's grandfather, who was literally the founder of his country. Grandfather Khama took over from his father in 1875, and immediately embarked upon a series of radical reforms. He prohibited strong drink, which was debauching his people; substituted education for witchcraft; became a Christian, and in 1885 accepted the protection of the British Crown. When Khama died in 1923, his son succeeded him, but the son lived only two years. Seretse, the next in line, was then only a boy, so the British appointed Tshekedi, Seretse's uncle, as regent. In 1949 Seretse married Ruth Williams, an English secretary, in London. After they returned to Serowe, he persuaded the Kgotla, the council of chiefs, to endorse him as the Paramount Chief. But Tshekedi, who questioned Seretse's fitness to rule, partly because he married a white woman, successfully influenced the British to exile him for five years. When I first met Seretse following his return from exile, he had been given the key post of Tribal Secretary. Under similar circumstances, many men would have been bitter. But Seretse never indulged in rancor. Instead he and Ruth became firm friends of Great Britain and the West.

After leaving the president's office, we called on The Honorable James Haskins, the minister of commerce, industry, and water, who had under his broad umbrella the Department of Wildlife and National Parks over which Tennant presided. With most of the country's economy concentrated in his ministry, Haskins was, of course, vitally interested in sources of revenue. There were six safari companies operating in the country, with an annual turnover of more than half a million dollars. The government received about $125,000 a year from hunting licenses alone. Tennant's department consisted of seven senior officers (game wardens), one ecologist, seventy-eight senior scouts and scouts. His budget ran to about $100,000 per year. On this, he had to police the Chobe National Park, an area of 4,000 square miles, and 500 square miles of Moremi Game Reserve. At the same time he had to control the utilization of game over the entire country. Until the time of our visit a license was required only for foreigners, with the result that vast numbers of game were shot and trapped by the tribesmen. In 1967 alone, 30,000 springbok hides were sold in the market. The new laws apply to everyone except the Bushmen, and are expected to reduce materially the killing of game for commercial purposes by tribesmen.

Most of these little seminaked people are now found in the central Kalahari Desert, where they pursue much the same primitive existence they have for ages past. During my journeys in Bechuanaland in 1959 and 1960, I visited several groups of Kung Bushmen, one of the last people on earth who still maintain themselves entirely from the land. With their tiny poisoned arrows they shoot the desert game, using all of the kill, even drinking the clear water found in the stomach cavity. They showed me how they made their poison from the pupa stage of certain bugs, and how they could draw water from under the sand with long bamboo poles, which they thrust into what they called their "sipping wells." They practiced a strange but often effective medicine, which they believed exists in all Bushmen and can be transferred from one person to another by means of putting both the donor and the recipient in a trance. This is produced by a wild dance which heats up the "medicine" and allows it to be transferred.

According to the police, there are only about 20,000 guns of all descriptions in the country. However, game can also be taken legally by means of traditional traps, so that the only really effective way to control the kill is to keep tabs on the skin buyers by regulating what they can purchase and export. The skin trade is thought to be the third major industry after cattle and crops. There will always be a big cropping of the grazing herds, but it will be supervised for the first time by not allowing the sale of skins unless they are taken on license.

There is now a four months' closed season for all game animals. Certain animals receive protection all year round. Among the most important of these are cheetah, rhino, hippo, and brown hyena. The brown hyena, although really in little danger of extinction, is nevertheless listed in the Red Book of the International Union for the Conservation of Nature as a species needing protection, especially in South Africa. In South-West Africa and Botswana, however, I have been told that, while fairly common, it is still accorded protection. Like all hyenas, the brown species kills livestock, with the result that it is undoubtedly becoming rare on farms. Although hyenas live mainly on the carrion left by the nobler beasts of prey, they have been known to hunt and kill healthy grazing animals. Surprisingly enough, hyenas have been clocked at forty miles an hour. Despite a reputation for cowardice, there have been instances where hyenas have attacked armed tribesmen. With their immensely powerful jaws and razor-sharp teeth, they can shear through a man's leg as if it were a sausage.

There are three species of hyena in the world today. They are found in India and the Near East, as well as in Africa. The striped hyena has the widest distribution, inhabiting India, Iran, and Asia Minor. The spotted species lives in Africa and over much of western Asia from the Mediterranean to Bengal. In Addis Ababa they invade the suburbs at night to clean up the refuse. The brown hyena is restricted to southern Africa.

It has been reported that one of the Christianized tribes of Botswana believes that the flesh and organs of the brown hyena are highly efficacious. They think the heart will impart courage, and the bones, if ground during a certain phase of the moon, will cure the bite of mad dogs. The people of some countries still believe the hyena is bisexual. I've heard this stated as a fact, even in the Transvaal. In fairness to the believers, however, it must be admitted that it is hard to tell the sexes apart; for externally, at least, there appears to be no difference at all. As a scavenger, the hyena plays an important part in cleaning the landscape and thus deserves protection. Lion and leopard are also protected, but they can be killed in defense of life and property.

The first general game survey of Botswana was made by Thane Riney and Peter Hill in 1962 for the International Union for the Conservation of Nature in association with the Food and Agriculture Organization of the United Nations. Beginning in 1965 Graham Child, a wildlife ecologist, also employed by FAO, made a two-year survey of the northeastern part of the country which included the Chobe area. Major Bruce Kinloch, M.C., under the auspices of the British Ministry of Overseas Development Fund, made a three months' survey in 1965. Lloyd Swift of World Wildlife Fund also visited Botswana in 1965 and spoke highly of the work being done there by Dr. Child. A bird survey has been made by Ray

Smithers of the Rhodesian Museum and he is shortly to complete a mammal survey.

Although Gaberones is a hot little town in March—my pocket thermometer registered 95 in the shade at high noon—the air is so dry that one hardly notices the heat. Consequently, Irene and I were able to walk about the town without undue effort. There is a supermarket that could easily have been located in our own familiar Easton, Maryland, and a fancy ladies' beauty parlor well patronized by all shades of local belles. There is, however, no barbershop for the men. The town contains a number of churches, and I was told that the London Missionary Society still operates in Botswana. This is the organization for whom David Livingstone sailed from England on December 8, 1840. After reaching the Cape, he trekked up to Kuruman, the mission in the wilds of Bechuanaland that Robert Moffat had established twenty years before. Livingstone, the first white man to visit Lake Ngami, had to cross part of the Kalahari Desert by oxcart to get there. Later he explored the Chobe River, the southern tributary of the Zambezi.

Livingstone noted in his diaries that even as early as 1853 elephants were becoming scarce because of overhunting for ivory. Though he made careful notes as to size and habits of these great beasts, he had no true idea of their longevity, for he said they lived 200 to 300 years. Touching on the firearms used in his day, Livingstone said that from four to six hardened bullets were necessary to kill the average bull elephant. All sizes of wildlife drew his attention, including ants, of which he classified fifteen species. He noted that the black ants were marauders who cut off the legs of the white ants so they could lug away the helpless victims and eat them at leisure. In a loftier vein, Livingstone believed that missionaries should cultivate an eye for the beautiful, saying that "we are forced to contemplate so much moral impurity and degradation that we should take every opportunity to delight in the green earth and the blue sky, the lofty mountain and the verdant valley, the glorious orbs of day and night and the starry canopy with all their celestial splendor."

Livingstone did not have a very high opinion of the tribal way of life in his day. He claimed that most of the tribesmen's thoughts were concentrated on eating, drinking, smoking wild hemp, and snuffing tobacco —behaving, in fact, like most of us. He noted sadly that the old women became the servants of their daughters. He admired King Seibtoane, however, who stopped the practice of wives' running away with men who were not their husbands. This he achieved by having his herald proclaim that on a certain day anyone who wished to could legally exchange mates. After that, there would be no further gallivanting, on pain of death.

According to Livingstone, the Bechuana villages would have been filthy without the attention of the scavenger beetle. He added that since Rome was a very dirty city, the Pope should import these valuable beetles to make his city sweet and clean. He also commented on a peculiar trait of the Hkoroe, the red-billed hornbill, whose mate seals herself up in a hole in a tree and is fed by her husband during her laying time. Livingstone declared this an example of conjugal devotion unequaled by any bird anywhere. He noted that female rhinos had a deeper attachment for their calves than elephants and considered the buffalo the most dangerous game, recording that many more natives were killed by them than by lions.

Livingstone did not comment on the tsetse fly, which may not yet have worked its way down into the areas he explored. Since then, however, it has been the scourge of southern Africa, carrying both the dread sleeping sickness for humans and the fatal nagana for domestic animals. Although game are carriers of the nagana virus, it doesn't affect them. In 1960 I saw great areas of the country where the trees had been felled in the belief that the tsetse could be stopped by denying them places to rest. Thousands of head of game were slaughtered for the same reason. Today, according to Tennant, who is also a veterinarian, spraying the breeding sites of tsetse is proving effective in controlling its spread.

Although Botswana is probably among the least-known nations of the world to most Americans, it enjoys special prestige in one of our fifty states. For, if one were to bore a hole through the earth from Gaberones, it would come out in the middle of Honolulu. This geographical coincidence has stimulated contact between the two cities, and a reporter from the Honolulu *Star Bulletin* came to Gaberones and wrote a series of articles on Botswana. Items on Hawaii have also appeared in the Botswana *Daily News*, a pleasant relief from the grim news headlined in the more worldly-oriented newspapers of South Africa.

234

From Gaberones Irene and I flew as guests of the Botswana government to Maun, accompanied by Tennant and Child. Leaving early, we flew over the limitless plains of the Kalahari, which was dotted with green trees because of the generous rains, and finally landed at the desert strip built by Anglo-American, the mining enterprise, just south of the Makarikari Pan. More than $700,000 worth of diamonds came from the original survey alone. When the mines go into full production early in 1971, the revenues will contribute substantially to the economy of Botswana.

There was little game on the southern side of the Makarikari, a vast interlocking set of salt pans, but on the northern reaches we dropped to a few hundred feet and surprised herd after herd of wildebeest, zebra, and springbok. There was also a number of ostrich flocks. Flying north from Makarikari, we sighted the road from Francistown to Maun. Soon after that we were over Nxai Pan, which has been renamed Paradise Pan by the Game Department. Here Tennant wanted to establish a small national park, and I can imagine no more desirable place. Giraffe, oryx, wildebeest, and springbok were grazing on the sweet grass around the pan, for the eternal problem of water in the Kalahari had been solved by sinking two bore holes. The area of the pan is only about twenty square miles, so that tourists can see it all in a day's drive.

Our line of flight skirted the vast area designated on the map as the Central Kalahari Game Reserve. This is also an area that Tennant wished to make into a national park, with the stipulation that the Kung Bushmen who still wander on its broad and desolate expanse will not be disturbed by tourists. Flying over the Kalahari recalled the accounts I have read of the times, only a scant century ago, when the Thirstland Trekkers, the Boers on their way to Angola, crossed those barren plains by oxcart. Then there were no bore holes, no roads, and only the stars to guide them. Even eight years before, when I flew in my military attaché's plane from Mafeking to Maun, we had no directional beam to guide us and had to stick closely to the Francistown-Maun road.

When we landed at Maun in the late morning—the distance from Gaberones is about 400 air miles—we were met by the resident game warden, Michael Slogrove, and driven to the camp of Bobbie Wilmot, a South African crocodile hunter, whom I met on my first shooting trip

Vultures, Botswana

Makarikari Pan, Botswana

with Pat Bromfield in 1959. Since then Wilmot has branched out from the pursuit of saurians and has built an attractive set of rondavels by the banks of what is appropriately named the Thamaklane (crocodile) River. Unfortunately, Robert Thomas, the district commissioner, who is an American lawyer on contract under the Syracuse Scheme, was away on safari. A parallel case would be for an Englishman to be hired by the U.S.A. to govern an Indian reserve in Montana.

While in Gaberones I had had a long and pleasant talk with the Honorable Amos Dambe, the minister of home affairs, who was with Lloyd on an epic afternoon when he had his dangerous tilt with a hippo on the Chobe River northeast of Maun. One of Lloyd's objectives in going to Maun was to look into the situation at the Moremi Wildlife Reserve, a game park established and administered by the Fauna Preservation Society of Ngamiland. My own brief sketch of the background of this tribal scheme may be helpful:

When I last visited Maun in 1961, an English couple named June and Robert Kay were endeavoring to promote a game park which would be run by the local Botswana tribe. The Regent of this tribe was Mrs. Moremi, an interesting woman who was trained as a nurse but who had been chosen, by the tribe and probably the British Commissioner, to run the Batawana tribe during the childhood of her son, Chief Lethslothere. In November, 1962, a park was proclaimed in the Okavango Swamps between the Kwaai and Mogohelo rivers, with Mrs. Kay as secretary. Aid was sought through appeals to World Wildlife Fund and the South African press. As a result, enough was donated by South Africans to get things started, appoint a game guard, and establish a camp at the Kwaai River entrance to the park. In April, 1963, Mrs. Kay went to London, where she interested Commander Peter Scott, my fellow member on the International Board of World Wildlife Fund, who helped in raising an initial grant of about $3,000, a great deal short of the $80,000 Mrs. Kay wanted, but at least a starter.

In August, 1963, H.R.H. Prince Bernhard of the Netherlands, the President of the International World Wildlife Fund, visited Maun and a Kgotla was assembled to do him honor, during which he addressed the tribe. In December, however, the trustees of the Fund voted against a grant for the Moremi Reserve, mainly because none of the game in it was in danger of extinction and the principal purpose of the Fund is to save rare and endangered species. By canvassing their own members and other friends of conservation, the Fauna Society was able to raise enough money to build up the game reserve staff to nine, buy some transport, make a few tracks through the reserve, and retain the services of Dr. Kenneth Tinley, the ecologist of the Game Department of South-West Africa, with whom Irene and I so much enjoyed talking on our recent trip to the Etosha Pan, in South-West, and whose report greatly impressed me.

In August, 1964, Mrs. Kay again went to London to try and help the World Wildlife Fund to promote a film of the Moremi Reserve. Some $6,000 was collected, but an agreement could not be reached with a producer. The funds were then turned over to the Reserve. After Mr. and Mrs. Kay resigned from the committee in April, 1965, the park underwent hard times, necessitating drastic reductions in staff. By 1966, however, the Tribe started to earn money from the renting of shooting rights to safari companies. At the end of 1967, the debts had been cleared and the society was in the black. The World Wildlife Fund subsequently did grant funds to make a film which hopefully will encourage further donations to the park.

Today two main problems face the society: the presence of the tsetse fly and lack of access roads. The government of Botswana has started a spraying campaign, however, and improvements on the road from Maun to Kasane are on the drawing boards. Other urgent needs are a boat and engine to patrol the waterways of the reserve; further training of the game guards; more basic camp facilities, and a film van, so that the conservation movie can be shown to school children of the Batawana tribe.

Chief Lethslothere, who in 1965 took over the leadership of the tribe from his mother, Mrs. Moremi, called a meeting of the society which Irene and I attended. He outlined most of the facts cited above and made a plea for help. I replied that whatever the World Wildlife Fund could do would be channeled through the Game Department of the Botswana Government. My personal opinion was that there were two inexpensive projects which World Wildlife Fund could aid. Tennant was anxious to send one or more of his men to the African Wildlife Leadership School at Maweka in Tanzania, where Africans are taught to look after their own game. It would be a sound investment, I think, if the Fund would provide about $3,000 to finance the travel and living expenses for one student for two years, or for two students for one year each. Another worthwhile project would be for the fund to provide a boat and outboard motor, which I was told would come to about $1,000.

As the sun was setting, Bobbie Wilmot gave us a memorable trip up the river. We got some superb photographs of a pair of fish eagles, usually the scariest of birds, who remained stationary until we came within twenty feet of them. Dwarf geese, jacana, and blue and goliath herons also showed little or no fear of us, the happy result of a complete absence of shooting on this section of the river. A family of five hippos lives on the stretch above Bobbie's camp, but unfortunately they were not to be seen. Nevertheless, there are hippos remaining in some numbers on the river. Wilmot told us that in 1956 he talked with a native who killed sixteen in one pool, far more than his entire clan could possibly have eaten before the meat spoiled. Regrettably, hippos are not always peaceful. Wilmot said that in the last few years he has had to shoot several that have attacked his boats.

All the birds of Botswana are protected by law except for the few game birds which can be shot on license. Hence with the exclusion of the francolin, guinea fowl, ducks, and geese, there is no legal shooting of any of the feathered dwellers of the country.

Wilmot's main business is still the hunting of crocodiles. At dinner one evening he told me something about his exotic means of making a living. Crocs are hunted at night when their eyes can be spotted in the beam of powerful lights. They are then shot in the head with a rifle and hauled on the bank and skinned. Those of nine to eleven feet bring the best prices. The giants of twenty feet are so scarred from mating wars that their skins are worth a great deal less. They take about ten years to reach eight feet and despite their tiny brains—about the size of golf balls—are extremely smart and wary. The mere fact that they have survived proves this, for they are hunted mercilessly by the natives. Crocs will eat almost anything. Wilmot has found a whole porcupine in the belly of a big bull croc, and so powerful are the stomach enzymes that the horns of an impala will be dissolved to the point where they can be bent like wires after a few days of digestion.

While most crocs do not normally attack humans, a number of natives are killed by them every year nevertheless. Wilmot once found the remains of a woman, two goats, and half a donkey in the interior of one especially epicurean croc. Since he started crocodile hunting in 1954, he has killed about 42,000 of them and of late years has averaged 2,000 skins a year. These are worth about twenty-five dollars for a prime skin. In the future, however, he is going to run a crocodile farm where he will raise his own stock.

We talked with Harry Selby, a partner in the safari firm of Kerr and Downey and one of the best-known and most reliable white hunters in Africa. He takes about thirty-six parties a year on the 5,000-square-mile shooting bloc which his firm rents north of Maun. Good firms like Kerr and Downey are a real help to Tennant because they are as much interested in conservation as he is. If the roan antelope grow scarce, Selby advises Tennant, and Tennant simply takes roan off the license.

To see Selby's shooting bloc as well as the Chobe National Park and the Moremi Reserve, we flew northeast to the Okavange swamps skirting the edge of the Moremi. Water was everywhere, with the land inundated by snakelike channels. By the side of a lagoon we saw our first lechwe. Under the palms a herd of sable antelope had gathered. Spur-winged geese floated on a little lake, and a bataleur eagle darted past us.

Northeast of the Moremi lies the Mababe Depression, a vast saucer-like piece of terrain which was dry for a hundred years until 1960, when water dammed from the Chobe River flooded it. Then in 1965, it dried again. But the heavy rains during 1967 in southern Angola led to another flooding, and when we passed it, the land was potted with water holes. Game, which always spreads when water is widely available, was still easy to spot. We flushed herds of impala, wildebeest, tweebe, giraffe, zebra, and buffalo and saw four small herds of elephant. The elephant of the Mababe do not carry important ivory, fifty pounds a side being the average. But there are exceptions. In 1960, while hunting with Pat Bromfield, I shot an old bull with 85- and 89-pound tusks. His last set of teeth were worn to paper thinness, so he could not have lasted another year. We also saw roan antelope, reed buck, kudu, wart hog, sitatunga, and a clan of baboons.

We did not have time to fly to the area of the border of Cape Province, South Africa, where Tennant hoped to establish a national park for oryx. In fact, there was a possibility that Botswana and South Africa might coordinate their efforts to make an international park there. I visited this remote and desolate part of Botswana in 1960 when I flew down to see the Camel Corps which patrols the Kalahari in those sandy regions. Established by the British during the days of the protectorate, the corps was still maintained by Colonel Bailey, who was Commissioner of Police for the Republic.

My net impression of Botswana was that it enjoys a stable government under a good president. If its economic problems can be solved, it will be an example to many of the newer nations of Africa. The development of its mineral resources by venture capital from abroad is, of course, the best hope for economic viability. Among the lesser sources of income, tourism could become important, and Tennant was doing a first-class job in conserving the game so that it will attract more people. His needs are many, perhaps the most pressing of them being a light plane to get around a parish the size of Texas.

CHAPTER XVII

The Little Kingdoms

Monarchy is not a popular form of government in Africa today, and only six of the fifty-one nations that compose the continent still support kings. Among these are the minute kingdoms of Lesotho and Swaziland, embedded in the Republic of South Africa. Both were former colonies of the British Crown. When I visited them last in 1961, they were known as the High Commission Territories, and were under the authority of Sir John Maud, Her Majesty's High Commissioner to the Union of South Africa. Since then Basutoland, as it was then called, has been given independence under the name of the Kingdom of Lesotho. Not long ago, Swaziland achieved similar status.

Slightly larger than the state of Maryland, Lesotho is an enclave entirely surrounded by South Africa. For all practical purposes it is almost completely dependent on the republic for a livelihood. Aside from exports of livestock and wool, which go to South African markets, the main source of income for the country is the wages that Basuto workers, laboring mostly in the South African mines, send home. There is also a small diamond field in operation, and when the Ox Bow hydroelectric scheme starts in a few more years another important source of income will be available. But in the meantime, the one million subjects of King Moshoeshoe II will continue to face lean times.

One of the few untapped means of making money is tourism. Hence an important objective in my going to the country was to try to interest the King and the Prime Minister in the possibility of proclaiming a game park that would attract people. There could not be a finer setting for a park, especially along the massif of the Drakensberg, whose peaks rise to 11,000 feet on the border of Natal. Less than a quarter of the country is in the lowland, which varies from 5,000 to 6,000 feet above sea level. There is adequate rainfall, and the temperature ranges compare favorably with those of Switzerland.

Our trip from Pietermaritzburg in Natal to Maseru was both precarious and time-consuming. In order to avoid a full day's drive, I chartered a twin-engined Piper Comanche. On the morning when we were scheduled to take off and fly over the Drakensberg to Maseru, the capital of Lesotho, the weather station at Durban reported that the ceiling was less than 500 feet, hardly a safe margin for attempting a flight over mountains two miles high. The next day we decided to try again even though the forecast was still ominous. However, instead of going over the mountains, we planned to make a long swing around them, keeping as much as possible to the low country of Natal and the Orange Free State. Dodging the thunder showers and flying below the cloud layer, we skimmed empty land and occasional towns. We passed over Ladysmith, where Winston Churchill reported in the Boer War, and finally, when the outlook deteriorated too badly, landed at Bethlehem, a farming town in the Free State. There I hired a taxi, so it wasn't until seven hours after our departure that we arrived at the border of Lesotho. Here we were met by Peter Jones, the political officer of our embassy and the son of my old friend, John Wesley Jones, then our ambassador to Peru.

Except for the addition of a number of new buildings, Maseru had changed little in seven years. The residence of the British commissioner, where I used to stay, had become the palace of the King. The Prime

Minister, Chief Leabua Jonathan, inhabited a considerably larger and grander establishment of an extraordinary semicircular architectural design. I recognized many familiar buildings from the colonial days, including the Archives, where I once spent a fascinating morning looking up the records of ritual murder, a method of acquiring personal power that has been brought to a high point of refinement by the Basuto. Since independence in 1966, such incidents have been officially ignored, but there is no reason to believe that they occur any less frequently now. The victim, who is often a close relative of the person who causes his death, must be made aware of why he or she is being murdered, and the body must sooner or later be found by the authorities. Only if all these requirements are met will the virtues and strengths of the unfortunate victim be transferred to the murderer.

The Basuto are a relatively recent people. Until the beginning of the eighteenth century the country was populated only by Bushmen and a great variety of game. Among the world's best primitive conservationists, the little people killed only what they could eat. They further demonstrated their respect and admiration for wildlife by painting sensitive pictures of animals on the walls of caves. Early in the seventeenth century small groups of Bantu from the lowlands began to invade the country. Today's stock is largely the result of intermarriage between these invaders and the indigenous Bushmen. It was not until 1818 that the Basuto, under the strong rule of Moshesh, a remarkably able and vigorous chief, became a united people. Those were the days when Shaka, the great Zulu warrior, ruled the low country. Many of the remnants of the tribes that he had crushed subsequently fled into the Drakensberg, where Moshesh organized them into a respectable fighting force usually capable of defending his mountain bastions. Inevitably, however, Moshesh clashed with the Boer farmers of the Orange Free State. In a series of wars that ensued, he lost most of his good farming land in the low country adjoining the mountains.

Realizing that he must have a powerful friend or perish, Moshesh appealed to Queen Victoria in 1868 to take over his country, saying plaintively that "we are lice in the Queen's blanket." The British dillydallied for a time, mainly because the government was unwilling to assume any financial responsibility. British control, which began in 1884, has had a profound and, I believe, mainly beneficial influence on the little country. It has been popular for some time now to criticize Britain's colonial empire, but most of the critics seem to be unaware that England still gives Lesotho about seven million dollars per annum, or approximately half the total cost of running the country. Furthermore, London is committed to continue to give Maseru this amount through 1970, and will, in all probability, continue to give a substantial amount of aid even after that. As she receives nothing in return, this is a handsome gesture.

One of the ablest of the long line of British civil servants who have dedicated most of their lives to Lesotho is James Hennessey, permanent secretary to the Prime Minister and the holder over a long period of time of many of the important jobs in the country. He and his wife, Pat, whom I knew when she served in the Royal Air Force in World War II, invited Irene and me to stay in their comfortable guest house. Along with our own people in the American embassy, they did a great deal to make my visit most worthwhile.

While the American Embassy in Maseru has a high-sounding title, it is in fact only a consular-sized operation with two substantive officers. The principal officer, or Chargé d'Affaires, was Richard Post, an energetic young man of thirty-seven, who, while establishing close relations with the Prime Minister and the other members of the Lesotho government, still managed to play polo and generally enjoy the sporting life of the country. He was ably supported by Peter Jones, who was at his first post after serving in the Marines in Vietnam.

During an hour's interview with the Prime Minister, Post and I discussed many matters of mutual interest with him. He declared himself solidly behind my suggestion that Lesotho proclaim a game reserve and said that the Motengo Valley, where the Ox Bow scheme will be developed, would be fine for it. I could not agree more, for the valley is lovely and spacious, with the advantage of being relatively easy to guard against poachers, because of the difficulties they would have in operating from the mountains around it. The Prime Minister said there would not be any trouble in alienating the land, but suggested that I also discuss the matter with the King, who has direct contact with the chiefs.

Land tenure in Lesotho is complicated. All land is held in trust for the Basuto people by the King and cannot be alienated without his personal permission. Grazing rights are communal, but arable land is allocated to families and individuals by the chiefs. It would be necessary, therefore, to have the King remove any cultivators who now farm the valley, as well as prohibit grazing by domestic cattle and sheep. The Prime Minister said that both Sir Seretse Khama, the Prime Minister of Botswana, and Jomo Kenyatta of Kenya, have offered him game. There is little doubt that South Africa would be glad to contribute fauna from her burgeoning excesses in her various parks. The matter really becomes one of fencing and paying the guards. Because this would certainly be a worthwhile project for the World Wildlife Fund, I wrote a letter to Anton Rupert, president of the African Appeal of the World Wildlife Fund, outlining the opportunity.

Just before the interview terminated, I urged the Prime Minister to pass a law protecting the lammergeyer, the rare bird that inhabits the peaks of the Drakensberg. Otherwise found only in the Himalayas, the Alps, and the mountains of Ethiopia, this huge predator, which resembles both an eagle and a vulture, has been reduced to limited numbers. It is uneatable, but since the young bring high prices in aviaries, the nests are sometimes raided. It also suffers from poisoned meat left for jackals. It is illegal to keep lammergeyers in captivity in South Africa. Consequently, if Lesotho also passes a protective law, its future will be brighter. The Prime Minister promised to do this as soon as I furnished him with the bird's scientific name, a description, and its habitat in his country.

I first met the King of Lesotho, Motlotlehi Moshoeshoe II, in 1960 when he had just returned from his studies at Oxford in order to claim the paramount chieftainship. This was not as easy as it might appear because the job was then held by a formidable woman named Mantsebo, who had ruled as Regent from the time the future king was two years old until he became twenty-two. With the help of a group of powerful chiefs who formed the Marema Tlou Party, which means Unity Chops Elephants, he was able to overcome Mantsebo's opposition and take over as Paramount Chief. I called on him at the Royal Seat, a modest establishment where the young Paramount, then known as Bereng Seeiso, received me in his study. He looked somewhat harassed, owing to his battle with the Regent or possibly to the fact that he had to look after some 300 relatives who were camped in huts about the palace. Another sobering

King Moshoeshoe II of Lesotho, Queen, Crown Prince, younger son and the author

thought may have been the fate of his namesake, Bereng, the eldest son of a previous Paramount Chief, Griffith. This Bereng was refused the Paramountcy by the chiefs who installed Mantsebo as Regent. He challenged her appointment in the High Court, but lost the case and immediately sought revenge in ritual murder. He was tried by the British and executed in 1949. I talked with the young Paramount about his duties as head of the Basuto nation and I received the impression that he wished to rule rather than reign. Perhaps significant was the picture above his desk of Moshesh, whose word was law to the people.

Eight years had left little mark on His Majesty, who still had his slim straight figure and engaging smile when Irene and I went to call on him and his Queen at the palace. He had, however, acquired a beard, a hirsute addition that some of his personal followers had also adopted. He told me he had heard of my wildlife mission to Lesotho and said he would

247

be delighted to help in any way he could. I explained the necessity of alienating sufficient land for a park as well as passing laws to preserve the wildlife. He said he did not think there would be any difficulties about this and also agreed that a valley in the Ox Bow scheme area would be a good site.

Horses are the best means of getting around the King's domain, and the native ponies are among the hardiest in Africa. In 1961 I made a four-day trek into the mountains to fish for trout, so I can attest to the pleasure of riding Basuto ponies. Partly Arab, due to importation of Arab stallions, they are agile, sure-footed and willing. Those of the Basuto Mounted Police are particularly sturdy. I was impressed with their quality when I was treated to a mounted review by the then commanding officer.

Trout fishing in Lesotho was introduced in 1935 when Major Harry Alston Smith, the officer commanding the Basutoland Mounted Police, Robert Forson, and seven Basuto policemen carried trout in four-gallon paraffin tins lashed to pack mules to the Mokhotlong River, a journey of ten days from Bushman's River at Giants Castle in Natal, where the trout were procured. Every half hour the water was replaced. By the time the Sanquebtu River was reached in Basutoland only seven fish survived. These brown trout, however, proved hardy enough to multiply and eventually to conquer and replace the indigenous yellow fish, a carp that can also show sport. The results have been ideal, for mountains cover two thirds of the country, with clear, sparkling streams running between them. Horses can be hired to reach the more remote fishing sites, and huts can be rented for camping. What more could an angler want?

Another pleasant occupation for the tourist in Basutoland is the study of rock paintings found in many of the caves of the Drakensberg Mountains. So far, more than 400 groups of paintings have been found. The majority—and by far the best—were done by the Bushmen in four fairly distinct periods. The earliest, dating from before 1600, depict human and animal figures, usually in reddish brown or maroon. The animals are typical of those which were plentiful throughout South Africa a century ago, and no extinct forms have been recognized. They include the eland, blesbok, springbok, and rhebok. A number of birds are also depicted, one of which looks like a lammergeyer. With the arrival of the first Bantu tribes about 1600, the Bushmen started to draw pictures of the newcomers, whose initiation ceremonies particularly fascinated them. Many of these paintings are beautifully shaded polychromes, in contrast to the crude work of the Bantu invaders. One sequence portrays a cattle raid where tiny Bushmen archers are defending their livestock from the black Bantu invaders armed with assagais and carrying oval shields. When the white man arrived, the Bushmen artist drew them with umbrellas on their horses and firing their guns.

Ritual murder also appears in the cave scenes. Painting in black with deep red shading, the artist depicts a tall figure with an animal's head standing beside a figure without a mask and carrying a spear. At their feet is a prostrate form. Another sequence records two masked figures, with blood dripping from their mouths, kneeling over a third figure lying on the ground. The men depicted were, of course, Bantu; the Bushmen did not practice ritual murder.

The Bushmen may, in fact, have been recording an act of cannibalism, a not uncommon occurrence in Basutoland before it was eliminated by Moshesh. In a fascinating old book called *The Basutos*, by the Reverend E. Casalis of the Paris Evangelical Mission House, published in London in 1861, there is an account of cannibalism. The incident, which was related to Casalis by a Basuto chief, runs as follows:

"One of the wives of the chief had fallen into the hands of the cannibals. He went to ransom her and arrived at an immense cavern surrounded by thorny bushes which the cannibals called home. The chief was horrified to see the ground littered with skulls and bones. The men had gone hunting and returned with a captive, shouting "Wah, wah," as Basutos do when driving oxen. The victim was a handsome young man, whom they promptly strangled. The dismembering was performed just as if they were slaughtering an ox. While this was going on, the chief heard screams from the rear of the cave and the words, "she is incorrigible—we must eat her!" After pleading, a cannibal woman convinced her cannibal husband she was more useful alive. With much parleying, the chief was able to ransom his wife for six oxen and, rejoicing, took her home with him. However, she had found friends among the cannibals and had acquired a taste for human flesh. She ran away to rejoin them."

The Paris Evangelical Mission, established in 1833, is still a potent force in the religious life of Lesotho. Today it runs 465 schools, as against 448 for the Roman Catholic Church and 148 for the English Church. A branch of the French Protestant Church, Paris Evangelical became the established church of Basutoland in 1964. The first Roman Catholic missionaries arrived in 1862 and established themselves at Tloutle, where in 1945 they founded the Pius XII College, which has since become the University of Basutoland, Bechuanaland and Swaziland.

Well treated by Moshesh, the Reverend Mr. Casalis was given a valley in which to live, some miles from Thaba Bosio, the chief's mountain stronghold. He was also supplied with a number of young men to help in establishing the mission. The country abounded in game, which Casalis shot for food and also enjoyed watching. Describing the bound of the springbok, he said, "The back forms a complete curve; the fawn-colored hair that covers the croup opens and discovers an undercoat of down of the most dazzling white. The head is turned slightly to one side with an air of defiance and disdainful coquetry." He saw vast herds of blesbok and gnu, which we call wildebeest. However, he preferred the flesh of the eland, for it tastes very much like good beef as I can attest myself. The former attacked their draft oxen and horses, while the latter made heavy inroads on their sheep. The black-maned lions, or *zwart leeuw*, as they were called by the Cape colonists, were the most ferocious.

Casalis described the same country that today harbors nothing more than a handful of wary rhebok and birds too small to be worth hunting. The verdant pastures on which the game of a century ago used to rejoice have been overgrazed to a point where parts of Lesotho are threatened by devastating erosion. The rainfall, averaging twenty-three inches a year, falls mostly between October and April, subjecting the land to floods. The country's total area of 11,716 square miles is populated by one and one-quarter million sheep, three-quarter million goats, almost a half million cattle, along with 200,000 horses, donkeys, and mules. Almost no general effort is made to restrict the communal grazing rights, with the result that the grass has no opportunity to recover. Soil-conservation efforts are, however, making considerable progress in some areas. More than four million trees have been planted to afforest Lesotho's barren hills.

Before flying out of Lesotho I made an aerial survey of the little country. Below us the mountains stretched to the horizon like a wind-tossed sea of peaks and valleys. Trout streams flashed in the sun, and here and there we saw the clusters of round huts that make up Basuto villages. Herds of sheep and cattle grazed on the stony slopes. There were almost no trees. More than a third of the population lives in these mountains without roads, telephones, and but few radios. Because all imports must come by mule or horse, it may take more than a week for supplies to reach an outlying post. Nor are the mountain tracks always open. In winter the snow drifts heavily; in summer the rains often make mountain streams impassable.

There is, in fact, only one vital need for which the mountain people must depend on the outside world—medical service—which can be supplied effectively only by air. I learned about the Lesotho Flying Doctor Service from Dr. Michael Moore, a forty-one-year-old Lesotho Government medical officer. Moore is a former Royal Air Force pilot who had previously served as a flying doctor in northern Nigeria. Operating from the Maseru airport in a tiny two-seater Piper Super Cub, he regularly visits seven mountain clinics, which usually consist of a badly lit hut doubling as a dispensary. In most cases, there is no radio contact with the clinic before he lands, so that the doctor does not know until he is over the strip whether it is usable. Funds for a two-way radio for all seven clinics are urgently needed. The doctor sees about 100 patients a month at each clinic, with the number steadily growing. He told me that if a second aircraft could be purchased it would be used to deliver drugs and medicine as well as to take a health assistant to the clinics to instruct the villagers on such subjects as basic sanitation, hygiene, and nutrition. Moore's work served as a good reminder to us that conservation also applies to people, so I made a point of noting that donations could be sent to Aeromed, P.O. Box 87, Maseru, Lesotho.

Our plans to visit Swaziland, the smallest but richest of the former High Commission territories, unfortunately had to be canceled owing to a combination of illness and pressure of time. However, since I had

251

visited Swaziland a number of times during my tour of duty in South Africa and have maintained contact during the interim with many of the leading personalities there, I feel it is worth including some notes about the country.

In most African nations there is only one man who counts. In Swaziland this man is Sobhuza II, Ngwenyama or King of the Amaswazi, who is admired both by the nation's 375,000 Swazis and her 10,000 Europeans. I remember vividly my first meeting with him at his European-style residence at Masundwini. He was dressed in a print toga over which he wore a blue-checked blanket. His woolly hair and long beard gave him a definite leonine appearance that went well with his name, for Ngwenyama means lion. This was in October, 1960, when the Belgian Congo had exploded and racial tensions were rising throughout southern Africa. The King, or Paramount Chief as he was then known, told me that he would never countenance such anarchy in Swaziland. Pursuing this subject further, he said he did not think Africa was ready for a universal franchise. He has not changed his view and only recently he was quoted as saying, "If only we could extricate Africa from this idea of one man, one vote, I am sure we would achieve our objectives."

Sobhuza has, in fact, been ruler of the Swazis since 1902, when he was a babe in arms, but it was not until 1922, when he reached his majority, that he was installed as Paramount Chief. This title was recently changed to King and has had even more significance since Swaziland achieved complete independence. Sobhuza's powers are semireligious and intimately connected with the fertility of the people and the land. In this he is closely dependent on his mother, the Ndlovukasi, or Lady Elephant, who annually renews his powers in a ceremony known as the Incwala, or First Fruit, which is held in December or January, depending on the phases of the moon. When I visited Sobhuza, his mother had recently died, and he substituted one of his older wives as Lady Elephant. This was no hardship, as he had nearly a hundred wives. When his daughters were married, they fetched a bride price of forty cows, as against ten for an ordinary girl. This practice, which is called *lobola*, not only imbues the husband with a sense of responsibility but makes the girl feel valuable.

Legend has it that the British bought Swaziland from a King for a case of gin and a brace of greyhounds. This is probably apocryphal, but during the long reign of King Mawati, which lasted from 1840 to 1868, white men began to enter Swaziland in significant numbers. The first recorded personal land concession was given by Mawati in September, 1860, to one Coenraad Vermaak, who in return for some thirty head of cattle and an annual rent of five pounds received 1,000 square miles of land and was made a chief over the Swazis on his estate. Mbandzani, a later King of the Swazis, blithely signed away concessions for almost every conceivable commodity and right in Swaziland, even giving to the white man the right to collect all taxes. He was, in fact, addicted to liquor and hounds and may have been the origin of the legend. The net of it was that the Swazis kept only about a third of their country. Not until 1960, under strong pressure from the British government, were the Swazis able to occupy 51.6 percent of the country's total area. Individual Europeans and other non-Swazi groups own the remaining 48.4 percent.

My particular interest in the little country concerns the Mlilwane Game Reserve, which has received some support and encouragement from the World Wildlife Fund. Dr. Anton Rupert has bought a 2,000-acre farm adjoining the park, and it will also be used as a game sanctuary. Because Swaziland has a much denser population than either Botswana or Lesotho, with land valuable both for crops and for the minerals that lie beneath, it is a wise precaution to set aside areas for wildlife at this time. All land occupied by the Swazis belongs, in theory, to the King, who apportions it to the various chefs. They in turn distribute it to their retainers. It is therefore easier to acquire European-owned property for parks in Swaziland.

CHAPTER XVIII

Wildlife of South Africa

South Africa's emblem is the springbok, the handsome little antelope that used to bound in countless thousands over the flowing veld and is still common enough to be seen in a wild state. More than any other peoples in Africa, South Africans honor and respect their game. In the early days the Boers lived on the wildlife. Only because these intrepid Dutch colonists could subsist on the land were the great treks possible. Today vast stretches of country have been turned into some of the continent's best-run game parks. Kruger, with 8,000 square miles, is bigger than Connecticut and Delaware together; Etosha Pan, with 38,000 square miles, is more than three times as large as Maryland. There is also a number of smaller parks where some of Africa's rarest animals are now carefully guarded: the Willem Pretorius Reserve in the Orange Free State, where the white-tailed gnus—which the Boers used to call black wildebeest— now number more than 850 head and are increasing; the Addo Elephant

National Park near Port Elizabeth in Natal, where this rare subspecies of elephant—reduced to only sixty individuals in 1960—has been bred to a herd of 120; and the famous Natal parks of Hluhluwe and Umfolozi, where the black and white rhinos have been so successfully cultivated that the excess population is exported to game reserves and zoos all over the world.

Reflecting this nationwide interest in conservation, South Africa has become the tenth nation to join the World Wildlife Fund. Thus one of my reasons for visiting the republic, where I spent two and a half memorable years as Ambassador, was to welcome South Africa to the international community of the Fund. President of the South African branch is Dr. Anton Rupert, the leading Afrikaans businessman of his country. Rupert kindly invited Irene and me to drive to his home in Stellenbosch, Cape Province, for lunch. This is the lovely vineyard-lined valley where Rupert lives near the grounds of the Stellenbosch University, the intellectual cradle of Afrikanderdom.

A friend of conservation who is proving his interest with hard cash, Dr. Rupert had already received pledges of about $130,000 on an annual basis from many of the leading firms of South Africa, and his campaign was just beginning. This is particularly impressive when it is realized that these pledges are not tax-exempt. How much money would we raise in America under these circumstances?

Among the projects to which the South African Wildlife Foundation, the registered name of the South African Appeal, has allocated funds is a permanent chair in wildlife management at the University of Pretoria. In Swaziland, the Foundation has purchased a farm of 2,760 acres, which will remain the property of the foundation but will be developed as part of the existing Mililwane Game Sanctuary. Other projects to be considered are help to the Moremi Reserve in Botswana; reintroduction of the white and black rhinos into areas where they once thrived; the creation of new game reserves in the Bantu Homelands; fencing of the National Gemsbok Park, part of which lies in Botswana and part in Cape Province; and a public-relations campaign to stimulate interest in conservation.

Although the South African Wildlife Foundation is a private organization, permission to form it had to be approved by the Cabinet. Conservation was therefore one of several matters that I discussed with the members of the government. These talks began with my official call on His Excellency James Fouché, State President of the Republic, at West Brook, the fine old Dutch mansion where the State Presidents have lived for decades. When I served in South Africa, Mr. Fouché, then Minister of Defense, was among the members of the cabinet whom I knew well and liked. A farmer from the Orange Free State, he has a love of the land and a respect for wildlife. He told me he approved highly of the foundation and wished it all success.

My next appointment was with the Honorable John B. Vorster, Prime Minister of South Africa. He had changed little physically since I last saw him, still a powerful man with a determined frown which sometimes dissolved in a disarming grin. We talked of the problems facing our two countries and the perplexed state of the world. He said frankly that he did not expect America to agree with his government's stand on the matter of race relations, but hoped we would refrain from constant criticism. He felt that both our countries were demonstrating their steadfast opposition to Communism, adding that South Africa was one of the few countries in the world where the American Embassy had not been assaulted by peace marchers. He was enthusiastic about the South African Wildlife Foundation and expressed envy of my trips to the game parks.

I also talked with Hilgard Muller, the able Minister of Foreign Affairs, whom I knew when he was South African High Commissioner in London and whom I had seen on his harried trips to the United Nations. Despite the pressure under which Muller operates, he always maintains a calm and detached viewpoint, not an easy state to achieve in his position. He agreed with me that the more international organizations such as the World Wildlife Fund that South Africa joins, the better it will be for all concerned. But the member of the cabinet who takes the greatest interest in wildlife is my old friend Ben Schoeman, senior minister after the Prime Minister and also Minister of Transport. An elephant hunter who walked through the middle of the herds to find a really fine tusker and never pulled a trigger unless he found one, Schoeman spends most of his vacation in the bush, so he knows the game areas of southern Africa better than most men. Today he has put up his heavy rifles and, aside from an occasional buck for the pot, never shoots at all. Keenly concerned with all phases of conservation, Schoeman arranged for me to see

256

all the parks my crowded schedule allowed. He also follows the conservation efforts of Botswana. Hence he was pleased to hear that efforts are now being made to establish a park for gemsbok that would lie partly in Cape Province and partly in Botswana.

Another old friend whom I was able to see was Sir de Villiers Graff, leader of the Opposition party.

While we devoted most of our time in Cape Town to urban appointments, we did manage a few trips to the hinterlands. Notable among these was a visit to the National Bontebok Park, some 130 miles out on the western Cape. Reduced to only seventeen survivors in 1931, this rare ungulate now has a thriving population of 211 in a carefully fenced and guarded reserve near the little town of Swellendam. The breed probably would not have survived at all but for the efforts of a number of gentleman farmers beginning in about 1864 when the Van der Byl, Van Breda, and Uys families started protecting small herds on their estates. It was from this nucleus that the government established a park for bontebok at Bredasdorp in 1931. The herd did not do well at Bredasdorp, however, so it was moved to Swellendam in 1960 and established in a five-and-one-half-square-mile park beneath the jagged peaks of the Langeberg Mountains.

Brown and black on the head, neck, and body, the bontebok has a white blaze on his face. Both sexes have horns. As for size, a bull weighs about 200 pounds. Recorded as a rare animal in the Red Book of the International Union for the Conservation of Nature, the bontebok is considered one of the scarcest survivors in the Boyidse family. The little reserve also contains some sixty vaal rhebok, a gray antelope, as well as rooibok hartebeest, eland, springbok, steinbok, and duiker. Nearby is the racecourse where the Swellendam Turf Club held their meets from 1848 to 1904, with fans from Cape Town coming by chartered sailing vessel. The district was also famous for its stud whose foundation was said to be a stallion captured from a British officer at the battle of Blauwberg in 1806. Along the boundary of the reserve comprised by the Breede River one can still see the tracks made by the ox wagons that trekked north across the drift, or ford, before the bridge was built in 1894. History in South Africa is recent and very much alive.

The residence of the American ambassador at Cape Town (the government of South Africa spends part of each year at the Cape and part at Pretoria, the capital, with the embassies following it), is at Wynberg, a wine-growing suburb on the flanks of Table Mountain. As Irene and I drove out to dine with William Rountree, our ambassador and good friend of many years, I remembered the day in 1960 when I had a frightening experience on this very same road. It was a time of considerable racial tension following the Sharpeville riots. There were rumors of a Bantu march from the locations into the city. Rounding one of the big curves in the road on my way to an important luncheon engagement at home, my Bantu driver, Xavier, and I saw a vast multitude of men approaching us. They spread across the road and its environs and far up the hill as well. What to do? To turn around and race back to Cape Town would be an admission of fear. To go toward them, on the other hand, might well be the end of us. Such a crowd could hoist my heavy Mercedes over and down the embankment with the greatest of ease. But it was too late to turn around, so we drove slowly toward the wall of humanity. Although the American flag was flying on my bumper, Xavier was not nearly so sure as I that it would be recognized and respected. Then the crowd, consisting entirely of ragged and angry Bantu, closed around the car and we found ourselves in a sea of people. I had wound up the windows, but we could clearly hear their cries of *uhuru*, or freedom. Surprisingly, despite the number and mood of the crowd, no one touched the car, and slowly the mob oozed around us and passed.

Since then there have been no major disturbances in South Africa, while Africans in other parts of the continent have been conducting outright wars. The Moslems of Nigeria have slaughtered the Ibo, the Congo has been rent by warring factions, and military coups have succeeded each other in dizzy succession in many newly independent countries. Critics of the South African regime claim that this peaceful period is due entirely to a highly efficient police force, which nips trouble in the bud. But the result of it is that South Africans of both races have been spared the bloodshed and property losses that have been plaguing many parts of the world, including the United States.

Many of the big farmers of the Cape protect game. We spent a very pleasant afternoon with Peter Barlow, who owns Rustenberg, a lovely farm lying under the peaks outside Stellenbosch. We saw part of his herd of vaal rhebok outlined against the sinking sun. He also gives sanctuary to the little grysbok and to two species of francolin, partridge, and guinea fowl. A troop of baboons lives high on his mountain slopes. At dinner we met Major Bruce Kinloch, one of the founders of the African Wildlife Leadership Foundation school at Mweka in Tanzania, which trains Africans to look after their own game. Kinloch, who served with the Gurkhas during the war and was later chief game warden of both Uganda and Tanzania, is now living in the Cape and writing books on conservation. Recently he made a survey of the Knysna elephant, a small herd that maintains itself in dense jungle at Knysna, 140 miles west of Port Elizabeth. He found seven elephants during his search and at one point took a remarkable picture of a charging bull. Almost shot out of existence in 1920 by Pretorius, the famous hunter, the Knysna elephants do not trust anyone and stick close to their almost impenetrable 200-square-mile reserve.

From Cape Town we flew along the Indian Ocean to Durban, Africa's biggest port and a throbbing testimony to the booming economy of the continent's first industrial power. We were met by an old friend Red Duggan, our consul general and a distinguished member of the Foreign Service. Soon after I first met him while he was Chargé d'Affaires in Dar-es-Salaam in 1961, he went blind, but so good was the job he had done with President Julius Nyerere of Tanzania that President Kennedy offered him the ambassadorship to that country. Uncertain how his blindness might affect his ability to handle the post, Red turned down the offer. Later, however, he accepted an appointment as consul general. We were in Zanzibar together just a few months before the Communists engineered the revolution that deposed the Sultan. In the old days, a British or an American gunboat would have made short work of such petty coups, but nowadays we seem to sit back and let the winds of change blow where they may.

The job of a diplomat is to report all shades of political opinion, and there were two men in Durban whom I found particularly stimulating on that score. One was Albert Luthuli, the Zulu chief who later won the Nobel Prize and has since died. The other was Alan Paton, the author and the then head of the Liberal Party. In the eight years since I had seen him last, Alan had aged. His wife, to whom he was completely devoted, had died during that time; and more recently the government had banned multiracial political parties, making it necessary for him either to dissolve the Liberal Party or restrict its membership to whites. He decided to dissolve.

A few weeks before we saw him, Alan had picked up two Africans who were thumbing a ride, only to have them beat him badly. Of course they did not know they were assaulting one of the best friends of the black man in South Africa. But none of these things had broken his spirit. During a long Chinese dinner to which Irene and I invited him, he kept up a lively account of his work. He was then considering writing (and has since written) a book about his life with his wife. It would be a new kind of autobiography. He warned us against too much bantering, saying when one member of the bantering team dies, the other deeply regrets the time wasted on it. He told us *Cry the Beloved Country* had now sold more than four million copies and has been translated into more than a score of languages. The result, he mentioned wryly, was that his correspondence had become so big that he had to have a secretary to keep up with it. The letters came from all over the world, hundreds of them from America alone. As for his freedom of movement, Alan is not banned by the government and can travel any place he wants in South Africa.

The next morning we were picked up at the hotel by Colonel Jack Vincent, the man who is rightly called the father of the Natal game parks. He drove us across the lovely rolling hills of Natal to Pietermaritzburg. On its outskirts lie the headquarters of the Natal Parks Board, with its own 200-acre estate. The headquarters building, designed under Colonel Vincent's direction, is the nerve center of the complex of thirty-one reserves totaling some 514,000 acres and occupying 2.2 percent of the entire area of Natal.

Born in England, Jack Vincent came to South Africa in 1923 to farm. But he was soon persuaded to join Admiral Hubert Lynes, the famous ornithologist, in a five-year survey of African birds, with special attention to the grass warblers. When World War II began, the admiral, although sixty-six years old, pestered the Admiralty until they gave him a destroyer, and he served on it with distinction. Vincent joined the Royal Natal Carabineers as a captain, fighting through Kenya, Ethiopia, and the

Western Desert. Later he went to the British Staff College. At the war's end he was a full colonel. He then joined the Natal Parks Board as chief executive officer and became its first director. After running the parks for fifteen years, he accepted an invitation in 1963 from the International Council for Bird Preservation which, along with the International Union for the Conservation of Nature, had its offices in Morges, Switzerland. Colonel Vincent subsequently started the Red Book of rare and endangered birds, which is now the "Bible" of bird conservationists. He was also the secretary of the Survival Service Commission, the international committee that decides on the rarity and need for protection of endangered species. I was pleased when I was recently elected to this board myself. Colonel Vincent returned to the Natal Parks Board as adviser in 1967.

When the colonel joined the Natal Parks Board it had a staff of fourteen rangers and a budget of $100,000 a year. This had since been increased to a staff numbering 178 Europeans and 498 Bantu and a budget amounting to well over a million dollars a year. Furthermore, so successful have the capturing programs for the various animals been that the board sells all its surpluses to parks, zoos, and conservation-minded landowners. Seldom does it have to shoot out the excess populations. To deter predators, especially jackals, the board maintains two packs of fox hounds that are hunted on horseback. The packs can be called on by any area of Natal where the jackal is a menace to game or even to farmers' sheep. I can imagine no nicer life than hunting hounds over the superb galloping fields of Natal. Kills average five brace of jacks a month, not a bad record for an "unstopped" country. Colonel Vincent, who used to hunt with the Southdown Hounds in England, inaugurated the packs.

The Pietermaritzburg and Mooi River sections of Natal are famous for their horses, and we passed Zulu tribesmen riding mounts that I would like to have myself. So popular are good horses among the tribes that *lobolas*, the bride price, which was formerly paid only in cattle, now often includes a horse complete with saddle and bridle.

One of the many advantages of traveling with Colonel Vincent is his instant and accurate recognition of birds. He pointed out the little red-footed falcon, which breeds in Siberia and was preparing for its long flight north. The lesser kestrel is also a visitor to Natal from the steppes of

Russian Asia. As we drove along we passed a family of red-winged francolin, and on the telephone wires above we spotted a bevy of European swallows that were late on their migration to the north. The males showed breeding plumage. It is autumn in South Africa in April, with winter just around the corner. The colonel pointed out a fine jackal buzzard, the first he had seen that year. We also saw a handsome Stanley bustard walking sedately along a field.

The objective of our trip was Giant's Castle, the 63,000-acre game reserve lying among the towering peaks of the Drakensberg Mountains on the border of Lesotho, the little kingdom of the Basutos which is completely surrounded by South Africa. At Bushman's River, a sparkling trout stream that rises in the mountains, we started climbing. By the time we reached the camp we were at an altitude of 6,000 feet. Berg cypresses lined the road up, and occasionally we saw Natal sugarbush, banks of lavender and white cosmos, and a species of protea with a pink flower. At the camp we were welcomed by Bill Barnes, the warden of Giant's Castle Game Reserve, and given a comfortable cottage for our stay.

In his garden, Barnes has a tame lammergeyer, the mysterious great bird that is classified between the eagles and the vultures. Well known to the ancients, the lammergeyer was the bird that Pliny held responsible for the death of the poet Aeschylus. It is in the habit of taking bones to great heights and dropping them in order to break them so that the marrow is exposed. Occasionally they will take up a turtle or a tortoise for the same reason. Pliny's bird mistook the bald, shining pate of the poet for a rock and dropped a heavy tortoise on it.

The lammergeyer is found in the Himalayas and in the Alps as well as in the mountains of Africa. There are two races of the bird—the northern, which occurs in Europe and Asia, and the southern, which inhabits the peaks of Ethiopia and Natal. None exist in either North or South America. Colonel Vincent drew our attention to its comparatively weak talons, scoffing at the often-told tales of lammergeyer carrying off babies and attacking men. Nevertheless, when the bird was fed we were amazed to see it swallow chunks of bone. In flight it has a wing span of more than seven feet. After Barnes's pet grows out of its new feathers— it was captured in Lesotho as a fledgling and easily tamed—it will fly away to join its mates in the eyries of Giant's Castle.

Barnes took us in two Land-Rovers for a tour of the highlands, where nothing but a Land-Rover or a goat could possibly have gone. The trail led straight up over rock ledges until we emerged on a vast land of grass-covered hills that runs up to the base of towering rock peaks. One of these is Giant's Castle, which rises to almost 11,000 feet, with slopes descending in both Natal and Lesotho. We saw a rich variety of game including oribi, mountain reed buck, vaal rhebok, red hartebeest, and blesbok. Blesbok, being very similar to the rare bonebok, can only be distinguished from them by less white on their rumps. The blesbok inhabits the area of summer rainfall, the bontebok that of winter rainfall. The blesbok are a great favorite with the farmers of Natal and the Orange Free State, so there is no chance that they will ever decline to the dangerous levels the bontebok once did.

Conservation education in Natal starts early, for Colonel Vincent's orders to his rangers were explicit on the importance of teaching the young to care about wildlife. Every ranger is encouraged to lecture to the schools in his district, with the result that the youngsters grow up with a keen interest in the wide and beautiful land in which they live. Trips to the reserves at reduced rates are given schoolboys and girls, enabling thousands of them to become familiar with the splendors of their natural heritage. Nor are older people neglected; they participate freely in conducted wilderness trail walks.

In order to promote a realization of the need for conservation of soil, water, and wildlife, the Wilderness Leadership School Trust was formed in 1963 in Durban. Up to the time of our South African mission the school had graduated 200 high-school boys and girls and seventy adults. Moreover, it was appealing for more funds to expand its operations. Colonel Vincent and others in Natal with whom I have discussed it think highly of the project, which might well interest the World Wildlife Fund both in South Africa and in Morges.

Early in the morning we drove over hair-raising trails—one was aptly named God Help Me Hill—to the foot of Giant's Castle. Although the altitude here was 7,500 feet, the castle itself towered another 3,000 feet above us. On the way we saw Langalibalele Pass, named after the Zulu chief who was defeated there in 1872 by a force of the Natal Carabineers, Colonel Vincent's old regiment of mounted infantry. We also passed a number of caves that the Bushmen decorated many years ago with their rock paintings. The last of these little aborigines were exterminated in Natal in 1884 when Chief Zeweei made his last stand at Sehonghong Cave.

Few birds inhabit the high mountains, but we saw two black eagles almost as big as a lammergeyer. These eagles prey on the dassies, the little rock hyrax, whose closest relation is the elephant. Other birds of prey we spotted consisted of a pair of jackal buzzards and a tawny-bodied rock kestrel. A covey of gray-wing francolin exploded before us, while a pair of white-necked ravens wheeled in the skies above the castle. At a stone blind, bird watchers can observe and photograph the lammergeyers and eagles during the winter months. Carcasses are left for the great birds to feast on only twenty feet away.

Among the many interesting flowers we noted in this alpine zone were mauve heather, pink everlasting, and yellow senecio. In the spring the mountain slopes are ablaze with hundreds of wildflowers. The only bushes that grow there are Leucsidea and Buddleia. The former has an aromatic smell, and the Basutos use it for head colds. One plant that had an unusual function was the *Ranunculus cooperi*, whose waterproof leaves were used by the Bushmen to line the water bags they made from buck stomachs.

From the mountain hut where we had tea we could see Majuba in the far distance. It was below this peak that the Boers defeated the British Army in 1902. A movie is being made of this battle, with a brigade of the South African Army choosing sides for the scrimmage. In a pool near the hut a new species of frog, *Rana umbraculata*, was discovered by a member of the parks board in 1960.

On the way back we ran over a berg adder, a small but poisonous snake that shares the chilly highlands with the Egyptian cobra. Farther along we saw a file of mounted game scouts silhouetted against the skyline. These were Zulus—very tough men indeed. Just how tough, the colonel gave me an example. When he was in charge of the Natal parks, Colonel Vincent received a report from the Umfolozi Game Reserve of an incident concerning a Zulu guard who was returning from duty. It seemed that as the Zulu rounded a corner on his route he came between a baby square-lipped rhino and its mother as the two were trotting by. With the toss of her head the mother caught the guard on her horns, throwing him into a nearby thorn tree. One horn penetrated his chest, the other his thigh. He remained unconscious in the tree for some time before falling to the ground after dark. The collision had occurred about 5 P.M. When the Zulu came to, he dragged himself to water to assuage his thirst from loss of blood and then crawled all that night and all the next day to camp, reaching his home some thirty-one hours after being wounded. He was subsequently rushed seventy miles to the hospital, by which time his lung could be plainly seen in the chest wound. About a month later the guard was back on duty. His only complaint was that he got a bit short of breath when he ran, so suggested he should be put on light duty. The incident described is virtually the only serious accident caused by the square-lipped rhinos and was pure accident. The species is not aggressive.

Brown trout were introduced into the Bushman's River in 1894 by John Parker, a British farmer from Maritzburg. Rainbow trout had been tried in other streams in 1888, but it was not until later that they were successfully reared. In 1912 the province of Natal took over the job of stocking the rivers. Today there are two provincial hatcheries, one for rainbows and one for browns. American native trout have never been successful. With this background well in mind, I accompanied Barnes to a lovely stretch of the Bushman's where a series of deep pools alternate with rapids. On the second cast with a little brown wet fly, I hooked a good fish, only to lose him later on a snag. In half an hour, however, Barnes and I had caught a nice mess, the best of which ran to a pound and a half. Rain forced us to quit, but I plan to return to Bushman's River some day to try for some of those five- and six-pounders that are some-times found in its dark pools. The Bushman's alone is forty miles long. The Little Tugela, which also runs partly in the game park, offers another fine stretch of fishing where the bags are all rainbows. The limit is ten trout over eight inches and the license is nominal. The season runs from August 1 to April 31.

The Giant's Castle camp affords room for forty-four people in attrac-tive cottages, with accommodations for twenty more in the huts on the mountains. Getting about requires a Land-Rover, unless you would rather ride one of the horses available for hire. Because no food can be bought at the camp—and as the nearest town is thirty miles away—it is necessary to come prepared. On that score, Mary Vincent, the colonel's good wife, did us all very well indeed.

From Giant's Castle we flew in a chartered plane to Maseru in Lesotho, taking off from there in a little Piper Comanche on the long trip to Exeter in the northern Transvaal. Studying the map as we flew over the Orange Free State and then the Transvaal, I found I could not locate Exeter, the grass strip near Kruger Park where we were to land. Exeter is the private landing field of Loring Rattray, a Durban industrialist who owns both the Mala Mala Game Reserve and the Exeter Farm and is also chairman of the 240-square-mile Sabi Sand Wildtuin which adjoins Kruger National Park. We finally did locate the Mala Mala strip on the map, but spotting it on the ground below was another thing. Our pilot had never been there before and was not even familiar with the Sand River, one of the local landmarks. We cruised for about an hour over the area where the Mala Mala field was supposed to be, but we failed to sight it. We then headed south in the hope of striking Skukuza, one of the airfields serving Kruger, and at last saw a little town with a strip which we thought must be it. On landing, however, we found barbed wire around the gas tanks. This, we realized, was not a public field. A few minutes later a government car shot onto the field carrying a brace of uniformed officers who promptly informed us that we had landed on a military airfield and, what is more, had approached it from Portuguese territory.

The town we had seen was not Skukuza at all, but Komatipoort, the border town between Portuguese Mozambique and South Africa. The officers were from the border patrol, and they wanted in no uncertain terms to learn what we were doing. When Winston Churchill escaped from Pretoria on a coal train to Mozambique during the Boer War, he was almost discovered here at Komatipoort, and I couldn't help feeling as he must have. We finally convinced the ardent young guards that we were indeed innocent and, after paying a five-dollar landing fee, we took off again. Our gas was then down to only half an hour's flying time, so we were lucky to spot the Sand River and next a dirt strip after fifteen minutes' flying along the railway. After landing we flagged down a Land-Rover whose driver was on his way to feed Loring Rattray's crocodiles in the river near Mala Mala.

Bontebok, Bontebok National Park, Cape Province, South Africa

Mala Mala used to belong to my friend Colonel William (Wac) Campbell, whom I visited in 1960 and where I shot a big black-maned lion. After Colonel Campbell's death, the 22,000-acre game farm was sold to Rattray. He has since turned it into the most attractive private resort in South Africa, with comfortable cottages, an air-conditioned dining room, and a staff of wardens to take the customers around the reserve with safety. Three quarters of the score of guests to which the camp is limited came from abroad, many of them of considerable prominence. Both Mala Mala and Exeter, where Rattray lives when he comes down from Durban, hold a large and varied quantity of game. Together they total about a quarter of the acreage included in the Sabi Sand Reserve.

The camp at Exeter, like that of Mala Mala, is on the bank of the Sand River. A lovelier spot in the low veld would be hard to find. Under the spreading branches of a huge and ancient Transvaal mahogany tree, one can sit in the evening and watch the game come to the river to drink. Hippos waddle from the pool to graze upon the lawn. All of the ungulates enjoy the lush grass of the river meadows in plain view of our chairs on the bank. As the sun set a mother giraffe and her calf wandered by, and a herd of impala infiltrated through the trees. Rattray and his wife have owned Exeter for thirty years. When they first came, they lived in a tent and had to walk in part of the way. The tent gave way to native huts, then to today's extremely comfortable camp.

The Sabi Sand Reserve, which is officially approved by the governor of the Transvaal, consists of the farms of an association of some forty-five owners who have agreed to help pay for the communal fencing—the Kruger fence defines one border, but they had to build an eight-foot barrier on the other borders—and pay the cost of guards. In order to shoot on their own farms the members must first obtain permission from Rattray, who is the chairman of the executive committee. He, in turn, requests permits from the Department of Nature Conservation. Some owners still shoot an occasional lion, and almost everyone has to crop the impala, which have increased to about 25,000 head. Rare species—nyala, sable, and white rhino—have been purchased from the surpluses at Umfolozi. There are also a few elephants, which have broken the Kruger fence.

The impala antelope, being a prolific breed and able to increase despite heavy depredation and drought, has to be strictly controlled. Censuses carried out by means of air, water-hole, and strip counts reflect approximately the following number of larger species in the preserve: 60 lion, 100 leopard, 10 cheetah, 40 Cape hunting dogs, 100 jackal, 15 elephant, 30 hippo, 550 giraffe, 900 kudu, 450 waterbuck, 25,000 impala, 200 bushbuck, 30 reedbuck, 14 nyala, 600 wart hog, 600 baboons, 300 vervet monkeys, 400 gray duiker, 200 steinbok, 40 klipspringer, 20 crocodile, and a wealth of other smaller species of mammals, reptiles, and birds that I need not mention here.

The habits of the lions on Exeter and Mala Mala are all well known to Rattray and his staff. Some of the beasts, it turned out, were not so loving toward their families as they might be. There was one old black-maned lion, for example, who proceeded to kill and eat his wife shortly after their honeymoon. On another occasion two old lions chased a lioness and did away with her, leaving only a few bits of skin. On the night we drove to the place where the lions are fed every night the scene was more congenial. Two old males, a brace of females, and four cubs all shared an impala with a minimum of discord.

Rattray not only cares about his game but has a great deal of affection for a staff of many years' standing. Jim and Tio, two grizzled Shangaan hunters who have been on Exeter since he bought it, are a mine of useful and interesting information about the animals, birds, and trees. They pointed out a marula tree, whose juicy fruit ferments in the stomach, making the bushveld inhabitants—man and animal—literally drunk. I have seen full-grown elephants wobbling around like sailors on the beach. Even the baboons appear to be tipsy. The Shangaans themselves do little work during the Marula season. There are many other more mundane varieties of trees, and Rattray, who is also in the lumber business, has had handsome furniture made of them.

Bird life in the low veld is prolific. In ten minutes we recognized a gray hornbill, Cape turtledove, black-headed oriole, black-collared barber, mourning dove, and glossy starling. Game birds were represented by flocks of guinea fowl and francolin, while high on a dead tree sat a batteleur eagle and an African hawk eagle.

Although South Africa has the best-run parks on the continent, the private parks of men like Rattray and his neighbors are an important addition to the conservation of wildlife. Furthermore, the idea is spreading so that more and more of the big landowners are becoming as proud of their herds of game as they are of their prize livestock.

Biggest of South Africa's national parks is Kruger, whose 8,000 square miles is the second-largest national park in the world after our Alaska National Park. The vast Etosha Pan is a provincial park of South-West Africa, hence it does not come under the authority of Rocco Knobel, Director of the National Parks. Knobel kindly met us at Skukuza, the headquarters of Kruger, and devoted a great deal of time and interest to our visit. He is not only responsible for the nine national parks with which the republic is dotted but also must look after a stream of visiting V.I.P.'s. We came after the Prime Minister of Luxembourg, and were in camp with the Minister of Education of Australia and with Avery Brundage, the then chairman of the Olympic Committee. Brundage had announced out of the blue that he was visiting South Africa and Kruger Park on the eve of the critical meeting in Switzerland where it might be decided whether or not the republic's team, even though integrated, was to be allowed to compete in the 1968 games at Mexico City.

Kruger, like several of the parks in America, owes its inception to the foresight of a statesman. In 1894, President Paul Kruger suggested to a meeting of the Volksraad, or Transvaal Parliament, that the time had come to do something toward saving the vast vanishing wildlife of the country. But it was not until 1898, a year before the outbreak of the Boer War, that the park was finally proclaimed. The original name was the Government's Game Reserve, with an area delineated as that lying between the Crocodile and Sabi rivers. After the war, the park was reproclaimed and considerably enlarged by the British. The famous Colonel James Stevenson-Hamilton became the first warden. Colonel Hamilton served until 1940, and I had the great pleasure of meeting his widow, who still visits the park and stays at Skukuza. In 1926 the National Parks Act renamed the reserve Kruger National Park.

Knobel, who has been Director of National Parks since 1953, enjoys a unique position among his colleagues in other countries, for his job is an autonomous one. That is, he is not responsible, as most park directors are, to a government ministry. The National Parks Board consists of a dozen members, four of whom are nominated by the four provinces of the republic, one by the South African Wildlife Protection Society, and the rest by the Minister of Lands. This arrangement gives him a great advantage in furthering his plans, for he can approach anyone from the Prime Minister on down without having to go through channels.

Knobel told me that Dr. Verwoerd, the Prime Minister who was assassinated in 1966, was a vitally important factor in the growth of the park system. It was largely due to his influence that the Cape Mountain Zebra Park and the Aughrabies Park were proclaimed. Dr. Verwoerd often visited the parks with his wife, who is still keen about wildlife. I paid my respects to her when I was in Pretoria.

Knobel's plans for the future include the addition of three more national parks. Under consideration is a park on the northern coast of Natal, where the province borders Mozambique. Although this area includes Lake Sibaya, the only large fresh-water lake in South Africa, it is virtually uninhabited, owing to the lack of water elsewhere in the region. The coast itself has an interesting tidal life as the southernmost coral beds in Africa lie along these shores. Another possible site for a

270

Rocco Knoble,
Director of South
Africa's national
parks and Irene
Crowe

national park is in Namaqualand in the vicinity of the town of Springbok.
A third is in the Cedarberg Mountains of Cape Province. The addition
of these parks to the present system would, of course, further increase
the board's budget, which now runs at $6,500,000. When Knobel took
over, the budget was only $500,000, and the staff consisted of sixty
Europeans and 400 nonwhites. It has since increased to 200 Europeans
and 1,200 non-Europeans. In fact, a whole township has been erected at
Skukuza to house both groups. It goes under the unofficial name of
Knobelville.

Born in what was then the High Commission Territory of Bechuanaland, Knobel was educated at Stellenbosch University at the Cape, where
one of his professors was Dr. Verwoerd. Later he did social work in
Johannesburg before taking over the national parks as director. At fifty-
four, Knobel had close personal ties with Dr. Vorster, the Prime Minister,
as well as with other ministers. In many ways, Knobel served as one of
the republic's best unofficial ambassadors. He was currently promoting
the project to have Kurt Steynberg, South Africa's leading sculptor, carve
a massive head of Kruger out of one of the park's granite knolls.

World Wildlife: the Last Stand

Knobel was an important factor in the formation of World Wildlife Fund in South Africa. Dr. Verwoerd, although an avid conservationist himself, was not against the idea, but he felt that any funds raised in the republic should only be spent there and in neighboring countries. Other members of the cabinet were divided, so the matter was postponed. It was due largely to Knobel's interest and urging that a favorable decision was reached at last. My own feeling is that not only is this a good thing for the cause of world conservation but also it is also particularly good for South Africa because the more international organizations she joins, the less her people will feel separated from the mainstream of world events. Furthermore, it is hoped that World Wildlife Fund will never be subjected to the political pressures that have made South Africa's participation in the Olympic Games so controversial.

Three officers run Kruger. The more than one million animals, and God knows how many birds, are under the control of Andrew Brynard, the chief conservator. A dedicated forty-year-old who was educated as a biologist, Brynard knows his job thoroughly and possesses a large degree of diplomacy as well. The park's 1,400 miles of roads, fifty of which are tarred, and an equal number trails, along with 120 windmills, reservoirs, and dams, are in charge of A. E. Kuschke, the chief engineer. The housing and feeding of more than 270,000 tourists a year come under H. C. Van der Veen, who has been with the park thirty-five years and had been the personal secretary of Colonel Stevenson-Hamilton. At the *brasivleis*, or barbeque dinner, that Knobel gave for us on the evening of our arrival we learned a great deal from Brynard and Van der Veen.

Although every effort is made to keep a balance between the predators and the grazing and browsing animals, some of the browsers are too big and breed too fast for the food supply and consequently have to be cropped. Therefore it is necessary to kill about 500 elephants a year. This is done, I hasten to point out, in the most painless manner possible. The elephants, selected by families, are first tranquilized by darts shot from helicopters. They are then dispatched by severing the juglar veins. The process is expensive, but in a park crowded with visitors no chances can be taken. The ivory, the skin and the meat are sold. I was told of elephant-skin shoes and coats which have been finished to a high degree of suppleness. The meat is processed both for human consumption and for pet food. It is noteworthy that maximum use is made of the harvest.

272

The man most directly involved with the scientific phases of the wild-life population is Dr. U. de V. Pienaar, a thirty-eight-year-old ecologist who has made a profound study of the park's inhabitants. In his office he showed us the crossbow—accurate up to thirty yards—of the type used for the tranquilizing of game. The elephants are shot in the hindquarters, and so powerful is the serum used that they are completely dormant in a few minutes. The carcasses are then hauled by truck to a processing plant. Some 500 buffalo are also culled each year as well as a quantity of the small buck, which are shot for food for the park workers. Pienaar said that the average increase in the elephant population is four percent per year, while the rate for the buffalo is seven percent. No predators have been shot since 1960 as every effort is being made to increase the park's estimated 1,000 lions along with the jackal, hyena, and wild-dog population.

Pienaar told us that by means of wide-angle cameras and helicopters a very accurate census of the animals is made. The March, 1968, count showed 6,093 elephant, 15,867 buffalo, 14,143 wildebeest, 14,710 zebra, 2,465 giraffe, 3,185 waterbuck, 5,150 kudu, 750 nyala, 1,860 reedbuck, 1,065 sable, 285 roan, 765 tsessebe, and 477 eland. A survey of the park's entire 8,000 square miles can be done in a week, so there is very little chance of the herds of larger animals moving and being counted twice. Small buck, of course, cannot be accurately counted, but Knobel estimated a population of at least a quarter million impala.

Before the coming of the white man and his deadly accurate rifles, the game was culled by drought. While this worked all right for the numerous animals such as impala and wildebeest, it was always hard on the rare species such as nyala, sable, and eland. By culling in the areas where there is not enough water, Pienaar is able to keep the rare species from perishing altogether through lack of grazing.

In order to make intimate studies of certain species, a one-square-mile enclosed area has been erected. The fence, elephant-proof and predator-proof, guarantees that the inmates will be completely undisturbed. An experiment was being made with ten roan antelope and will be continued with nyala, tsessebe, and sable. So tame were the roan in the enclosure that one could approach them.

Law enforcement in the park comes under Brynard, and we learned that penalties for violations by white men are much stiffer than for those by nonwhites. This applies to tourists as well as poachers. I was told of the case of four white men caught poaching eland in the Kalahari Gemsbok Park who lost their new Land-Rover, four expensive guns, and a $5,000 fine. The following year they were caught again. This time, however, they were lucky enough to be in the Botswana part of the park, which is patrolled by Knobel's men under an arrangement with the Botswana authorities. Because there was no extradition treaty between Botswana and South Africa, the men simply posted bond, then skipped into South Africa. If they had been caught for a second time in the republic, they might well have been sent to jail for five years.

Tourists sometimes take stupid chances, too. One man and his wife threw oranges at a lion and another couple drove between a cow elephant and her calf. She promptly pushed their little car back a dozen yards, penetrating the hood with her tusks. Fines for this kind of thing are severe. The same holds for driving faster than the park's regulation twenty-five miles per hour.

Kruger has two sets of roads, the broad highways where the tourists jockey for position beside the animals and a complex of jungle trails which are sandy and barely wide enough for a Land-Rover. Here the park officials and the scientists can observe wildlife virtually undisturbed. Luckily for me, I have never been restricted to seeing Kruger from the highway, for this can sometimes be a harrowing experience. On Easter weekend when we visited the park there were almost 10,000 tourists crowding the roads, and a perfectly decent man on the streets of Johannesburg or Cape Town becomes a domineering hog when it comes to watching game. He refuses to let his neighbor pass even though he has exhausted his roll of film, and he moves on slowly only when the lion has settled behind a boulder out of sight. Both Knobel and Brynard took us for drives into the bush on the quiet byways, so we saw a variety of games even though the recent heavy rains had made it unnecessary for the animals to congregate at the rivers and water holes. One observation made to us apropos of this was that while all varieties of humanity will try to live together, animals prefer to stay with their own particular kind. An example of this is the impala and the nyala, which feed together during the day. As soon as evening falls, however, the impala drift to the open country, while the nyala wander into the bush.

Van der Veen, while he was working for Colonel Stevenson-Hamilton, knew Sakubona, the Shangaan ranger whose tale appears in one of the colonel's books. It seems that Sakubona, who was retired for old age, was returning home one night full of liquor when he saw a lioness lying in the path. He shouted at her, "Child, why do you block the path of the Colonel's best tracker?" The lioness was unmoved, and Sakubona smacked her on the head with his knobkerrie. She bit him badly in the leg, but he finally escaped, owing, he thought, to the fact the lioness got drunk herself from biting him. No one believed the story until an examination of the tracks convinced the doubters otherwise.

Another famous game guard who was a personal friend of Van der Veen was Harry Wolhuter, an Englishman who started in the park under Colonel Stevenson-Hamilton and became known all over the low veld for his adventure with lions. Wolhuter was returning to camp on horseback one evening when two lionesses suddenly appeared on the trail. Before he could escape, one of them charged and leaped on his horse. The horse shied, dislodging the lion and throwing Wolhuter. The other lion then grabbed him by the shoulder and started dragging him along the ground. Despite the intense pain, Wolhuter kept his senses and slowly reached down for his sheath knife in his belt. When the lioness stopped for a moment, he stabbed her twice in the chest and once in the throat. As the lioness gasped out her life, Wolhuter dragged himself to a little tree, climbed into its branches—which were barely ten feet above the ground —and tied himself on with his belt. He then fainted from loss of blood.

In the meantime the other lion had lost the horse and returned to the scene. She could easily have leaped up and dragged Wolhuter out of the tree had it not been for the bravery of Wolhuter's little fox terrier, which attacked furiously every time she approached the tree. The riderless horse galloped back to camp, where a rescue party came for Wolhuter. He was then carried by litter more than 100 miles to the nearest hospital and after three months' treatment miraculously survived.

Years later when Wolhuter was in Sheffield, England, where his life-saving sheath knife had been made, he told the clerk at the store there about what he owed the knife. The clerk replied, "Oh, that is nothing, sir. These knives are often used in England to kill sheep."

Our last day at Kruger was spent in the company of Avery Brundage, a cheerful octogenarian with a high degree of courage and dedication, who had been president of the International Olympic Committee for the previous sixteen years and was then undoubtedly facing the greatest crisis in his long association with the games. The committee had voted to invite South Africa to compete in the Olympiad to be held in Mexico City in the summer of 1968, but the black African countries, egged on and abetted by the Communists, threatened to pull out of the games unless South Africa was barred. The facts that most of the black African states did not even belong to the Olympic Committee and only three of the others were prepared to send athletes were apparently not relevant. Mexico, in the meantime, was afraid that she would have no competitors, and more important still, the whole question of the integrity of the Olympics was at stake. If political considerations were going to control membership, the whole concept of the games would be irrevocably damaged.

Avery Brundage, President of the International Olympic Committee, and the author at Kruger Park

Brundage and Reginald Honey, Q. C., the South African member of the committee, were really more concerned over this matter of basic principle than they were over the effort to oust South Africa. Honey made a moving speech at dinner in which he praised Brundage for his devotion to the Olympic ideals and for his firm stand against the Communists and others who were attempting to wreck the games. As Honey, like Brundage, was over eighty, it was a heartening thing to see these two men fighting the good fight for the torch lit so many centuries ago by the ancient Greeks.

While Brundage, Honey, Irene, and I were enjoying Knobel's hospitality and admiring the game, the world press was having a fit. In fact, it was only by the most heroic efforts that reporters were barred from tracking us down among the lions and elephants. Every South African paper headlined the story, and the phone lines were jammed trying to get more facts—or any facts. For all Brundage had said when he was caught by the press at Jan Smuts Airfield was that in view of the confusion in the world of humans, he thought it would be salubrious to contemplate the world of wildlife for a few days.

We left Kruger and its hospitable director with real regret, proceeding to Johannesburg for a round of final engagements before returning to America. We stayed with C. S. (Punch) Barlow, an ornithologist and an enthusiastic member of the South African World Wildlife Fund and an old friend from my former days in his country. At Punch's invitation I attended a meeting of the South African Foundation and was able to get in a few licks for conservation as well as discuss other matters relevant to the foundation's public-relations campaign in the United States. Tourism is, of course, a major industry in South Africa, as most people come to see the animals. I also talked with Gerard Jooste, former ambassador to the United States and now adviser to the Prime Minister on foreign affairs. Always a keen conservationist, Jooste is interested in ways by which South Africa can help her poorer neighbors. Aid for conservation is certainly one of these ways.

Appendix I

World Wildlife Fund Projects orginated by the author.

Project No. 49: Mesopotamian Fallow Deer
Project No. 125: Fauna of the Falkland Islands
Project No. 129: Arabian Oryx
Project No. 132: Promotion of nature conservation in Australasia
Project No. 172: Fellowship for Hunter Han-ting Eu, Taiwan
Project No. 179: Thylacine, or Tasmanian "Wolf"
Project No. 180: Birds of the Fiji Islands
Project No. 191: Promotion of nature conservation in Ceylon, India, Sikkim, and Bhutan
Project No. 216: Promotion of nature conservation in North Africa
Project No. 272: Promotion of nature conservation in Central America and Mexico
Project No. 300: Green Turtle Research Station at Tortuguero, Costa Rica
Project No. 310: Wildlife of Bhutan
Project No. 314: Promotion of nature conservation in southern Africa
Project No. 316: White-winged dove protection program, Mexico
Project No. 395: Wilderness Leadership School, Durban, South Africa —Grant for 1968-1970
Project No. 397: Namib Desert Golden Mole Research and conservation program.

Appendix II

CONVENTION ON NATURE PROTECTION AND WILDLIFE
PRESERVATION
IN THE WESTERN HEMISPHERE
PREAMBLE

The governments of the American Republics, wishing to protect and preserve in their natural habitat representatives of all species and genera of their native flora and fauna, including migratory birds, in sufficient numbers and over areas extensive enough to assure them from becoming extinct through any agency within man's control; and

Wishing to protect and preserve scenery of extraordinary beauty, unusual and striking geologic formations, regions, and natural objects of aesthetic, historic or scientific value, and areas characterized by primitive conditions in those cases covered by this Convention; and

Wishing to conclude a Convention on the protection of nature and the preservation of flora and fauna to effectuate the foregoing purposes, have agreed upon the following Articles:

Article I

Description of terms used in the wording of this Convention.

1. The expression *National Parks* shall denote:

Areas established for the protection and preservation of superlative scenery, flora, and fauna of national significance which the general public may enjoy and from which it may benefit when placed under public control.

2. The expression *National Reserves* shall denote:

Regions established for conservation and utilization of natural resources under government control, on which protection of animal and

281

plant life will be afforded in so far as this may be consistent with the primary purposes of such reserves.

3. The expression *Nature Monuments* shall denote:

Regions, objects, or living species of flora or fauna of aesthetic, historic or scientific interest to which strict protection is given. The purpose of nature monuments is the protection of the specific object, or a species of flora or fauna, by setting aside an area, an object, or a single species, as an inviolate nature monument, except for duly authorized scientific investigations or government inspection.

4. The expression *Strict Wilderness Reserves* shall denote:

A region under public control characterized by primitive conditions of flora, fauna, transportation and habitation wherein there is no provision for the passage of motorized transportation and all commercial developments are excluded.

5. The expression *Migratory Birds* shall denote:

Birds of those species, all or some of those individual members may at any season cross any of the boundaries between the American countries. Some of the species of the following families are examples of birds characterized as migratory: Charadriidae, Scolopacidae, Caprimulgidae, Hirundinidae.

Article II

1. The Contracting Governments will explore at once the possibility of establishing in their territories national parks, national reserves, nature monuments, and strict wilderness reserves as defined in the preceding article. In all cases where such establishment is feasible, the creation thereof shall be begun as soon as possible after the effective date of the present Convention.

2. If in any country the establishment of national parks, national reserves, nature monuments, or strict wilderness reserves is found to be impractical at present, suitable areas, objects, or living species of fauna or flora, as the case may be, shall be selected as early as possible to be transformed into national parks, national reserves, nature monuments, or strict wilderness reserves as soon as, in the opinion of the authorities concerned, circumstances will permit.

3. The Contracting Governments shall notify the Pan American Un-

ion of the establishment of any national parks, national reserves, and of the legislation, including the methods of administrative control, adopted in connection therewith.

Article III

The Contracting Governments agree that the boundaries of national parks shall not be altered, or any portion thereof be capable of alienation, except by the competent legislative authority. The resources of these reserves shall not be subject to exploitation for commercial profit.

The Contracting Governments agree to prohibit hunting, killing, and capturing of members of the fauna and destruction or collection of representatives of the flora in national parks except by or under the direction or control of the park authorities, or for duly authorized scientific investigations.

The Contracting Governments further agree to provide facilities for public recreation and education in national parks consistent with the purposes of this Convention.

Article IV

The Contracting Governments agree to maintain the strict wilderness reserves inviolate, as far as practicable, except for duly authorized scientific investigations or government inspection, or such uses as are consistent with the purposes for which the area was established.

Article V

1. The Contracting Governments agree to adopt, or to propose such adoption to their respective appropriate lawmaking bodies, suitable laws and regulations for the protection and preservation of flora and fauna within their national boundaries, but not included in the national parks, national reserves, nature monuments, or strict wilderness reserves referred to in Article II hereof. Such regulation shall contain proper provisions for the taking of specimens of flora and fauna for scientific study and investigation by properly accredited individuals and agencies.

2. The Contracting Governments agree to adopt, or to recommend that their respective legislatures adopt, laws which will assure the protection and preservation of the natural scenery, striking geological formations, and regions and natural objects of aesthetic interest or historic or scientific value.

Article VI

The Contracting Governments agree to cooperate among themselves in promoting the objectives of the present Convention. To this end they will lend proper assistance, consistent with national laws, to scientists of the American Republics engaged in research and field study; they may, when circumstances warrant, enter into agreements with one another or with scientific institutions of the Americas in order to increase the effectiveness of this collaboration; and they shall make available to all the American Republics equally through publication or otherwise the scientific knowledge resulting from such cooperative effort.

Article VII

The Contracting Governments shall adopt appropriate measures for the protection of migratory birds of economic or aesthetic value or to prevent the threatened extinction of any given species. Adequate measures shall be adopted which will permit, in so far as the respective governments may see fit, a rational utilization of migratory birds for the purpose of sports as well as for food, commerce, and industry, and for scientific study and investigation.

Article VIII

The protection of the species mentioned in the Annex to the present Convention is declared to be of special urgency and importance. Species included therein shall be protected as completely as possible, and their hunting, killing, capturing, or taking shall be allowed only with the permission of the appropriate government authorities in the country. Such permission shall be granted only under special circumstances, in order to further scientific purposes, or when essential for the administration of the area in which the animal or plant is found.

Article IX

Each Contracting Government shall take the necessary measures to control and regulate the importation, exportation, and transit of protected fauna or flora or any part thereof by the following means:

1. The issuing of certificates authorizing the exportation or transit of protected species of flora or fauna, or parts thereof.

2. The prohibition of the importation of any species of fauna or flora or any part thereof protected by the country of origin unless accom-

panied by a certificate of lawful exportation as provided for in Paragraph 1 of this article.

Article X

1. The terms of this Convention shall in no way be interpreted as replacing international agreements previously entered into by one or more of the High Contracting Powers.

2. The Pan American Union shall notify the Contracting Parties of any information relevant to the purposes of the present Convention communicated to it by any national museums or by any organizations, national or international, established within their jurisdiction and interested in the purposes of the Convention.

Article XI

1. The original of the present Convention in Spanish, English, Portuguese, and French shall be deposited with the Pan American Union and opened for signature by the American Governments on October 12, 1940.

2. The present Convention shall remain open for signature by the American Governments. The instruments of ratification shall be deposited with the Pan American Union, which shall notify their receipt and the dates thereof, and the terms of any accompanying declarations or reservations, to all participating Governments.

3. The present Convention shall come into force three months after the deposit of not less than five ratifications with the Pan American Union.

4. Any ratification received after the date of the entry into force of the Convention shall take effect three months after the date of its deposit with the Pan American Union.

Article XII

1. Any Contracting Government may at any time denounce the present Convention by a notification in writing addressed to the Pan American Union. Such denunciation shall take effect one year after the date of the receipt of the notification by the Pan American Union, provided, however, that no denunciation shall take effect until the expiration of five years from the date of the entry into force of this Convention.

2. If, as the result of simultaneous or successive denunciations, the

number of Contracting Governments is reduced to less than three, the Convention shall cease to be in force from the date on which the last of such denunciations takes effect in accordance with the provisions of the preceding Paragraph.

3. The Pan American Union shall notify all of the American Governments of any denunciations and the date on which they take effect.

4. Should the Convention cease to be in force under the provisions of Paragraph 2 of this article, the Pan American Union shall notify all of the American Governments, indicating the date on which this will become effective.

PAN AMERICAN CONVENTION
ANNEX

The list of species to be included in the Annex of the Convention from various countries can be procured from the Pan American Union. The United States officially listed the following species:

Woodland Caribou	*Rangifer carbou sylvestris*
Sea Otter	*Enhydra lutris*
Manatee	*Trichechus latirostris*
Trumpeter Swan	*Cygnus buccinator*
California Condor	*Gymnogyps californianus*
Whooping Crane	*Grus americana*
Eskimo Curlew	*Phaeopus borealis*
Hudsonian Godwit	*Limosa haemastica*
Puerto Rican Parrot	*Amazona vittata*
Ivory-Billed Woodpecker	*Campephilus principalis*

Index